TOWER HAMLETS

91 000 001 682 79 8

KT-473-531

DESERT ISLAND DISCS
FLOTSAM & JETSAM

TOWER HAMLETS
Idea Stores & Libraries
WITHDRAWN

www.**transworldbooks**.co.uk

DESERT ISLAND DISCS
FLOTSAM & JETSAM

Fascinating facts, figures and miscellany
from one of BBC Radio 4's
best-loved programmes

MITCHELL SYMONS

BANTAM PRESS

LONDON · TORONTO · SYDNEY · AUCKLAND · JOHANNESBURG

TOWER HAMLETS LIBRARIES	
91000001682798	
Bertrams	25/10/2012
791.447	£14.99
THISBO	TH12001254

TRANSWORLD PUBLISHERS
61–63 Uxbridge Road, London W5 5SA
A Random House Group Company
www.transworldbooks.co.uk

Published by arrangement with the BBC
in 2012 by Bantam Press
an imprint of Transworld Publishers

Copyright © Mitchell Symons 2012

Mitchell Symons has asserted his right under the Copyright,
Designs and Patents Act 1988 to be identified as the author of this work.

A CIP catalogue record for this book
is available from the British Library.

ISBN 9780593070079

The BBC logo is a trade mark of the British Broadcasting Corporation
and is used under licence. BBC logo © BBC 1996. BBC Radio 4 logo © 2008.

This book is sold subject to the condition that it shall not,
by way of trade or otherwise, be lent, resold, hired out,
or otherwise circulated without the publisher's prior
consent in any form of binding or cover other than that
in which it is published and without a similar condition,
including this condition, being imposed on the
subsequent purchaser.

Addresses for Random House Group Ltd companies outside the UK
can be found at: www.randomhouse.co.uk
The Random House Group Ltd Reg. No. 954009

The Random House Group Limited supports the Forest Stewardship Council (FSC®), the
leading international forest-certification organization. Our books carrying the FSC label are
printed on FSC®-certified paper. FSC is the only forest-certification scheme endorsed by
the leading environmental organizations, including Greenpeace. Our paper procurement
policy can be found at www.randomhouse.co.uk/environment.

Design by Hugh Adams, AB3 Design
Typeset in Sabon, Caslon Open, and Trajan.
Printed and bound in Great Britain by
Clays Ltd, Bungay, Suffolk

2 4 6 8 10 9 7 5 3 1

MIX
Paper from
responsible sources
FSC® C016897

To Penny, Jack and Charlie,
my three favourite castaways

CONTENTS

INTRODUCTION

'I don't want to achieve immortality through my work . . . I want to achieve it through not dying,' said Woody Allen.

Alas, Roy Plomley is no longer with us, but he achieved his immortality on the strength of a high-concept idea he came up with more than 70 years ago. There was nothing new in asking people to nominate their favourite records (the book and the luxury came later): what really made the programme unique was the desert island. The combination of the two meant that the music took on huge importance. This was it: there was no going back to the record shop. Your choices defined you.

And that's where we, the listeners, came in.

How much did we really know about politicians, film stars or, indeed, our fellow citizens?

Their choice of music – revealed in the course of an interview in which they were often (and not deliberately) caught offguard – told us much more than mere words could ever have done.

Whether it was Dame Edith Evans choosing *Rawhide* (by Frankie Laine), Noël Coward selecting *The Hole In The Ground* (by Bernard Cribbins) as his favourite record or even Jeffrey Archer asking for *It's Hard To Be Humble* by Mac Davis, *Desert Island Discs* has never lost its ability to surprise and delight the listener.

As the writer of fun reference books, I had often made lists of such interesting choices. I had also put together lists of people who had chosen their own records, unusual luxuries selected and people who had requested a specific song (e.g., *My Way*). This was, obviously, a painstaking job but one which, as a fan of trivia and the programme, I relished.

And then two things happened.

First, the creation of a fantastic website – www.bbc.co.uk/ desertislanddiscs. Now, *everything* was available, all the choices of records, books and luxuries with links to other guests who had made the same or similar choices.

Then, almost simultaneously, I was invited to compile this book to celebrate the seventieth anniversary of this illustrious programme, first broadcast in January 1942.

I thought I'd died and gone to heaven.

Yup, that's the sort of man I am, but then who else would you want to do a book like this?

Precisely.

Paradoxically, the existence of such a brilliant site that was available to everyone was problematical. If this book was to be of any value, it couldn't just replicate the site. Obviously, I would be using it as my primary source (though I would also draw upon newspaper libraries and my own celebrity database) but it was important to derive – rather than merely reprint – from it.

So it was that I found the two people (Arthur Askey and Sir David Attenborough) who had been on the show four times, the 12 three-time guests and 225 two-timers (so to speak).

Then there were the 84 husbands and wives (separately rather than together), the 10 fathers and sons, the 10 fathers and daughters, the eight pairs of brothers, the eight pairs of sisters and the seven pairs of brother and sister.

Something interesting emerged through these lists. Of all the husbands and wives, only three pairs had been on in the past 17 years: Alison Steadman (1995) and Mike Leigh (1997), Harold Evans (April 2000) and Tina Brown (December 2000), and Meera Syal (2003) and Sanjeev Bhaskar (2008). I should add, for the sake of rigorous accuracy, that they may not have been married at the time of their appearances.

Sir Terence Conran (1996) and Jasper Conran (1995) were the most recent father and son; Nigel Lawson (1989) and Nigella Lawson (2003), the most recent father and daughter; Sir Lew Grade (1987) and Sir Bernard Delfont (1991), the most recent brothers; and the writers A. S. Byatt (1991) and Margaret Drabble (2001) the most recent sisters.

The programme has cast its net much wider in recent years. In its first 40 years, it clearly drew from a much smaller group of people. This explains why so many of them were invited back so often.

Similarly, I managed to find six fathers-in-law and sons-in-law, six mothers-in-law and sons-in-law, nine brothers-in-law and sisters-in-law, seven pairs of cousins and four uncles and nephews. I even managed to find a grandmother and grandson (Dame Gladys Cooper and Sheridan Morley) and an uncle and niece (Christopher Lee and Dame Harriet Walter).

However, in every instance, I was careful not to use the word 'all'. Whereas I was confident that I had indeed found all the husbands and wives who had appeared, I couldn't be so sure with brothers-in-law and sisters-in-law.

You will notice the absence of the word 'all' in much of the rest of the book. This is *not* due to uncertainty but rather because it was essential to make the book as readable as possible.

Let me explain.

If I compile a list of people who have chosen a specific song, I only use the names I think readers will know. It might be interesting to discover that someone you've heard of has chosen a song as one of their eight most important records; it most certainly *isn't* interesting to discover that someone you've *never* heard of has done so.

So how do I know who you – or other readers – 'know'?

I've tried to select the names I think *most people* will recognize. Note: I don't say 'everyone' or 'no one' – just 'most people'. Having spent my entire career making that call of who is known to most people and who isn't, I'm confident that I've got it right here.

Most of the time.

Apart from choosing the avenues I wanted to explore – and most of them were, if you like, self-selecting – I haven't editorialized at all.

Of course, that's absolutely right. Although I'm the author, this isn't 'my' book: it's a *Desert Island Discs* book. You've almost certainly bought it for the subject matter rather than the author.

I haven't even raised a metaphorical eyebrow.

So let me do so now.

When it comes to the most popular (non-classical) music acts, there's no surprise that The Beatles (chosen 252 times), Frank Sinatra (240), Bing Crosby (166), Louis Armstrong (136) and Noël Coward (131) are the most successful. However, I am surprised by how few castaways chose otherwise immensely popular acts . . . and vice versa. Let me remind you here that the cut-off date for this book is 29 January 2012, the seventieth anniversary of the very first programme.

So it was that John McCormack (with 40) was chosen by more castaways than Carole King, Madness, Santana, Steely Dan, The Moody Blues, Hank Williams, The Carpenters, The Doors, Electric Light Orchestra and The Small Faces *put together*!

Similarly, I find it hard to believe that 10cc, Cream, Duran Duran,

Chris Isaak, Sade, Status Quo, Tom Petty And The Heartbreakers, Steve Winwood and Frank Zappa were all chosen just once each and that *not one of* The Allman Brothers, America, Crowded House, Bo Diddley, Fairport Convention, The Four Tops, The Hollies, The Isley Brothers, Joe Jackson, Manfred Mann, Simple Minds, Sly And The Family Stone and The Style Council *was chosen at all*!

I'm not particularly knowledgeable about classical music but I'm useful with a database and so I faithfully recorded the most popular composers (all fairly predictable) and works. In addition, I included the results of the BBC's own 2011 survey of listeners' choices, and it was interesting to compare and contrast the aggregated choices of the guests with those of the listeners. The former are more highbrow and esoteric; the latter more populist and mainstream.

When it came to the luxuries and books, I aimed for eclecticism. With the luxuries, some guests were scrupulously honest and chose things that would enhance their lives on the desert island. Others . . . well, I would draw your attention to the 'Unique Luxuries Chosen' on page 230. I particularly liked Benjamin Zephaniah's request for the law of the land (so he could break it) and Felix Dennis's choice of a very long stainless-steel shaft to encourage pole-dancing mermaids.

As for the book choices, it's quite clear that some guests use the programme as an opportunity to show off their erudition – hence the 'popularity' of Tolstoy, Proust and Joyce. As with the music choices, it's at least worth pondering some surprises. Proust alone was selected by more castaways (48) than Evelyn Waugh, Ernest Hemingway, John Steinbeck, John Buchan, G. K. Chesterton, Agatha Christie, D. H. Lawrence, J. D. Salinger, Kingsley Amis, Saul Bellow, Anthony Burgess, Albert Camus, J. P. Donleavy, John Fowles, Laurie Lee, Harper Lee, Doris Lessing, George MacDonald Fraser, V. S. Naipaul, George Orwell, Kurt Vonnegut and John Wyndham *put together*.

Meanwhile, it's extraordinary to think that not one of the novels by Martin Amis, J. G. Ballard, Truman Capote, Joseph Conrad, William Golding, Günter Grass, Graham Greene, Ian McEwan, Iris Murdoch, Boris Pasternak, Terry Pratchett, Philip Roth, Aleksandr Solzhenitsyn, Muriel Spark, John Updike or Keith Waterhouse was chosen at all.

That's Graham Greene – as in the finest writer of the twentieth century (I know, I'm editorializing here). It is true that his brother, the former director-general of the BBC Sir Hugh Greene (1983), did choose, as a record, an excerpt from Greene's *In Search of a Character: Two African Journals*, a work of non-fiction. But *still*. It is extraordinary.

Oh well, there's always time.

Finally, a brief note about the castaways and their titles: throughout the book a title or honorific is given only when the castaway had already been awarded it at the time of their appearance on the programme. You will find a full list of the *Flotsam & Jetsam* castaways at the end of the book.

Desert Island Discs will continue to run for as long as there are people willing to share their choices and listeners who are keen to listen to them.

Here's to the next 70 years!

Mitchell Symons

CASTAWAYS

THE PRESENTERS

Roy Plomley (1942–1985)

Michael Parkinson (1986–1988)

Sue Lawley (1988–2006)

Kirsty Young (2006–present)

THE ANNIVERSARY GUESTS

The very first guest was Vic Oliver, on 29 January 1942.

The tenth-anniversary guest was actress Jeanne de Casalis, on 29 January 1952.

The twentieth-anniversary guest was actor Sir John Gielgud, on 29 January 1962.

The thirtieth-anniversary guest was opera singer Stuart Burrows, on 29 January 1972.

The fortieth-anniversary guest was musician Paul McCartney, on 30 January 1982.

The fiftieth-anniversary guest was Prime Minister John Major, on 26 January 1992.

The sixtieth-anniversary guest was Viscount Linley, on 3 February 2002.

The seventieth-anniversary guest was naturalist Sir David Attenborough, on 29 January 2012.

THE FIRST TEN CASTAWAYS
(IN 1942)

Vic Oliver (Comedian)

James Agate (Critic)

Commander Campbell (Mariner and Explorer)

C. B. Cochran (Showman)

Pat Kirkwood (Actress)

Jack Hylton (Bandleader)

Captain Dingle (Explorer)

Joan Jay (Fashion Glamour Girl)

The Rev. Canon W. H. Elliott
(Precentor of the Chapels Royal)

Arthur Askey (Comedian)

THE TWO PEOPLE WHO
WERE ON FOUR TIMES

Arthur Askey (1942, 1955, 1968, 1980)

Sir David Attenborough (1957, 1979, 1998, 2012)

ALL THE PEOPLE WHO WERE ON THREE TIMES

Petula Clark (1951, 1982, 1995)

Michael Crawford (1971, 1978, 1999)

Sir David Frost (1963, 1971, 2005)

Robertson Hare (1951, 1959, 1972)

Stanley Holloway (1951, 1962, 1975) – already 60 on the first occasion

Barry Humphries (1973, 2009 and as Dame Edna Everage 1988)

Dame Celia Johnson (1945, 1954, 1975)

Sir Charles Mackerras (1959, 1975, 1999)

Sir John Mills (1951, 1973, 2000)

Sir John Mortimer (1968, 1982, 2001)

Peter Ustinov (1951, 1956, 1977)

Sir Terry Wogan (1983, 1988, 2012)

ALL THE PEOPLE WHO WERE ON TWICE

Kingsley Amis (1961, 1986)

Julie Andrews (1964, 1992)

John Arlott (1953, 1975)

Sir Frederick Ashton (1959, 1981)

Richard Attenborough (1952, 1964)

Isobel Baillie (1955, 1970)

Dame Beryl Bainbridge (1986, 2008)

(ALL THE PEOPLE WHO WERE ON TWICE – *cont.*)

Dame Janet Baker (1968, 1982)

Dame Joan Bakewell (1972, 2009)

Jill Balcon (1945, 2007)

John Barry (1967, 1999)

Richard Rodney Bennett (1968, 1997)

Stan Barstow (1964, 1986)

Tony Bennett (1972, 1987)

Sir John Betjeman (1954, 1975)

John Bird (1968, 2000) (actor and comedian)

Cilla Black (1964, 1988)

Peter Blake (1979, 1997)

Sir Arthur Bliss (1959, 1972)

Claire Bloom (1955, 1982)

Dirk Bogarde (1964, 1989)

Sir Chris Bonington (1973, 1999)

Sir Adrian Boult (1960, 1979)

Julian Bream (1961, 1983)

Richard Briers (1967, 2000)

Raymond Briggs (1983, 2005)

Dave Brubeck (1959, 1999)

Dora Bryan (1956, 1987)

Sir Arthur Bryant (1960, 1979)

Marti Caine (1979, 1991)

Ian Carmichael (1958, 1979)

Robert Carrier (1965, 1987)

Jackie Charlton (1972, 1996)

George Chisholm (1963, 1982)

John Cleese (1971, 1997)

John Clements (1951, 1964)

Sebastian Coe (1981, 2009)

Joan Collins (1961, 1989)

Fay Compton (1952, 1974)

Billy Connolly (1977, 2001)

Dame Gladys Cooper (1952, 1967)

Ronnie Corbett (1971, 2007)

Cicely Courtneidge (1951, 1957)

Quentin Crewe (1984, 1996)

Sinéad Cusack (1983, 2002)

John Dankworth (1957, 1986)

Sir Robin Day (1969, 1990)

Cecil Day-Lewis (1960, 1968)

Dame Ninette de Valois (1966, 1991)

Dame Judi Dench (1972, 1998)

Monica Dickens (1951, 1970)

David Dimbleby (1974, 2008)

Sacha Distel (1971, 2004)

Ken Dodd (1963, 1990)

Sir Anton Dolin (1955, 1982)

Diana Dors (1961, 1981)

Sir Anthony Dowell (1975, 1998)

Margaret Drabble (1968, 2001)

Jimmy Edwards (1951, 1961)

Mary Ellis (1954, 1982)

Gwen Ffrangcon-Davies (1962, 1988)

Dame Gracie Fields (1951, 1961)

(ALL THE PEOPLE WHO WERE ON TWICE – *cont.*)

Sir Ranulph Fiennes (1983, 1994)

Michael Flanders (1965, and 1958 with Donald Swann)

Bruce Forsyth (1962, 1996)

Dick Francis (1967, 1998)

Lady Antonia Fraser (1969, 2008)

Sir John Gielgud (1962, 1981)

Hermione Gingold (1952, 1969)

Tito Gobbi (1958, 1979)

Rumer Godden (1975, 1996)

Stewart Granger (1945, 1981)

Frederick Grisewood (1945, 1960)

Sir Alec Guinness (1960, 1977)

Henry Hall (1952, 1968)

Sir Peter Hall (1965, 1983)

Joan Hammond (1951, 1970)

Sheila Hancock (1965, 2000)

Robert Hardy (1978, 2011)

Earl of Harewood (1965, 1981)

Rolf Harris (1967, 1999)

Tom Harrisson (1943, 1972)

Lord Healey (1978, 2009)

Sir Robert Helpmann (1953, 1978)

Sir Alan P. Herbert (1955, 1970)

Jack Higgins (1981, 2006)

Graham Hill (1963, 1974)

Susan Hill (1974, 1996)

Earl Hines (1957, 1980)

Thora Hird (1968, 1989)

Valerie Hobson (1945, 1954)

Michael Holroyd (1977, 2000)

Sir Michael Hordern (1967, 1987)

Kenneth Horne (1961, and 1952 with Richard Murdoch)

Elizabeth Jane Howard (1972, 1995)

Frankie Howerd (1959, 1982)

Bobby Howes (1945, 1954)

Sir Fred Hoyle (1954, 1986)

David Hughes (1956, 1970)

Richard Ingrams (1972, 2008)

Jeremy Irons (1986, 2006)

Glenda Jackson (1971, 1997)

Clive James (1980, 2000)

P. D. James (1982, 2002)

Eileen Joyce (1945, 1955)

Thomas Keneally (1983, 2007)

Deborah Kerr (1945, 1977)

Pat Kirkwood (1942, 1955)

Robin Knox-Johnston (1970, 1990)

Dame Cleo Laine (1958, 1997)

Sir Osbert Lancaster (1955, 1979)

Evelyn Laye (1954, 1969)

C. A. Lejeune (1942, 1957)

Alvar Liddell (1945, 1969)

John Lill (1970, 2001)

Sir Andrew Lloyd Webber (1973, 1999)

Margaret Lockwood (1951, 1972)

(ALL THE PEOPLE WHO WERE ON TWICE – *cont.*)

Elizabeth, Countess of Longford (1979, 2002)

Jacques Loussier (1967, 1987)

Joanna Lumley (1987, 2007)

Moura Lympany (1957, 1979)

Dame Vera Lynn (1951, 1989)

Humphrey Lyttelton (1956, 2006)

Lorin Maazel (1971, 2005)

George MacDonald Fraser (1978, 2001)

Sir Fitzroy MacLean (1962, 1981)

Dame Alicia Markova (1958, 2002)

George Martin (1982, 1995)

James Mason (1961, 1981)

Sir Peter Maxwell Davies (1983, 2005)

Sir Robert Mayer (1965, 1979)

Kenneth McKellar (1961, 1977)

Sir Ian McKellen (1971, 2003)

Virginia McKenna (1966, 2004)

Yehudi Menuhin (1955, 1977)

Sir Jonathan Miller (1971, 2005)

Spike Milligan (1956, 1978)

Warren Mitchell (1967, 1999)

Bob Monkhouse (1998, and 1955 with Denis Goodwin)

Gerald Moore (1951, 1967)

Kenneth More (1956, 1969)

Dr Desmond Morris (1968, 2004)

Jan Morris (1983, 2002)

Peggy Mount (1968, 1996)

Castaways

Malcolm Muggeridge (1956, 1981)

Frank Muir (1976, and 1960 with Denis Norden)

Barbara Mullen (1946, 1971)

Richard Murdoch (1961, and 1952 with Kenneth Horne)

Boyd Neel (1952, 1963)

Peter Nichols (1981, 2000)

John Julius Norwich (1975, 1997)

Sir Trevor Nunn (1968, 2003)

Edna O'Brien (1987, 2007)

John Ogdon (1967, 1989)

Vic Oliver (1942, 1955)

John Osborne (1959, 1982)

Alan Parker (1986, 2000)

Sir Peter Pears (1969, 1983)

Paco Peña (1978, 1999)

Siân Phillips (1979, 1997)

John Piper (1970, 1983)

Roy Plomley (1942, 1958)

Dame Joan Plowright (1981, 2006)

Dennis Potter (1977, 1988)

Dilys Powell (1957, 1991)

Michael Powell (1942, and 1980 with Emeric Pressburger)

André Previn (1967, 1996)

James Prior (1975, 1987)

Anthony Quayle (1957, 1976)

Steve Race (1959, 1971)

Frederic Raphael (1981, 2006)

Sir Simon Rattle (1978, 2008)

(ALL THE PEOPLE WHO WERE ON TWICE – *cont.*)

Ralph Reader (1944, 1961)

Sir Michael Redgrave (1945, 1955)

Brian Reece (1953, 1961)

Beryl Reid (1963, 1983)

Sir Tim Rice (1976, 2004)

Sir Ralph Richardson (1953, 1979)

John Ridgway (1986, and 1966 with Chay Blyth)

Sir Brian Rix (1960, 2009)

Alec Robertson (1957, 1972)

Sir Bobby Robson (1986, 2004)

Patricia Routledge (1974, 1999)

Lord Sainsbury (1992, 2004)

Vidal Sassoon (1970, 2011)

John Schlesinger (1967, 1991)

Peter Scott (1951, 1961)

Ronald Searle (1959, 2005)

Sir Harry Secombe (1956, 1997)

Phyllis Sellick (2002, and 1963 with her husband, Cyril Smith)

Athene Seyler (1956, 1988)

David Shepherd (1971, 1999)

Donald Sinden (1956, 1982)

Stephen Sondheim (1980, 2000)

Sir Stephen Spender (1962, 1989)

Terence Stamp (1987, 2006)

Tommy Steele (1957, 1969)

James Stewart (1974, 1983)

Castaways

Christopher Stone (1952, 1957)

Eric Sykes (1957, 1997)

Jimmy Tarbuck (1972, 2004)

Barbara Taylor Bradford (1985, 2003)

Dame Maggie Teyte (1951, 1968)

Irene Thomas (1979, 1997)

Terry Thomas (1956, 1970)

Sir Michael Tippett (1968, 1985)

Paul Tortelier (1964, 1984)

Dame Eva Turner (1956, 1982)

Sir Laurens van der Post (1959, 1996)

Sir William Walton (1965, 1982)

Elsie and Doris Waters (1958, 1972)

Elisabeth Welch (1952, 1990)

Fay Weldon (1980, 2010)

Sir Arnold Wesker (1966, 2006)

Katharine Whitehorn (1966, 2005)

June Whitfield (1973, 1990)

Emlyn Williams (1942, 1975)

Kenneth Williams (1961, 1987)

Baroness Shirley Williams (1986, 2006)

Barbara Windsor (1970, 1990)

Sir Norman Wisdom (1953, 2000)

Ernie Wise (1990, and 1966 with Eric Morecambe)

Victoria Wood (1987, 2007)

David Wynne (1964, 1997)

Franco Zeffirelli (1978, 2003)

ALL THE HUSBANDS AND WIVES WHO HAVE APPEARED ON THE SHOW

The two people in question were not necessarily married to each other *at the time of* their appearance. The first one to appear on the programme is listed first.

Pat Kirkwood (1942 and 1955) and Hubert Gregg (1966)

Vic Oliver (1942 and 1955) and Sarah Churchill (1966)

Jill Balcon (1945 and 2007) and Cecil Day-Lewis (1960 and 1968)

Stewart Granger (1945) and Jean Simmons (1975)

Dame Celia Johnson (1945, 1954 and 1975) and Peter Fleming (1951)

Sir Michael Redgrave (1945 and 1955) and Rachel Kempson, Lady Redgrave (1989)

Cicely Courtneidge (1951 and 1957) and Jack Hulbert (1952)

Kay Hammond (February 1951) and John Clements (March 1951 and 1964)

Peter Scott (1951 and 1961) and Elizabeth Jane Howard (1972 and 1995)

Richard Attenborough (1952 and 1964) and Sheila Sim (1953)

Hermione Gingold (1952 and 1969) and Eric Maschwitz (1956)

Sonnie Hale (1952) and Jessie Matthews (1954)

Sonnie Hale (1952) and Evelyn Laye (1954 and 1969)

Esmond Knight (1952) and Nora Swinburne (1953)

Roger Livesey (1952) and Ursula Jeans (1955)

Anna Neagle (1952) and Herbert Wilcox (1955)

Dame Sybil Thorndike (1952) and Sir Lewis Casson (1965)

Pamela Kellino (1953) and James Mason (1961 and 1981)

Margaret Leighton (1954) and Laurence Harvey (1955)

Castaways

Margaret Leighton (1954) and Michael Wilding (1961)

Claire Bloom (1955 and 1982) and Rod Steiger (1999)

Barbara Kelly (May 1955) and Bernard Braden (December 1955)

Sir Osbert Lancaster (1955 and 1979) and Anne Scott-James (2004)

Leslie Caron (1956) and Sir Peter Hall (1965 and 1983)

Bebe Daniels (1956) and Ben Lyon (1958)

Janette Scott (1956) and Mel Tormé (1976)

John Dankworth (1957 and 1986) and Dame Cleo Laine (1958 and 1997)

Peter Sellers (1957) and Britt Ekland (1994)

Moira Shearer (1957) and Ludovic Kennedy (1971)

John Osborne (1959 and 1982) and Mary Ure (1961)

John Osborne (1959 and 1982) and Jill Bennett (1969)

Ronald Searle (1959 and 2005) and Kaye Webb (1993)

Anthony Newley (1960) and Joan Collins (1961 and 1989)

Michael Somes (1960) and Antoinette Sibley (1974)

Kingsley Amis (1961 and 1986) and Elizabeth Jane Howard (1972 and 1995)

Coral Browne (1961) and Vincent Price (1969)

Roy Hay (1961) and Frances Perry (1980)

Hattie Jacques (1961) and John Le Mesurier (1973)

Pamela Hansford Johnson (1962) and C. P. Snow (1975)

Sir Stephen Spender (1962 and 1989) and Natasha Spender (2007)

Group Captain Leonard Cheshire (1963) and Sue Ryder (1987)

Dorothy Squires (1963) and Roger Moore (1981)

Sir Peter Hall (1965 and 1983) and Maria Ewing (1999)

Sheila Hancock (1965 and 2000) and John Thaw (1990)

Earl of Harewood (1965 and 1981) and Marion Stein (1973)

(HUSBANDS AND WIVES WHO HAVE APPEARED ON THE SHOW – *cont.*)

MacDonald Hastings (1965) and Anne Scott-James (2004)

Hayley Mills (1965) and Roy Boulting (with John Boulting, 1974)

Harold Pinter (1965) and Lady Antonia Fraser (1969 and 2008)

Sir William Walton (1965 and 1982) and Susana Walton (2002)

Virginia McKenna (1966 and 2004) and Denholm Elliott (1974)

Lilli Palmer (1966) and Rex Harrison (1979)

Katharine Whitehorn (1966 and 2005) and Gavin Lyall (1976)

André Previn (1967 and 1996) and Anne-Sophie Mutter (1986)

Jeremy Thorpe (1967) and Marion Stein (1973)

Margaret Drabble (1968 and 2001) and Michael Holroyd (1977 and 2000)

Sir Trevor Nunn (1968 and 2003) and Janet Suzman (1978)

Dr Roy Strong (1970) and Julia Trevelyan Oman (1971)

Robert Bolt (1971) and Sarah Miles (1990)

Maggie Smith (1972) and Robert Stephens (1979)

Lord Longford (1975) and Elizabeth, Countess of Longford (1979 and 2002)

Julia Foster (1976) and Bruce Fogle (2001)

Billy Connolly (1977 and 2001) and Pamela Stephenson (1982)

Shirley Conran (1977) and Sir Terence Conran (1996)

Jacqueline du Pré (1977) and Daniel Barenboim (2006)

Jane Grigson (1978) and Geoffrey Grigson (1982)

Josephine Barstow (1979) and Terry Hands (1981)

Roald Dahl (1979) and Patricia Neal (1988)

Earl of Snowdon (1980) and Princess Margaret (1981)

Timothy West (1980) and Prunella Scales (1992)

Jeffrey Archer (1981) and Mary Archer (1988)

Castaways

Daniel Massey (1981) and Penelope Wilton (2008)

Sinéad Cusack (1983 and 2002) and Jeremy Irons (1986 and 2006)

Madhur Jaffrey (1985) and Saeed Jaffrey (1997)

Phil Edmonds (1986) and Frances Edmonds (1987)

Maureen Lipman (1986) and Jack Rosenthal (1998)

Jeremy Lloyd (January 1987) and Joanna Lumley (September 1987 and 2007)

Jane Asher (1988) and Gerald Scarfe (1989)

Anita Dobson (1988) and Brian May (2002)

Neil Kinnock (1988) and Glenys Kinnock (1994)

Lady Lucinda Lambton (1989) and Sir Peregrine Worsthorne (1992)

John Major (1992) and Dame Norma Major (2000)

Lord Norman Tebbit (1992) and Lady Margaret Tebbit (1995)

Alison Steadman (1995) and Mike Leigh (1997)

Harold Evans (April 2000) and Tina Brown (December 2000)

Meera Syal (2003) and Sanjeev Bhaskar (2008)

~~~~~~

Vivien Leigh (1952) and Dame Joan Plowright (1981 and 2006) were both married to Sir Laurence Olivier.

Pamela Brown (1953) lived with Michael Powell (1942 and 1980 – the latter appearance was with film producer Emeric Pressburger) until her death in 1975.

Nigel Balchin (1954) and Michael Ayrton (1955) were both married to Elisabeth Walshe.

Peter Sellers (1957) and Sir David Frost (1963, 1971 and 2005) were both married to Lynne Frederick.

Cyril Connolly (1966) and George Weidenfeld (1990) were both married to Barbara Skelton.

Maya Angelou (1987) and Germaine Greer (1988) were both married to Paul du Feu.

ALL THE FATHERS AND SONS WHO HAVE APPEARED ON THE SHOW

Ted Kavanagh (1951) and P. J. Kavanagh (1974)

Ted Ray (1952) and Robin Ray (1974)

Richard Dimbleby (1958) and David Dimbleby (1974 and 2008)

Kingsley Amis (1961 and 1986) and Martin Amis (1996)

Robert Morley (1962) and Sheridan Morley (1974)

MacDonald Hastings (1965) and Max Hastings (1986)

Raymond Postgate (1968) and Oliver Postgate (2007)

Marquess of Bath (1975) and Marquess of Bath (2001)

Earl of Snowdon (1980) and Viscount Linley (2002)

Sir Terence Conran (1996) and Jasper Conran (1995)*

* This is the only example of a father going on the show *after* his son had been on.

ALL THE FATHERS AND DAUGHTERS WHO HAVE APPEARED ON THE SHOW

Bobby Howes (1945 and 1954) and Sally Ann Howes (1951)

Sir Michael Redgrave (1945 and 1955) and Vanessa Redgrave (1964)

Sir Michael Redgrave (1945 and 1955) and Lynn Redgrave (1970)

Sir John Mills (1951, 1973 and 2000) and Hayley Mills (1965)

Nigel Balchin (1954) and Dr Penelope Leach (1992)

Sir Michael Balcon (1961) and Jill Balcon (1945 and 2007)*

Lord Longford (1975) and Lady Antonia Fraser (1969 and 2008)*

Lord Longford (1975) and Rachel Billington (1983)

Eric Thompson (1975) and Emma Thompson (2010)

Nigel Lawson (1989) and Nigella Lawson (2003)

* The daughter went on the show *before* her father.

ALL THE MOTHERS AND SONS WHO HAVE APPEARED ON THE SHOW

Lady Diana Cooper (1969) and John Julius Norwich (1975 and 1997)

Shirley Conran (1977) and Jasper Conran (1995)

Princess Margaret (1981) and Viscount Linley (2002)

Anne Scott-James (2004) and Max Hastings (1986)*

* This is the only example of a mother going on the show *after* her son.

ALL THE MOTHERS AND DAUGHTERS WHO HAVE APPEARED ON THE SHOW

Thora Hird (1968 and 1989) and Janette Scott (1956)

Elizabeth, Countess of Longford (1979 and 2002) and Lady Antonia Fraser (1969 and 2008)

Elizabeth, Countess of Longford (1979 and 2002) and Rachel Billington (1983)*

Rachel Kempson, Lady Redgrave (1989) and Vanessa Redgrave (1964)

Rachel Kempson, Lady Redgrave (1989) and Lynn Redgrave (1970)

* This is the only example of a mother going on the show *before* her daughter.

ALL THE PAIRS OF BROTHERS WHO HAVE APPEARED ON THE SHOW

Peter Fleming (1951) and Ian Fleming (1963)

Richard Attenborough (1952, 1964) and Sir David Attenborough (1957, 1979, 1998, 2012)

Sir John Gielgud (January 1962, 1981) and Val Gielgud (November 1962)

William Douglas-Home (1964) and Sir Alec Douglas-Home (1977)

David Kossoff (1964) and Alan Keith (1971)

Sir Andrew Lloyd Webber (1973 and 1999) and Julian Lloyd Webber (1981)

Edward Fox (1979) and James Fox (1983)

Sir Lew Grade (1987) and Sir Bernard Delfont (1991)

ALL THE PAIRS OF SISTERS WHO HAVE APPEARED ON THE SHOW

Isabel Jeans (1953) and Ursula Jeans (1955)

Hermione Baddeley (1959) and Angela Baddeley (1974)

Joan Collins (1961, 1989) and Jackie Collins (1986)

Vanessa Redgrave (1964) and Lynn Redgrave (1970)

Sarah Churchill (1966) and Mary, Lady Soames (1992)

Margaret Drabble (1968 and 2001) and A. S. Byatt (1991)

Lady Antonia Fraser (1969 and 2008) and Rachel Billington (1983)

Not two, but *three* sisters who have appeared on the show: Jessica Mitford (1977), the Duchess of Devonshire (with her husband in 1982) and Diana, Lady Mosley (1989).

ALL THE PAIRS OF BROTHER AND SISTER WHO HAVE APPEARED ON THE SHOW

Binnie Hale (October 1952) and Sonnie Hale (November 1952)

Sir Compton Mackenzie (February 1952) and Fay Compton (May 1952 and 1974)

Jack Warner (1953) and Elsie and Doris Waters (1958 and 1972)

Yehudi Menuhin (1955 and 1977) and Hephzibah Menuhin (1958)

Stirling Moss (1956) and Pat Moss (1963)

Anna Massey (1961) and Daniel Massey (1981)

Lord Rothschild (1984) and Miriam Rothschild (1989)

FATHERS-IN-LAW AND SONS-IN-LAW WHO HAVE APPEARED ON THE SHOW

Eric Barker (1957) and Anthony Hopkins (1985)

Sir Michael Balcon (1961) and Cecil Day-Lewis (1960)*

Sir Stephen Spender (1962 and 1989) and Barry Humphries (1973 and 2009)

Lord Longford (1975) and Harold Pinter (1965)*

Roy Dotrice (1977) and Edward Woodward (1974)*

David Puttnam (1984) and Loyd Grossman (1997)

* In each case, the son-in-law went on the show *before* the father-in-law.

Clement Freud (1967) was the father of Emma Freud, the partner of Richard Curtis (1999).

MOTHERS-IN-LAW AND SONS-IN-LAW WHO HAVE APPEARED ON THE SHOW

Dorothy Dickson (1952) and Anthony Quayle (1957 and 1976)

Dame Gladys Cooper (1952 and 1967) and Robert Morley (1962)

Thora Hird (1968 and 1989) and Mel Tormé (1976)

Elizabeth, Countess of Longford (1979 and 2002) and Harold Pinter (1965)

Maureen O'Sullivan (1974) and André Previn (1967 and 1996)*

Natasha Spender (2007) and Barry Humphries (1973 and 2009)*

* In each case, the son-in-law went on the show *before* the mother-in-law.

GRANDMOTHER AND GRANDSON WHO HAVE APPEARED ON THE SHOW

Dame Gladys Cooper (1952 and 1967) and Sheridan Morley (1974)

BROTHERS-IN-LAW AND SISTERS-IN-LAW WHO HAVE APPEARED ON THE SHOW

Roger Livesey (1952) and Isabel Jeans (1953)

Binnie Hale (1952) and Jessie Matthews (1954)

Binnie Hale (1952) and Evelyn Laye (1954 and 1969)

Diane Cilento (1960) and Peter Shaffer (1979)

Anthony Newley (1960) and Jackie Collins (1986)

Lord Longford (1975) and Anthony Powell (1976)

Patrick Lichfield (1981) and the Duke of Westminster (1995)

Maurice Saatchi (1995) and Nigella Lawson (2003)

Sir Terence Conran (1996) and Antonio Carluccio (2008)

Nick Hornby (2003) and Robert Harris (2010)

Louis Kentner (1962) shared a mother-in-law – Evelyn Suart – with Yehudi Menuhin (1955, 1977).

UNCLES AND NEPHEWS WHO HAVE APPEARED ON THE SHOW

Leslie Howard (1942) and Alan Howard (1981)

Alec Waugh (1975) and Auberon Waugh (1986)

Sir Lew Grade (1987) and Michael Grade (1992)

Sir Bernard Delfont (1991) and Michael Grade (1992)

UNCLE AND NIECE WHO HAVE APPEARED ON THE SHOW

Christopher Lee (1995) and Dame Harriet Walter (2011)

COUSINS WHO HAVE BEEN ON THE SHOW

Margaret Rutherford (1953) and Tony Benn (1989)

Terry Thomas (1956, 1970) and Richard Briers (1967, 2000)

Ernest Thesiger (1959) and Wilfred Thesiger (1979)

Ian Fleming (1963) and Christopher Lee (1995)

Earl of Harewood (1965, 1981) and Princess Margaret (1981)

Sir Ranulph Fiennes (1983, 1994) and Ralph Fiennes (1999)

Antony Sher (1987) and Ronald Harwood (2000)

Christabel Bielenberg (1992) and Viscount Rothermere (1996)

GROOMS AND BEST MEN WHO HAVE BEEN ON THE SHOW

GROOM	BEST MAN
Spike Milligan (1956, 1978)	George Martin (1982, 1995)
Tommy Steele (1957, 1969)	Lionel Bart (1960)
Rowan Atkinson (1988)	Stephen Fry (1988)
Marco Pierre White (1991)	Michael Winner (2005)
Chris Evans (2005)	Danny Baker (2011)
Howard Jacobson (2011)	Melvyn Bragg (1976)

OTHER CONNECTIONS BETWEEN CASTAWAYS

The daughter of Dame Daphne du Maurier (1977) married the son of Viscount Montgomery of Alamein (1969).

While in prison, T. Dan Smith (1968) was involved in amateur dramatics and encouraged fellow prisoner Leslie Grantham (1989) to pursue a career as a professional actor. (Grantham was later to star in the BBC soap opera *EastEnders*.)

The GP father of Nicholas Parsons (2007) delivered Margaret Thatcher (1978).

David Tennant (2009) was born David John McDonald but had to change his name because there was another David McDonald already on the books of the actors' union Equity. So he adopted the professional name 'Tennant' – inspired by Neil Tennant (2007) of the Pet Shop Boys, after reading a copy of *Smash Hits* magazine.

Barbara Pym (1978)'s career was revived in 1977 when two prominent writers, Lord David Cecil (1969) and Philip Larkin (1976), nominated her as the most underrated writer of the century.

Hammond Innes (1972) bequeathed Celia Imrie (2011) his London house. He'd been a friend of her mother.

In 1959, Lord Soper (1966) was preaching at a meeting in Ballymena, Northern Ireland, which was also attended by the Rev. Ian Paisley (1988). A Bible was hurled from the crowd and hit Lord Soper on the head after he described Paisley as an 'intellectual rabbit'. Paisley was subsequently fined for disturbing the peace.

(OTHER CONNECTIONS BETWEEN CASTAWAYS – *cont.*)

After Sir John Gielgud (1962 and 1981) was arrested for 'persistently importuning male persons for immoral purposes', Edward Chapman (1968) started a petition to force him to resign from Equity. Sir Laurence Olivier reportedly threw Chapman out of his dressing room when he asked him to sign the petition.

Sir A. J. Ayer (1984) was the stepfather of Nigella Lawson (2003).

Jane Asher (1988) was engaged to Paul McCartney (1982).

PAIRS OF CASTAWAYS WHO DIED ON THE SAME DAY

Jim Laker and Otto Preminger – 23 April 1986

Cecil Day-Lewis and Margaret Rutherford – 22 May 1972

Bernard Miles and Dame Peggy Ashcroft – 14 June 1991

Benny Green and Maureen O'Sullivan – 22 June 1998

Sir John Gielgud and Barbara Cartland – 21 May 2000

Alistair Cooke and Hubert Gregg – 30 March 2004

Patricia Neal and Jack Parnell – 8 August 2010

CASTAWAYS' UNUSUAL OCCUPATIONS

Dr Gwen Adshead (2010), Forensic Psychotherapist

Valentine Britten (1956), BBC Gramophone Librarian

John Brooke-Little (1974), Richmond Herald of Arms

Peter Bull (1983), Actor, Teddy Bear Expert

Charlie Cairoli (1976), Clown

Stanley Dangerfield (1975), Dog Show Judge

Vivian de Gurr St George (1954), Piccadilly Shoeblack

Fred Dibnah (1991), Steeplejack

Lieutenant-Colonel Sir Vivian Dunn (1971), former Music Director of Royal Marines

Percy Edwards (1957), Animal Imitator

Eileen Fowler (1974), Physical Exercise Instructor

Oleg Gordievsky (2008), KGB Colonel

Rev. John Graham (2011), Crossword Compiler

Dr W. Grey Walter (1961), Roboticist

Rosina Harrison (1976), Lady Astor's Lady's Maid

Christopher Hopper (1966), Manager of the Royal Albert Hall

Maurice Jacobson (1969), Music Festivals Adjudicator

Heather Jenner (1967), Owner of a Marriage Bureau

C. A. Joyce (1971), Prison Worker

Harry Loman (1973), Stage-door Keeper

Emily MacManus (1966), Retired Matron

Robert Marx (1965), Underwater Archaeologist

Alan Pegler (1969), Owner of the *Flying Scotsman*

Philippe Petit (2005), High-wire Artist and Acrobat

(CASTAWAYS' UNUSUAL OCCUPATIONS – *cont.*)

Nicolai Poliakoff (1963), Coco the Clown

Percy Press (1974), Punch and Judy Puppeteer

T. R. Robinson (1963), Horologist

Clive Stafford Smith (2004), Death-row Lawyer

Doris Stokes (1985), Medium

Irene Thomas (1979 and 1997), *Brain of Britain* Radio Personality

Stanley Unwin (1962), Inventor of Nonsense Language, Comedian

Leslie Welch (1955), Memory Expert

Barbara Woodhouse (1980), Dog Trainer

Maurice Woodruff (1971), Psychic, Clairvoyant, Astrologer

Lavinia Young (1964), Matron of
Westminster Hospital

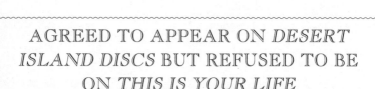

AGREED TO APPEAR ON *DESERT ISLAND DISCS* BUT REFUSED TO BE ON *THIS IS YOUR LIFE*

Danny Blanchflower (1960): he later explained, 'I consider this programme [*This Is Your Life*] an invasion of privacy.'

Richard Gordon (1971): on hearing the words 'This is your life', he replied, 'Oh balls, it's not,' but he did agree to go on the show the following week.

Roger Moore (1981): 'I couldn't bear to think of all those cross ex-wives.'

LIVED FOR AT LEAST 60 YEARS AFTER (FIRST) GOING ON THE PROGRAMME

Pat Kirkwood, 1942 (died 2007)

Jill Balcon, 1945 (died 2009)

Deborah Kerr, 1945 (died 2007)

Nova Pilbeam, 1945

Petula Clark, 1951

Sally Ann Howes, 1951

Jean Kent, 1951

Dame Vera Lynn, 1951

LIVED FOR AT LEAST 50 YEARS AFTER (FIRST) GOING ON THE PROGRAMME

Larry Adler, 1951 (died 2001)

Phyllis Calvert, 1951 (died 2002)

Constance Cummings, 1951 (died 2005)

Sir John Mills, 1951 (died 2005)

Peter Ustinov, 1951 (died 2004)

Richard Attenborough, 1952

Dulcie Gray, 1952 (died 2011)

Elisabeth Welch, 1952 (died 2003)

Googie Withers, 1952 (died 2011)

Belita, 1953 (died 2005)

Duncan Carse, 1953 (died 2004)

Jean Carson, 1953 (died 2005)

Peggy Cummins, 1953

Yolande Donlan, 1953

Moira Lister, 1953 (died 2007)

Sheila Sim, 1953

Richard Todd, 1953 (died 2009)

Lizbeth Webb, 1953

Sir Norman Wisdom, 1953 (died 2010)

(LIVED FOR 50 YEARS AFTER GOING ON THE PROGRAMME – *cont.*)

Claire Bloom, 1955

Max Bygraves, 1955

Christopher Chataway, 1955

Dora Bryan, 1956

Humphrey Lyttelton, 1956 (died 2008)

Stirling Moss, 1956

Donald Sinden, 1956

Sir David Attenborough, 1957

Tommy Steele, 1957

Eric Sykes, 1957 (died 2012)

Blanche Thebom, 1957 (died 2010)

Harry Belafonte, 1958

Ian Carmichael, 1958 (died 2010)

Dame Beryl Grey, 1958

Edmundo Ros, 1958 (died 2011)

Elizabeth Seal, 1958

Wendy Toye, 1958 (died 2010)

Chris Barber, 1959

Dave Brubeck, 1959

Judy Grinham, 1959

Sir Charles Mackerras, 1959 (died 2010)

Ronald Searle, 1959 (died 2011)

Joan Sutherland, 1959 (died 2010)

Sylvia Syms, 1959

Shirley Bassey, 1960

Diane Cilento, 1960 (died 2011)

John Freeman, 1960

Anne Heywood, 1960

Herbert Lom, 1960

Sir Bernard Lovell, 1960 (died 2012)

Denis Norden, 1960

Cliff Richard, 1960

Sir Brian Rix, 1960

Pat Suzuki, 1960

Marty Wilde, 1960

The Beverley Sisters, 1961

Julian Bream, 1961

Joan Collins, 1961

Ann Haydon-Jones, 1961

Barbara Jefford, 1961

Leslie Phillips, 1962

~~~~~~~~

Anna Massey died on 3 July 2011, precisely one week before the fiftieth anniversary of her appearance on the show, 10 July 1961.

PEOPLE WHO WERE OVER 90 WHEN THEY (LAST) WENT ON THE SHOW

The music patron Sir Robert Mayer appeared in 1979, three days before his hundredth birthday. He went on to live to 105. The only other *Desert Island Discs* castaway to reach such a great age was the harpist Sidonie Goossens, who appeared on the show in 1955 and went on to live until 2004. Born in 1899, she not only lived to 105, but also lived in three centuries.

Sir Robert Mayer, 99 in 1979

Athene Seyler, 99 in 1988

Gwen Ffrangcon-Davies, 97 in 1998

Cecil Lewis, 93 in 1991

Naomi Mitchison, 93 in 1991

Lord Shinwell, 93 in 1978

Kitty Godfree, 91 in 1987

Lord Healey, 91 in 2009

Dame Alicia Markova, 91 in 2002

Betty Driver, 90 in 2011

Lewis Gilbert, 90 in 2010

Rev. John Graham, 90 in 2011

Tony Iveson, 90 in 2011

June Spencer, 90 in 2010

Dame Fanny Waterman, 90 in 2010

Sir Adrian Boult appeared on the programme for the second time on the eve of his ninetieth birthday in 1979.

Sir Laurens van der Post appeared on the programme for the second time a month before his ninetieth birthday (and, indeed, his death) in 1996.

Luise Rainer appeared on the programme at the age of 89 in 1999 and lived beyond her hundredth birthday.

PEOPLE WHO WERE UNDER 30 WHEN THEY (FIRST) WENT ON THE SHOW

Petula Clark, 18 in 1951

Janette Scott, 18 in 1956

Hayley Mills, 19 in 1965

Jill Balcon, 20 in 1945

Lillian Board, 20 in 1969

Adam Faith, 20 in 1961

Judy Grinham, 20 in 1959

Cliff Richard, 20 in 1960

Tommy Steele, 20 in 1957

Marty Wilde, 20 in 1960

Cilla Black, 21 in 1964

Sally Ann Howes, 21 in 1951

Pat Kirkwood, 21 in 1942

Geraldine McEwan, 21 in 1953

Daley Thompson, 21 in 1980

Ann Haydon-Jones, 22 in 1961

Belinda Lee, 22 in 1957

Ann Mallalieu, 22 in 1968

David Wilkie, 22 in 1976

Shirley Bassey, 23 in 1960

Joe Bugner, 23 in 1973

John Conteh, 23 in 1975

Robin Cousins, 23 in 1981

Anna Massey, 23 in 1961

Anne-Sophie Mutter, 23 in 1986 (her 23rd birthday)

Simon Rattle, 23 in 1978

Rita Tushingham, 23 in 1965

Virginia Wade, 23 in 1969

Claire Bloom, 24 in 1955

Robbie Brightwell, 24 in 1964

Christopher Chataway, 24 in 1955

Sebastian Coe, 24 in 1981

David Frost, 24 in 1963

June Paul, 24 in 1958

Clodagh Rodgers, 24 in 1971

Shirley Abicair, 25 in 1956

Leslie Caron, 25 in 1956

Alma Cogan, 25 in 1957

Steve Davis, 25 in 1983

Wing Commander Guy Gibson, 25 in 1944

Sir Andrew Lloyd Webber, 25 in 1973

Elizabeth Seal, 25 in 1958

Sylvia Syms, 25 in 1959

Chay Blyth, 26 in 1966

Will Carling, 26 in 1992

Diane Cilento, 26 in 1960

Gareth Edwards, 26 in 1973

Castaways

David Gower, 26 in 1984

David Hughes, 26 in 1956

John Lill, 26 in 1970

Stirling Moss, 26 in 1956

Jamie Oliver, 26 in 2001

Pat Smythe, 26 in 1955

John Williams, 26 in 1968

Mai Zetterling, 26 in 1951

Boy George, 27 in 1989

Julian Bream, 27 in 1961

Peggy Cummins, 27 in 1953

John Curry, 27 in 1977

Evelyn Glennie, 27 in 1993

Laurence Harvey, 27 in 1956

Anne Heywood, 27 in 1960

Frank Ifield, 27 in 1965

Lynn Redgrave, 27 in 1970

Vanessa Redgrave, 27 in 1964

Barry Sheene, 27 in 1977

Don Thompson, 27 in 1960

June Thorburn, 27 in 1959

Mary Ure, 27 in 1961

Julie Andrews, 28 in 1964

Chris Barber, 28 in 1959

Chris Brasher, 28 in 1957

Jim Clark, 28 in 1964

Joan Collins, 28 in 1961

Margaret Drabble, 28 in 1968

Valerie Hobson, 28 in 1945

Lucy Irvine, 28 in 1984

Lang Lang, 28 in 2010

Sara Leighton, 28 in 1966

Pat Moss, 28 in 1963

Anthony Newley, 28 in 1960

Sir Trevor Nunn, 28 in 1968

Alan Pascoe, 28 in 1976

Captain John Ridgway, 28 in 1966

June Ritchie, 28 in 1966

Tommy Simpson, 28 in 1966

Jenny Agutter, 29 in 1982

Richard Attenborough, 29 in 1952

Jean Carson, 29 in 1953

Leslie Crowther 29 in 1962

Diana Dors, 29 in 1961

Noel Edmonds, 29 in 1978

Georgie Fame, 29 in 1973 (three days before his thirtieth birthday)

Tony Greig, 29 in 1976

Nigel Kennedy, 29 in 1986

Eartha Kitt, 29 in 1956

Gary Lineker, 29 in 1990

Moira Lister, 29 in 1953

Millicent Martin, 29 in 1963

Alan Minter, 29 in 1980

John Osborne, 29 in 1959

Wayne Sleep, 29 in 1977

Pat Suzuki, 29 in 1960

Kenneth Tynan, 29 in 1956

Marco Pierre White, 29 in 1991

CLOSE TO DEATH

David Penhaligon died on 22 December 1986. The show he had pre-recorded was transmitted after his death on 22 March 1987.

John Ogdon died on 1 August 1989. The show he had pre-recorded was transmitted after his death on 24 September 1989.

DIED THE SAME YEAR

Wing Commander Guy Gibson VC, February 1944 (died September 1944)

Professor Francis Camps, June 1972 (died July 1972)

Dr Jacob Bronowski, January 1974 (died August 1974)

BBC Director-General Sir Ian Trethowan, March 1990 (died December 1990)

Sir Laurens van der Post, November 1996 (died December 1996)

Elizabeth, Countess of Longford, June 2002 (died October 2002)

Sacha Distel, February 2004 (died July 2004)

Betty Driver, January 2011 (died October 2011)

DIED THE FOLLOWING YEAR

Leslie Howard, 1942 (died 1943)

Elisabeth Schumann, 1951 (died 1952)

Tod Slaughter, 1955 (died 1956)

Dennis Brain, 1956 (died 1957)

Billy Mayerl, 1958 (died 1959)

Agnes Nicholls, 1958 (died 1959)

Ian Fleming, 1963 (died 1964)

Tommy Simpson, 1966 (died 1967)

Lillian Board, 1969 (died 1970)

Sir Alan P. Herbert, 1970 (died 1971)

William Hardcastle, 1974 (died 1975)

Graham Hill, 1974 (died 1975)

Natalie Wood, 1980 (died 1981)

Princess Grace of Monaco, 1981 (died 1982)

Sir Douglas Bader, 1981 (died 1982)

Sir Anton Dolin, 1982 (died 1983)

Sir William Walton, 1982 (died 1983)

Kenneth Williams, 1987 (died 1988)

Jean Rook, 1990 (died 1991)

Ronald Eyre, 1991 (died 1992)

Oliver Postgate, 2007 (died 2008)

Alan Sillitoe, 2009 (died 2010)

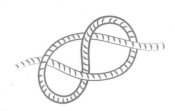

PEOPLE WHO WERE
CAST AWAY TOGETHER

Denis Compton and Bill Edrich (1951)

Michael Denison and Dulcie Gray (1952)

Richard Murdoch and Kenneth Horne (1952)

Bob Monkhouse and Denis Goodwin (1955)

Michael Flanders and Donald Swann (1958)

Elsie and Doris Waters (1958, 1972)

Ronnie Boyer and Jeanne Ravel (1959)

Frank Muir and Denis Norden (1960)

Michaela and Armand Denis (1960)

The Beverley Sisters (1961)*

Fanny and Johnnie Cradock (1962)

Frank Launder and Sidney Gilliat (1962)

Cyril Smith and Phyllis Sellick (1963)

Dorita and Pepe (1964)

Eric Morecambe and Ernie Wise (1966)

John Ridgway and Chay Blyth (1966)

Bob and Alf Pearson (1966)

Nina and Frederik (1966)

John and Roy Boulting (1974)

Raymond Mander and Joe Mitchenson (1978)

The Amadeus String Quartet (1978)

Dick Clement and Ian La Frenais (1979)

Beaux Arts Trio (1981)

The Duke and Duchess of Devonshire (1982)

N. Busch, J. Kuchmy, M. Parry and M. Wilson, members of the London Philharmonic Orchestra (1982)

Cindy Buxton and Annie Price (1983)

Albert and Michel Roux (1986)

Peter Fluck and Roger Law (1987)

* The Beverley Sisters – Joy, Babs and Teddy – all share the same birthday, 5 May. Joy was born on 5 May 1929 and her twin sisters were born on the same day in 1932.

~~~~~~~

Ventriloquist Peter Brough was cast away with Archie Andrews (1952), his 'dummy'.

ROYALS WHO HAVE APPEARED ON THE SHOW

Prince Chula Chakrabongse of Thailand (1960). He chose a private recording of a Thai wedding overture. His book was *Who's Who* and his luxury was a family photo album.

The Earl of Harewood, first cousin to the Queen, appeared twice, in 1965 and 1981. On his first appearance his book choice was an encyclopaedia, and on his second, he chose an anthology of poetry. On both occasions he chose a typewriter as his luxury item.

Princess Grace of Monaco (1981). Her book was *Plays* by George Kelly (her uncle) and her luxury was a pillow.

Lord Lichfield (1981). His book was a book with blank cork pages and his luxury was an astronomical telescope.

Princess Margaret (1981). Her book was *War and Peace* by Leo Tolstoy and her luxury was a piano.

Princess Michael of Kent (1984). Her book was *Histories* by Herodotus and her luxury was an oriental cat.

The Duchess of Kent (1989). She is the only castaway ever to choose The Beatles song *Maxwell's Silver Hammer*. Her book was a do-it-yourself manual and her luxury was a lamp with solar batteries.

Viscount Linley (2002). He appeared as David Linley and is the only castaway ever to choose a Serge Gainsbourg song – *Aux Armes Et Cetera*. His book was *The Art of Looking Sideways* by Alan Fletcher, and his luxury was a guitar.

OCCUPATIONS OF THE CASTAWAYS THROUGH THE DECADES

Some castaways appear in more than one category.

1940s

Academia and Education – 1

Art, Fashion and Design – 2

Business – 1

Medicine, Science and Engineering – 2

Military and Law – 5

Music – 5

Nature and Conservation – 1

Politics and Public Service – 3

Religion and Philosophy – 2

Sport – 2

Stage, Screen and Radio – 37

Travel and Exploration – 3

Writing – 15

1950s

Academia and Education – 1

Art, Fashion and Design – 8

Business – 3

Food and Drink – 1

Medicine, Science and Engineering – 2

Military and Law – 1

Music – 120

Nature and Conservation – 9

Politics and Public Service – 4

Prizewinner or Record Breaker – 3

Sport – 23

Stage, Screen and Radio – 258

Travel and Exploration – 7

Writing – 46

1960s

Academia and Education – 23

Art, Fashion and Design – 21

Business – 19

Food and Drink – 5

Medicine, Science and Engineering – 14

Military and Law – 11

Music – 140

Nature and Conservation – 13

Politics and Public Service – 25

Prizewinner or Record Breaker – 5

Religion and Philosophy – 7

Royal or Aristocracy or Peer – 1

Sport – 47

Stage, Screen and Radio – 246

Travel and Exploration – 11

Writing – 98

1970s

Academia and Education – 25

Art, Fashion and Design – 26

Business – 6

Food and Drink – 4

Medicine, Science and Engineering – 16

Military and Law – 8

Music – 131

Nature and Conservation – 12

Politics and Public Service – 23

Prizewinner or Record Breaker – 1

Religion and Philosophy – 2

Sport – 34

Stage, Screen and Radio – 208

Travel and Exploration – 9

Writing – 133

1980s

Academia and Education – 17

Art, Fashion and Design – 24

Business – 18

Food and Drink – 8

Medicine, Science and Engineering – 11

Military and Law – 6

Music – 100

Nature and Conservation – 5

Politics and Public Service – 42

Prizewinner or Record Breaker – 5

Religion and Philosophy – 6

Royal or Aristocracy or Peer – 6

Sport – 24

Stage, Screen and Radio – 164

Travel and Exploration – 8

Writing 122

1990s

Academia and Education – 21

Art, Fashion and Design – 29

Business – 31

Food and Drink – 12

Medicine, Science and Engineering – 32

Military and Law – 11

Music – 64

Nature and Conservation – 8

Politics and Public Service – 61

Prizewinner or Record Breaker – 6

Religion and Philosophy – 8

Royal or Aristocracy or Peer – 2

Sport – 18

Stage, Screen and Radio – 124

Travel and Exploration – 9

Writing – 121

2000s

Academia and Education – 23

Art, Fashion and Design – 33

Business – 25

Food and Drink – 9

Medicine, Science and Engineering – 29

Military and Law – 11

Music – 64

Nature and Conservation – 8

Politics and Public Service – 40

Prizewinner or Record Breaker – 19

Religion and Philosophy – 7

Royal or Aristocracy or Peer – 1

Sport – 13

Stage, Screen and Radio – 144

Travel and Exploration – 7

Writing – 136

2010s

Academia and Education – 5

Art, Fashion and Design – 7

Business – 11

Food and Drink – 1

Medicine, Science and Engineering – 4

Military and Law – 2

Music – 10

Nature and Conservation – 1

Politics and Public Service – 7

Religion and Philosophy – 1

Royal or Aristocracy or Peer – 1

Sport – 7

Stage, Screen and Radio – 33

Travel and Exploration – 1

Writing – 26

SEXES OF THE CASTAWAYS
THROUGH THE DECADES

1940s

Male 45 (69 per cent)

Female 20 (31 per cent)

1950s

Male 271 (67 per cent)

Female 134 (33 per cent)

1960s

Male 404 (76 per cent)

Female 129 (24 per cent)

1970s

Male 384 (74 per cent)

Female 135 (26 per cent)

1980s

Male 327 (73 per cent)

Female 124 (27 per cent)

1990s

Male 294 (71 per cent)

Female 120 (29 per cent)

2000s

Male 304 (73 per cent)

Female 113 (27 per cent)

2010s

Male 61 (66 per cent)

Female 31 (34 per cent)

FIRSTS

The first programme was recorded in a bomb-damaged Maida Vale studio on 27 January 1942 and broadcast two evenings later.

The first castaway was the comedian Vic Oliver. Plomley's first choice, the philosopher Dr C. E. M. Joad, famous for *The Brains Trust*, had said he was busy.

Oliver was prime minister Winston Churchill's son-in-law. He appeared twice on the programme, but in his first appearance his choices were:

Frédéric Chopin: *Étude in C minor*
Haydn Wood: *Roses of Picardy*
Hildegarde: *Love is a Dancing Thing*
Pyotr Ilyich Tchaikovsky: *Marche Slave*
Jack Hylton and His Orchestra: *Happy Days Are Here Again*
New Light Symphony: *Parade of The Tin Soldiers*
Bebe Daniels: *I Give You My Heart*
Richard Wagner: *Ride of The Valkyries* (from *Die Walküre*)

In those days, castaways were not invited to choose a book or a luxury. The first castaway to choose a luxury was *Chitty Chitty Bang Bang* actress Sally Ann Howes in 1951. She chose garlic.

The first castaway to choose a book was actor and director Henry Kendall three weeks later. He chose *Who's Who in the Theatre*.

In November 1951, the actress Kathleen Harrison became the first castaway to choose a novel – Charles Dickens's *The Pickwick Papers*.

In 1992, John Major became the first, and only, serving prime minister to appear on the show.

FIRST GUESTS

Michael Parkinson's first guest was Alan Parker.

Sue Lawley's first guest was Quintin Hogg (Lord Hailsham).

Kirsty Young's first guest was Quentin Blake.

LAST GUESTS

Roy Plomley's last guest was Sheila Steafel.

Michael Parkinson's last guest was Brendan Foster.

Sue Lawley's last guest was Dame Joan Plowright.

ONLYS

Three castaways have chosen *By The Sleepy Lagoon* – the theme music to *Desert Island Discs* – but only James Agate chose the version performed by Eric Coates and his orchestra, which is, of course, the one used on the programme.

The only time a castaway has been allowed to take a living person as a luxury was when Dame Edna Everage insisted on taking her bridesmaid, Madge Allsop. According to the presenter, Sue Lawley, 'I reminded her that the luxury had to be an inanimate object. She assured me that Madge was exactly that. So I allowed it.'

Percussionist Evelyn Glennie is the only profoundly deaf person to have been a guest on the programme. (Lord Ashley was also profoundly deaf until he received a cochlear implant in 1993, which restored much of his hearing before he went on the programme in the same year.)

(ONLYS – *cont.*)

Dorothy Dickson With Orchestra was chosen just twice – and by a single castaway, Sir Hugh Greene.

Hans Werner Henze was chosen just twice, and by the same castaway, Sir William Walton.

George Duke was chosen just twice, and by the same castaway, Steve Davis.

Only two people have chosen Dame Cleo Laine and her daughter Jacqueline Dankworth on separate records in the same programme. One was trade unionist Bill Morris, the other was Dame Cleo herself.

Frank Oz, the voice of Miss Piggy on *The Muppet Show*, was the only person to choose Mose Allison, and chose three of his records.

The only castaway to choose silence as a record was Ian McMillan, who chose John Cage's *4' 33"* which is, of course, 4 minutes 33 seconds of silence. It was also his favourite record. Only a few seconds were played – during which Ian McMillan's stomach was heard to rumble.

The only time Roy Plomley broke his strict rule of not influencing his guests' choices was when a writer – never named by Plomley – told him that he was tone deaf and so couldn't pick a single record. So, after discovering the writer had a good sense of rhythm and enjoyed dancing, he got him to name his favourite dances – foxtrot, waltz, etc. – and asked the researchers to find pleasant examples of them.

Shami Chakrabarti is the only castaway to have chosen Harper Lee's *To Kill a Mockingbird*.

Simon Cowell is the only castaway to have chosen Jackie Collins's *Hollywood Wives*.

Thomas Keneally is the only Booker prizewinner to have been on the programme twice.

Sarah Vaughan is the only woman to have requested golfing equipment (clubs and balls) as a luxury.

Leslie Crowther is the only castaway to have requested music by The Black And White Minstrels.

Lady Soames is the only woman to have requested (Havana) cigars as a luxury.

Michael McIntyre is the only person to have chosen the song *Bewitched, Bothered And Bewildered*.

Bill Nighy is the only castaway to have chosen two Rolling Stones songs (*Gimme Shelter* and *Winter*).

Jack Higgins is the only castaway to have chosen three Fred Astaire songs.

Rex Harrison is the only castaway to have chosen four Benny Goodman records. He was also the only castaway to choose music by Barney Bigard – and, indeed, he selected two of his records.

Colin Montgomerie is the only castaway to decline a luxury on the basis that he felt he'd had a 'wonderful and fortunate lifestyle'. He said, 'I've had all the luxuries, and if it all ends tomorrow, I've had a great time at it.'

WHEN *DESERT ISLAND DISCS* MADE THE NEWS

Desert Island Discs has often made the news, but perhaps even more so in recent years. Maybe it is because Roy Plomley's successors are more hard-hitting, or because the castaways are prepared to reveal more about themselves. Or maybe it is just because newspapers have so many more pages to fill? In any event, here are some ways in which the programme has made the news – sometimes even the headlines – in recent years.

When former *Daily Mirror* (and *News of the World*) editor Piers Morgan appeared on the programme in 2009, he was asked a question about the unscrupulous methods of tabloid newspapers – including phone taps, taking secret photos and raking through dustbins. In his reply, he admitted, 'A lot of it was done by third parties rather than the staff themselves. That's not to defend it because you were running the results of their work. I'm quite happy to be parked in the corner [in the role of] tabloid beast and to have to sit here and defend all the things we used to get up to. I make no pretence about the stuff we used to do. I simply say the net of people doing it was very wide and certainly comprised the high and the low of the newspaper market.'

This was pretty unremarkable at the time but, in the light of Morgan's elevation to CNN's star interviewer and the phone hacking scandal (and his appearance before the Leveson Inquiry), his interview with Kirsty Young was subjected to much examination by the press.

In 2011, tenor Alfie Boe shocked the opera establishment by declaring on *Desert Island Discs* that he found watching opera boring.

In 2010, Emma Thompson talked of experiencing depression after her divorce from Kenneth Branagh and also told of how her grandmother had been raped during the Second World War when working as a servant.

There was a huge furore after the journalist Lynn Barber (2010) admitted to sleeping with 'probably 50 men' during two terms at Oxford (and, as Kirsty Young pointed out, the Oxford terms are short).

Mary Portas had therapy after her 2010 appearance on the programme in which she spoke in depth for the first time about her childhood and the early deaths of her parents. 'I had therapy after I did *Desert Island Discs* because when you go into the public eye it's the first time you have to keep explaining your life. It was quite a shock. People had started to ask me about my family and it made me think, "Have I really, really dealt with this?" So I did that, dealt with all that fear you carry into adulthood.'

When John Humphrys (2008) talked about his time reading the *Nine O'Clock News* on BBC TV, he commented that it was 'no job for a grown man. Or woman.'

In 1996 Sue Lawley asked the then unmarried Gordon Brown about his sexuality. 'People want to know whether you're gay or whether there's some flaw in your personality that you haven't made a relationship.' Brown replied that he hoped to marry one day but that a relationship 'just hasn't happened'.

In 2010, Nick Clegg admitted he was a secret smoker and was accused of promoting cigarettes.

In 2008 novelist Dame Beryl Bainbridge opined that women were inferior to men, which led to much comment in the papers.

In 2012, it emerged that *War Horse* would (probably) not have been turned into a critically acclaimed play and a blockbuster film had it not been for *Desert Island Discs*. Dr Rosemary Morris listened to Michael Morpurgo on the programme in 2004 and was so fascinated by his life story that she bought his books – including *War Horse*, a children's story that had been published 22 years previously. Dr Morris's son Tom was the associate director of the National Theatre and was looking for something for the Handspring Puppet Company to do. She suggested *War Horse* and within three years it had become a hit play at the National Theatre.

REVELATIONS ON THE PROGRAMME

When asked what the Velvet Underground sounded like, founder member of the band John Cale (2004) replied, 'Painful.'

Debbie Harry (2011) revealed that she felt sorry she had never had children.

Gyles Brandreth (2011) revealed that he kept his marriage a secret from his parents for two years because he regarded it as a purely private matter between him and his wife.

Martin Clunes (2011) revealed he was routinely bullied by pupils and beaten by teachers after being 'bundled off' to boarding school.

Jack Lemmon (1989) revealed that his mother was so keen to continue playing her bridge game that he ended up being born in an elevator.

Fay Weldon (2010) said that she believed she has psychic powers. 'There is a degree of second sight, I think, on occasion.'

David Walliams (2009) admitted dark thoughts. 'I can't stand being on my own. I hate it. I have a pathological fear of [it] . . . When I'm with my own thoughts I start to unravel myself and I start to think real dark thoughts, self-destructive thoughts. If somebody said to me you have to spend a weekend on your own, in your house, I wouldn't be able to hack it.'

Miriam Margolyes (2008) revealed that she blamed herself for her mother's death, having come out to her mother as a lesbian just a few days before her mother suffered the severe stroke from which she never recovered. She said, 'Yes, I do believe it caused the person I loved the most in the world a pain she could not bear.'

Harvey Goldsmith (2009) revealed that legendary trumpeter Miles Davis threatened to kill him because of a watermelon. 'I was bringing Miles Davis over to Europe and I thought I would lay on this buffet. I had this huge tray of watermelon and I thought that would be fantastic. I had it all laid out on a bed of ice and he walked into the room and I could see there was fire coming out of his eyes and I thought he was actually going to knock me flying. Watermelon is a statement of slavery and I didn't know this at all and it was something that Americans looked at as the worst insult you could possibly do to somebody.'

James Nesbitt (2008) spoke about his mother's Alzheimer's disease, and called for more support for sufferers' families. 'It has such a devastating impact on a family, particularly on my father, and it is very hard to find the necessary help.'

Yoko Ono (2007) revealed she allowed John Lennon to decide whether or not to abort their son Sean. 'I thought, well, I should let John decide whether I should keep it or not.' When Kirsty Young asked why she made that decision, she replied, 'I didn't want to burden him with something he didn't want.'

When Janet Street-Porter (2008) chose Otis Redding's *That's How Strong My Love Is*, she recalled that it was 'an orgasmic moment' when she first heard it.

Sir Michael Caine (2009) revealed that he makes 'the best roast potatoes in the world'.

Len Goodman (2011) revealed that he still takes the bus to the *Strictly Come Dancing* studio. 'They offer me a car but I can't be doing with it. Sitting there like Little Lord Fauntleroy. It's not my cup of tea.'

Jimmy Tarbuck (2004) revealed that John Lennon once spiked his drink with drugs. 'You'd leave your drinks around, or you'd nod off or something. Then John would drop speed in your drink. You'd be high as a kite for days. But Lennon just thought it was all hysterically funny. He was a good lad. One of the lads – a good laugh.'

Iain Duncan Smith (2002) revealed that his father was once chatted up by Marilyn Monroe. 'I'm told nothing happened, but that's what my mother tells me, so I'm not quite certain.'

Jon Snow (2011) revealed that he cries on location. 'It's a good thing, because otherwise you bottle it up and come home bonkers.'

PROGRAMME CONTROVERSIES

The greatest controversy was when Diana, Lady Mosley, the widow of the fascist leader Sir Oswald, appeared in 1989. Lady Mosley was reminiscing about her friend Hitler, and how she and her husband felt when they discovered that Hitler's version of anti-Semitism was to exterminate the Jews. Lady Mosley recalled they didn't discover this for a long time and it was years before she could believe it. When Sue Lawley asked, 'Do you believe it now?' Lady Mosley replied, 'I don't really, I'm afraid, believe that six million people were . . . I think it's just not conceivable. It's too many, but you see whether it's six or whether it's one, really makes no difference morally. It's equally wrong. I think it was a dreadfully wicked thing myself.' Later in the interview Lady Mosley describes Hitler as 'fascinating'.

In 1994, when newsreader Trevor McDonald was invited to be on the show, the Commission for Racial Equality highlighted how few black and Asian guests had appeared on the programme before him.

In 2002 Gordon Ramsay told Sue Lawley that he'd played first-team football for Rangers: 'I got my first team games. I was with the first team squad. I played three first team games.'

It was later reported that, according to the club, he was just a trialist: 'He trained with us for a few months but then got injured.'

Lauren Bacall (1979) was a difficult guest. When Roy Plomley asked her to pick just one of her eight records, she exploded. 'What is this? You said I had eight records. Now you're saying I only have one?'

Kirsty Young often asks castaways about what they are wearing, especially if it is relevant to their work, achievements and identity. However, the appearance of Gok Wan in 2010 provoked accusations of dumbing down, which were not mitigated by Kirsty asking him to 'take me through what you are wearing'. The BBC later confirmed it had received ten formal complaints about his interview, while scores more debated the issue on internet message boards.

When Morrissey (2009) talked about suicide and described 'self-destruction' as 'honourable', there were complaints from the friends and families of people who had committed suicide.

Wendy Richard (1995) didn't like being asked anything other than anodyne questions. She stopped Sue Lawley four times in the course of the recording and was distressed when she wasn't allowed to take her pet Cairn terrier to the island as a luxury. 'She asked why the dog was such a life-and-death business,' said the actress, 'and I told her the truth: because she is my best friend. I had to take my tapestries instead. I emerged feeling wretched.'

In 2011, Martin Sheen caused eyebrows to be raised when he described his son Charlie's addiction to be 'as dangerous as cancer'.

PROGRAMME FUN

When programme researchers invited Alistair MacLean on the show, they were expecting the best-selling author of books such as *Where Eagles Dare* and *The Guns of Navarone*. Unfortunately, by mistake, they invited Alastair MacLean, the European director of tourism for Ontario, Canada, who was unknown to radio listeners in Britain. Ever the gentleman, Roy Plomley covered up the error and the interview went ahead anyway, although it was never broadcast.

A frequently told tale about the programme goes as follows: when Roy Plomley asked the French actress Brigitte Bardot what she had chosen as her luxury, she replied, 'A peeenissss.'

Plomley, astonished, had enough presence of mind to say, 'Most interesting, and why precisely, may I ask?'

'Well,' said Bardot, 'it's what the world needs most, isn't it? 'Appiness.'

Great story – except that Brigitte Bardot was *never* on the programme and so it *never* happened. In fact, the only time it did happen was in a Peter Sellers film, *There's a Girl in my Soup*. However, one suspects that it's ascribed to *Desert Island Discs* because it illustrates Roy Plomley's unflappability.

Roy Plomley also demonstrated his poise off air. He once recalled:

> I was summoned to the office of a senior BBC administrator, who gave me a glass of sherry and announced: 'We're going to send you to a desert island. I'll come over to you every evening after the six o'clock news and ask you how you're getting on. When can you leave?'
>
> 'I've a better idea,' I replied. 'I've more experience of asking questions than you. You go to the island and I'll come over to you after the six o'clock news.' It was not mentioned again. My idea of an island is Manhattan.

Alfred Wainwright (1988) only agreed to go on the show on condition that Sue Lawley went to Manchester to record the programme, as he refused to go to London. (Apparently, he was intrigued to see if her legs were as good as people had said.) Also, he wanted a friend to drive him to the studio – as he didn't drive – and on the way they had to stop at Harry Ramsden's for fish and chips. His *Desert Island Discs* book choice was just as eccentric: two photographs – one of his wife and one of the 1928 Blackburn Rovers FC team.

Margaret Rutherford (1953) said she'd be perfectly happy as a castaway because she would turn herself into a mermaid. She explained that, for recreation, she adored putting on her floral bathing costume and diving into the freezing depths of the Hampstead Heath Lido. 'There is something so cleansing mentally and emotionally in feeling yourself weightless in water,' she said.

When David Dimbleby (2008) was asked by Kirsty Young for his luxury, he replied, 'I'll take you.' Understandably, this wasn't allowed under the rules and so he chose a collection of drawing books, pencils and varnish instead.

Lord Hailsham chose *I Do Like To Be Beside The Seaside* – and, in the words of his interviewer, Sue Lawley, was 'pompomming along to it as he sat in the studio'.

When Betty Kenward, a magazine journalist with a reputation for snobbery, was on the show in 1974, Roy Plomley asked her why she never mentioned 'working-class people'. She replied, 'My dear, I'm never introduced to them.'

Jack Straw appeared on the show in 1998 – not long after his son had been exposed in a tabloid sting operation selling cannabis in a pub. He asked his children to select a record to remind him of family life during his desert island exile. They selected *History* by The Verve, which includes the line, 'I've got a skinful of dope' – although the music fades before this particular line is aired on the programme.

Legend has it that Margaret Thatcher chose Rolf Harris's *Two Little Boys* because it illustrated the importance of sharing. The only problem with this story is that she never chose this record.

~~~~~~

TRIVIA

Eric Coates's *By The Sleepy Lagoon* has always been the show's theme tune. For added atmosphere, the sound of herring gulls was added. However, it turns out the herring gull is never found anywhere near tropical islands. So they were briefly replaced by (more authentic) sooty terns before, by popular demand, the herring gulls were reintroduced. *By The Sleepy Lagoon* was inspired by a view from Bognor Regis.

Most people have a list of the discs they would take to an island if invited on to the show. A. A. Gill (2006) said that he'd been planning his list since the age of 12, while Graham Norton (2004) knew his eight records the moment he was asked (his favourite being *Islands In The Stream*, on which he once duetted with Dolly Parton).

Patrick Stewart was so keen to appear on the show that he claimed to have carried around a list of his eight choices. Fortunately for him, he was on the show in 2005. The former home secretary Herbert Morrison, who was said to have kept a permanent selection in his top pocket in case he got the call, never did get to appear. Nor, to date, has his grandson, Peter Mandelson.

James Ellroy (2010) chose works by just three composers: Beethoven (5), Bruckner (2) and Sibelius (1).

Enoch Powell (1989) chose works by just three composers: Wagner (4), Beethoven (3) and Haydn (1).

Baroness Maria von Trapp (1983) chose works by just three composers: Mozart (4), Schubert (3) and Bach (1).

Sir Osbert Lancaster chose the same song (on the same programme) sung by two different artists (the song was *Alabama Song* and he chose versions by Noël Coward and Gertrude Lawrence and by Lotte Lenya). Sir John Mills did the same with the song *Blue Skies*, choosing versions by Benny Goodman and Paul Whiteman.

Castaways

When David Cameron (2006) picked *This Charming Man* by The Smiths, the group's guitarist, Johnny Marr, was angry enough to tell the future prime minister to stop saying that he's a fan of the group.

Alan Bennett's diary for 2009, published in the *London Review of Books*, contained an interesting entry for 20 February. 'It's years since I was on *Desert Island Discs* but these days I'd find it much easier to choose the eight records I don't want than those that I do. I don't ever want to hear again: Mussorgsky's *Pictures At An Exhibition*, Rimsky-Korsakov's *Scheherazade*, Schubert's *Fifth Symphony*, Beethoven's *Pastoral Symphony* or Mozart's *40th Symphony*. And it isn't that I've heard them too often. I just don't care for any of them.'

Dame Peggy Ashcroft loved Johann Sebastian Bach's *Brandenburg Concerto No. 5 in D major* so much that she requested no fewer than *three* excerpts from it.

Of all the castaways who appeared on the show twice or more, the shortest time between two appearances is five years – a distinction shared by Christopher Stone (1952, 1957), Peter Ustinov (1951, 1956) and Sir Terry Wogan (1983, 1988).

Other people who reappeared within ten years are Cicely Courtneidge (1951, 1957), Michael Crawford (1971, 1978), Sir David Frost (1963, 1971), Robertson Hare (1951, 1959), Dame Celia Johnson (1945, 1954), Cecil Day-Lewis (1960, 1968), Valerie Hobson (1945, 1954), Bobby Howes (1945, 1954), Brian Reece (1953, 1961) and James Stewart (1974, 1983).

Of all the castaways who appeared on the show twice or more, the *longest* time between two appearances is 62 years – in the case of Jill Balcon (1945, 2007).

Michael Mansfield QC rejected the Bible in favour of *The Rights of Man* by Thomas Paine.

Some castaways are not great readers. Showjumper Harvey Smith told Roy Plomley: 'I've never read a book in my life and I don't intend to start for you, sir', while Jamie Oliver admitted, 'I don't read books', and instead requested notepaper and pens to write recipes.

A listener wrote in to criticize the emphasis on famous guests and offered himself instead. 'As a retired Post Office worker,' he wrote, 'I think I qualify and I enclose a list of my eight records. I am available most days except Thursdays, when I go to Old Time dancing.'

In a 2006 survey, *Desert Island Discs* was chosen as the second best British radio show – behind *I'm Sorry I Haven't a Clue* and ahead of *Woman's Hour, The Archers* and *Just a Minute*.

T. Dan Smith (1968), Jeffrey Archer (1981) and Gary Glitter (1981) went on the programme before going to prison, while Robert Maxwell (1987) faced public disgrace later in his life.

George Clooney (2003) chose Tolstoy's *War and Peace* as his book, 'as there may not be toilet paper . . . and that's a huge book'.

Maria Aitken (1989) found the experience of being on the programme a bit like 'talking to God', while Geraldine James (2004) said that recording the programme was like 'making your own radio obituary'.

Rev. Ian Paisley chose eight records that were unique to him – though some of the songs (*Danny Boy, Amazing Grace*) were chosen by other castaways, but by different singers.

Heston Blumenthal and Dame Kelly Holmes each chose seven artists who were not chosen by any other castaway.

Steve Davis and Georgie Fame each chose six artists who weren't chosen by any other castaway.

Garrison Keillor chose two records by the Huddersfield Choral Society.

Mary Poppins author P. L. Travers picked seven poems and an excerpt from Shakespeare's *Cymbeline* as her 'music'.

Both times that Barry Humphries was on he chose Randolph Sutton singing *On Mother Kelly's Doorstep*. The only other person to choose a Randolph Sutton song was Humphries's hero and mentor Sir John Betjeman, who asked for Sutton singing *When Are You Going To Lead Me To The Altar, Walter?*

Imran Khan chose three songs by Nusrat Fateh Ali Khan.

Arthur Askey requested a mixture of pop music he would be 'glad to leave behind'.

In Tom Stoppard's play *The Real Thing*, Henry, a playwright, is worrying about his imminent appearance on *Desert Island Discs* and what to choose: the music he likes or the music that will make him look good. When his wife advises him to simply pick his eight all-time greats, Henry becomes flustered by his dilemma. Can he *really* maintain his intellectual credibility – critiquing the likes of Jean-Paul Sartre and the post-war existentialists – if he chooses the Crystals singing *Da-Doo-Ron-Ron*?

In 1996, *Absolutely Fabulous* featured Edina (Jennifer Saunders) being interviewed by Sue Lawley (in an off-camera cameo) for *Desert Island Discs*. All of Edina's music choices were Lulu songs.

MUSIC

PEOPLE WHO CHOSE THEIR OWN RECORDS

CHOSE 8 . . .

On her first appearance on the show (1957), Moura Lympany didn't choose any of her own recordings. However, on her second appearance (1979), she chose eight pieces of music that all featured her as the pianist:

Felix Mendelssohn: *Piano Concerto No. 1 in G Minor*

Sergey Vasilievich Rachmaninov: *Prelude in G Major*

Aram Khachaturian: *Piano Concerto in D Flat Major*

Alan Rawsthorne: *Piano Concerto No. 16*

Wolfgang Amadeus Mozart: *Piano Concerto No. 21 in C Major*

Frédéric Chopin: *Prelude in E Minor*

Franz Schubert: *Piano Quintet in A Major 'Trout'*

Sergey Vasilevich Rachmaninov: *Piano Concerto No. 3 in D Minor*

CHOSE 7 . . .

Elisabeth Schwarzkopf (1958) chose seven tracks featuring her singing:

Johannes Brahms: *Ihr Habt Nun Traurigkeit* (from *German Requiem*)

Johann Strauss II: *Vienna Blood Waltz*

Richard Wagner: *Selig Wie Die Sonne* (from *Die Meistersinger von Nürnberg*)

Wolfgang Amadeus Mozart: *An Chloe*

Hugo Wolf: *Elfenlied* (from *Mörike Lieder*)

Giuseppe Verdi: *Tutto Nel Mondo È Burla* (from *Falstaff*)

Engelbert Humperdinck: *Hansel And Gretel*

The only item she chose on which she didn't perform was Richard Strauss's Prelude to *Der Rosenkavalier*, performed by the Philharmonia Orchestra and conducted by Herbert von Karajan.

CHOSE 6 . . .

Sir Peter Pears (1969 and 1983) selected Franz Schubert's *Im Dorfe* from *Winterreise* (which he chose on both occasions), *The Foggy, Foggy Dew*, Philip Rosseter's *Sweet Come Again*, Charles Dibdin's *Tom Bowling* and Benjamin Britten's *The Sprig of Thyme*. Each piece of music featured him as a soloist.

Jule Styne (1978) chose six songs he'd co-written: *People, Let It Snow, Three Coins In The Fountain, Guess I'll Hang My Tears Out To Dry, Don't Rain On My Parade* and *All I Need Is The Girl.*

CHOSE 5 . . .

Sir Norman Wisdom (1953 and 2000) chose *Don't Laugh At Me 'Cos I'm A Fool, Follow A Star, Falling In Love, Narcissus* and *Writing A Song.*

Louis Armstrong (1968) selected *Blueberry Hill, Mack The Knife, Bess, You Is My Woman Now, Stars Fell On Alabama* and *What A Wonderful World.*

Zubin Mehta (1984) chose five records which featured him conducting: Richard Strauss's *Symphonia Domestica,* Mozart's *Sinfonia Concertante in E Flat Major*, Schubert's *Symphony No. 5 in B Flat Major*, Stravinsky's *The Rite of Spring* and Vivaldi's *Concerto for Four Violins in B Minor, Op. 3/10.*

CHOSE 4 . . .

Ambrose (1965) chose his orchestra playing *Copenhagen, The Moon Was Yellow, When Gimble Hits The Cymbal* and *When Day Is Done*.

Stephen Sondheim (1980 and 2000) selected his works *The Ballad of Sweeney Todd* (on both his appearances), *Finishing The Hat* and *The Advantages of Floating In The Middle of The Sea*).

Sir William Walton, who appeared in 1965 and 1982, chose his compositions *Old Sir Faulk (Foxtrot)* (from *Façade*), *Violin Concerto in B Minor, Belshazzar's Feast* and *Symphony No. 2*.

Leopold Stokowski (1957) chose four discs which featured him conducting: Johann Sebastian Bach's *Chorale Prelude* (*Nun Komm, Der Heiden Heiland*), Beethoven's *Symphony No. 7 in E Major*, Debussy's *Sirènes (*from *Nocturnes)*, and Tchaikovsky's *Again, As Before, Alone (Solitude), Op. 73/6*.

CHOSE 3 . . .

Rolf Harris (1999) chose *Ego Sum Pauper (I Give You My Heart)* with him singing with the Dowlais Male Voice Choir, *Gendarmes Quartet*, and his hit song *Two Little Boys*.

Paddy Moloney (1999) selected three songs featuring The Chieftains, the band he founded: *Full of Joy, Coast of Malabar* and *Long Journey Home*.

Tex Ritter (1956) chose a selection of songs – all with a cowboy theme, and with him taking the vocal lead: *The Chisholm Trail, Rye Whiskey*, and *Do Not Forsake Me, O My Darling* from the film *High Noon*.

John Eliot Gardiner (1992) chose three records on which he'd been the conductor: Jean-Philippe Rameau's *Les Boréades*, Johann Sebastian Bach's *St Matthew Passion – Peter's Denial* and Handel's *Solomon*.

CHOSE 2 . . .

Arthur Askey appeared four times on the programme, 1942, 1955, 1968 and 1980, and he selected two songs which featured him singing: *Band Waggon* (1942), and *The Proposal*, which he performed with Richard Murdoch.

Billy Cotton (1959) chose two songs featuring him conducting his famous band: *Dambusters March* and *I've Got A Loverly Bunch of Coconuts*.

Sacha Distel (1971 and 2004) selected a recording of him singing on each appearance: *To Wait For Love* (1971) and *My Funny Valentine* (2004).

Sir David Frost (1963, 1971 and 2005) chose recordings of interviews he conducted for his appearance in 1971: Bobby Kennedy, whom he interviewed that year, and an excerpt from *The Frost Report On Everything* – also that year. (During his appearance on the programme in 1963 he chose Millicent Martin singing *That Was The Week That Was*, theme song of the television show he presented.)

Lionel Hampton (1983) chose *Stardust*, played by the Lionel Hampton Allstars, and *Jodo* by the Lionel Hampton Orchestra. He also featured on Louis Armstrong's version of *Memories of You*, another of his selections.

Woody Herman (1984) conducted the music on two of his choices: *I've Got You Under My Skin* by Frank Sinatra, and *I Got It Bad And That Ain't Good*.

Stanley Holloway (1951, 1962 and 1975) performed with Elsa Macfarlane on two pieces of music he chose: *Memory Street* (in 1951) and *Down Love Lane* (in 1962).

Ralph Kohn (2004) was the soloist on two of his choices: Raffaello Rontaini's *Se Bel Rio / If A Beautiful Brook*, and Bach's *Cantata No. 211: Schweigt stille – hat man nicht mit seinen Kindern*.

Lupino Lane (1957) chose *An Elephant Never Forgets* and *Me And My Girl*, performed with Teddie St Denis.

George Lloyd (1995) chose two of his compositions: Sybil's aria from Act 3 of *John Socman* and the final section of his *Fourth Symphony*.

Joe Loss (1963) selected two pieces of music which featured his orchestra: *Begin The Beguine* and *In The Mood*.

Dame Vera Lynn (1951 and 1989) selected two songs that she'd sung, both in 1989: *Room 504* and *Heart of Gold*.

George Mitchell (1962) chose two pieces of music by his choir/minstrels: *Wimoweh* and *Side By Side*.

(CHOSE TWO – *cont.*)

Dudley Moore (1969) selected two of his songs: *Little Miss Britten* (from *Beyond The Fringe*) and *Lilian Lust* from the film *Bedazzled*.

Luciano Pavarotti (1976) chose Gaetano Donizetti's *Pour Mon Âme* (*Qual Destino*) from *The Daughter of The Regiment* (the Luciano Pavarotti Orchestra), and Gaetano Donizetti's *Era d'Amor l'Immagine* from *Maria Stuarda*, featuring himself as the soloist.

André Previn (1967 and 1996)'s choices featured him conducting Ralph Vaughan Williams's *Symphony No. 5 in D Major* and Richard Strauss's *Don Quixote* – both in his 1996 appearance.

Edmundo Ros (1958) chose his orchestra playing *Could It Be?* and *Canción Cubana*.

Artur Rubinstein (1971) selected two pieces featuring him as soloist: Franz Schubert's *Piano Sonata No. 21 in B Flat Major* and Frédéric Chopin's *Nocturne in E Flat Major*.

Claude-Michel Schönberg (2003) selected *At The End of The Day* and *The Prologue* – both from *Les Misérables*, which he composed.

Sandie Shaw (2010) chose two of her songs: *Coconut Grove* and *Bananas* with Herbie Flowers and Roger Cook.

Gloria Swanson (1981) chose two songs featuring her singing: *I Love You So Much I Hate You* and *Love*.

John Tavener (1994) selected two of his compositions: *Akathist of Thanksgiving* and *Blessed Duet* (from *Mary of Egypt*).

Sir Michael Tippett (1968 and 1985) chose two of his compositions: *Symphony No. 2* (in 1968) and *Song No. 2* from *Songs for Dov* (in 1985).

John Tomlinson (1998) selected two pieces featuring himself as the soloist: Wagner's *Wotan's Farewell* from *Die Walküre* and Mozart's *Riconosci In Quest' Amplesso* from *The Marriage of Figaro*.

CHOSE ONE OF THEIR OWN RECORDINGS

Includes pieces castaways wrote, or in which they sang or played.

Joan Baez (1993), *Diamonds And Rust*

(7th) Marquess of Bath: *Love Words* (written as Lord Weymouth)

Hylda Baker (1969), *Give Us A Kiss*

Harry Belafonte (1958), *Scarlet Ribbons*

Richard Rodney Bennett (his 1997 appearance), theme from *Tender Is The Night*

Tony Bennett (his 1972 appearance), *Smile*

The Beverley Sisters (1961), *Cottage For Sale*

Cilla Black (her 1964 appearance), *Anyone Who Had A Heart*

Mel Brooks (1978), *Springtime For Hitler*

Dave Brubeck (1999), *The Way You Look Tonight*

Grace Bumbry (1977), Jules Massenet's *Pleurez, Mes Yeux* from *Le Cid*

Max Bygraves (1955), *You're A Pink Toothbrush*

John Cale (2004), *Some Kinda Love* by the Velvet Underground

Patrick Cargill (1971), *The Blood Donor* – the sketch in which he played the doctor opposite Tony Hancock

(CHOSE ONE OF THEIR OWN RECORDINGS – *cont.*)

George Chisholm (1982), *Blue Turning Grey Over You*

Petula Clark (her 1995 appearance), *Tell Me It's Not True*

Eric Coates (1951), *Valse* – although he *didn't* choose *By The Sleepy Lagoon*, his version of which has been the theme tune to *Desert Island Discs* throughout its history

C. B. Cochran (1941), *C. B. Cochran Medley* by C. B. Cochran, Edward Cooper and Elisabeth Welch

Alma Cogan (1957), *You, Me And Us*

Aaron Copland (1958), his *Symphony No. 3*

Professor Brian Cox (2011), *King of Spades* by Dare, a band of which he was a member

Noël Coward (1963), love scene from *Private Lives* with Gertrude Lawrence

Michael Crawford (1999), *Eternal Love*

David Croft (1993), *Friends*

Andrew Cruickshank (1966), his reading of the *New English Bible: Letters of Paul to the Colossians*

Sinéad Cusack (her 1983 appearance), *Demewer But Dangerous* with Jonathan Hyde

Paul Daniel (1998), Sir William Walton's *Symphony No. 1 in B Flat Minor: 4th movement*, in which he'd been the conductor

Chris de Burgh (1998), *The Simple Truth*

Charlie Drake (1958), *Tom Thumb's Tune*

Jacqueline du Pré (1977), Johannes Brahms's *Cello Sonata No. 2 in F Major* – also featuring her husband, Daniel Barenboim

Clive Dunn (1971), *Grandad*

Jimmy Edwards (1961), *I've Never Seen A Straight Banana*

Dame Edna Everage (1988), *My Bridesmaid And I*

Adam Faith (1961), *What Do You Want?*

Gwen Ffrangcon-Davies (her 1988 appearance), *Fair Is The Moonlight* from *The Immortal Hour*

Dame Gracie Fields (her 1961 appearance), *The Holy City*

Renée Fleming (2005), *River*

Ken Follett (2001), *I'm Your Hoochie Coochie Man*

George Foreman (2003), *Little Girls*, a song he wrote, sung by the Vienna Boys' Choir

George Formby (1979), *Leaning On A Lamp Post*

Gary Glitter (1981), *Rock And Roll, I Gave You The Best Years of My Life*

Tito Gobbi (his 1979 appearance), *La Montanara*

Princess Grace of Monaco (1981), *The Proud Horse* from *Venus and Adonis* by William Shakespeare, read by her and Richard Pasco

Stéphane Grappelli (1972), *Gary* with Marc Hemmeler and Jack Sewing

Deryck Guyler (1970), *Home Again* with Tommy Handley

Marvin Hamlisch (1983), *Dreamers*

John Lee Hooker (1995), B. B. King's *You Shook Me* – featuring B. B. King and John Lee Hooker

Bob Hope (1961), *Thanks For The Memory*, sung with Shirley Ross

Frankie Howerd (his 1959 appearance), *Song And Dance Man*

Engelbert Humperdinck (2004), *All This World And The Seven Seas*

Maxwell Hutchinson (1991), *Lacrimosa* (*Requiem In A Village Church*)

Jeremy Irons (his 1986 appearance), *All For The Best* with David Essex and others

Sidney James (1960), *Sunday Afternoon At Home*, from *Hancock's Half Hour*, in which he co-starred

Karl Jenkins (2006), *Benedictus* from *The Armed Man: A Mass for Peace*

Glynis Johns (1976), *Send In The Clowns*

Miriam Karlin (1967), *Do You Love Me* with Topol

Desert Island Discs: Flotsam & Jetsam

(CHOSE ONE OF THEIR OWN RECORDINGS – *cont.*)

Stubby Kaye (1984), *Howdy Friends And Neighbors*

Stan Kenton (1956), *The House of Strings*

Ben Kingsley (1986), *Eagle Dance*

Dame Cleo Laine (her 1997 appearance), *Winter*

Fran Landesman (1996), *White Nightmare*

Lang Lang (2010), *The Yellow River In Wrath* from *The Yellow River Piano Concerto*

John Laurie (1976), Robert Burns's *My Love Is Like A Red, Red Rose*

Robert Lindsay (1992), *Hold My Hand*

Tasmin Little (2001), Jean Sibelius's *Violin Concerto in D Minor*

Hugh Lloyd (1965), *The Blood Donor* – the sketch in which he played opposite Tony Hancock as a fellow blood donor

Sir Andrew Lloyd Webber (his 1999 appearance), *Pie Jesu* from *Requiem*

Humphrey Lyttelton (his 2006 appearance), *Big Bill Blues*

Shirley Maclaine (1983), *If My Friends Could See Me Now*

George Martin (his 1995 appearance), *Old Boston*; he also chose several recordings he had produced

Mary Martin (1977), *I've Gotta Crow*, from *Peter Pan*, with her daughter Heller Halliday

Brian May (2002), *We Will Rock You*

Kenneth McKellar (1961), *The Flowers of The Forest*

Yehudi Menuhin (his 1977 appearance), Béla Bartók's *Violin Concerto No. 2*

Bernard Miles (1982), *The Race For The Rhinegold Stakes*

Sir John Mills (his 2000 appearance), *Ever The Best of Friends*

Ron Moody (1975), *Rinkety Tink*

Music

Christy Moore (2007), *A Stitch In Time*

Graham Norton (2004), *Islands In The Stream* – his duet with Dolly Parton

John Ogdon (his 1989 appearance), Sergey Rachmaninov's *Tarantella*

Antonio Pappano (2004), Puccini's *E Ben Altro Il Mio Sogno!* from *Il Tabarro*

Alan Price (1982), *House of The Rising Sun* with The Animals

Vincent Price (1969), *America The Beautiful*

Thomas Quasthoff (2009), Bach's *Cantata No. 82: Ich Habe Genug – Schlummert Ein*

Pauline Quirke (1996), *What'll I Do?* with Linda Robson

Sir Simon Rattle (his 2008 appearance), Gustav Mahler's *Symphony No. 9 in D Major – 1st Movement*

Ted Ray (1952), *Jack The Giant Killer* with his son Andrew

Sir Michael Redgrave (his 1945 appearance), *Youth's The Season* (from *The Beggar's Opera*)

Paul Robeson (1958), *Steal Away*

John Rutter (2005), conducting The Cambridge Singers singing *Keep Me As The Apple of An Eye* from *The Office of Compline*

Andras Schiff (1999), opening of Mozart's *Sonata in C Major* for four hands, with George Malcolm, his teacher

Phyllis Sellick (her 1963 appearance), Rachmaninov's *Romance*, with her husband Cyril Smith as the other soloist

Victor Silvester (1958), *They Didn't Believe Me*

Leonard Slatkin (2000), conducting the St Louis Symphony Orchestra, playing *Danny Boy*

Dorothy Squires (1963), *Roses of Picardy* with Russ Conway

Isaac Stern (1972), Johannes Brahms's *String Quintet No. 2 in G Major*

James Stewart (1983), *Rolling Stone* with Henry Fonda

Desert Island Discs: Flotsam & Jetsam

(CHOSE ONE OF THEIR OWN RECORDINGS – *cont.*)

Doris Stokes (1985), *Voices In My Ear*

Joan Sutherland (1959), Donizetti's *Lucia Di Lammermoor*

Chris Tarrant (2001), *Bucket of Water Song* by The Four Bucketeers – he was a member of the group, which started out on the popular children's television programme *Tiswas*

Jack Teagarden (1957), *Junk Man*

Michael Tilson Thomas (1997), Richard Strauss's *Ein Heldenleben,* with him conducting the London Symphony Orchestra

Paul Tortelier (in his 1984 appearance), *Variations On A Theme of Rossini* – with 'Madame' Tortelier

Stan Tracey (1999), *Stompin' At The Savoy*

Sophie Tucker (1963), *Some of These Days*

Frankie Vaughan (1958), *We Are Not Alone*

Sir Arnold Wesker (his 2006 appearance), *Shone With The Sun* – written with Ben Till for the Eurovision Song Contest

Barbara Windsor (her 1990 appearance), *Sparrows Can't Sing*

Ernie Wise (his solo appearance in 1990), *Bring Me Sunshine* with Eric Morecambe

CASTAWAYS WHO CHOSE A RECORD WITH WHICH THEY WERE ASSOCIATED

Lindsay Anderson (1980): Alan Price singing *Poor People*, which was part of the soundtrack to *O Lucky Man* which Anderson directed.

Sir David Attenborough (his 2012 appearance): Francisco Yglesia playing *Pajaro Campana (The Bell Bird)*, which was the theme music to his TV series *Zoo Quest*.

Peter Blake (his 1979 appearance) chose *Sgt Pepper*, for which he designed the album cover.

Richard Branson (1989): Mike Oldfield's *Tubular Bells*, which his company, Virgin Records, produced.

John Cleese (his 1997 appearance): Monty Python's *The Meaning of Life*.

Colin Cowdrey (1968): John Arlott and Richie Benaud commentating on 'Cowdrey's 100 (highlights of the 1950 Fifth Test Match, England v. South Africa)'.

David Edgar (2006): the original cast recording of *The Journey To Portsmouth* in *The Life And Adventures of Nicholas Nickleby*, which he had adapted from the Charles Dickens book.

Gordon Jackson (1975): Ray Martin And His Orchestra performing *The Edwardians* which was from *Upstairs, Downstairs*, the TV series in which he starred.

Clive James (his 2000 appearance): *Laughing Boy* (Pete Atkin) – a song he co-wrote with Pete Atkin.

Bill Kenwright (1998): *Tell Me It's Not True* from *Blood Brothers*, which he'd produced on stage.

Herbert Kretzmer (2003): *She*, which he co-wrote with Charles Aznavour.

Richard Lester (1968): the opening theme to *The Knack*, a film he directed.

(CHOSE A RECORD WITH WHICH THEY WERE ASSOCIATED – *cont.*)

Andrea Levy (2011): the theme music from the TV series of her book *Small Island*.

Arthur Lowe (1970): *Who Do You Think You Are Kidding Mr Hitler?* by Bud Flanagan (the theme song to *Dad's Army*). This was also chosen by Wendy Richard (1995), who occasionally appeared in *Dad's Army*.

Sir Cameron Mackintosh (2001): several songs from shows he had produced.

Jimmy McGovern (1996): the theme from *Brookside*, a series he wrote for.

Ruth Prawer Jhabvala (1999): the end titles from *Shakespeare Wallah*, for which she wrote the screenplay.

Otto Preminger (1980): several songs from films he had directed.

Ralph Reader (1961): *These Are The Times* from *The Gang Show*, which was produced by him.

Vikram Seth (2012): Mark Padmore performing *Thoughts While Travelling At Night*, for which he wrote the libretto (translated from the Chinese poet Du Fu).

James Stewart (1974 and 1983): The Glenn Miller Orchestra performing *Moonlight Serenade*. Stewart played Miller in the film *The Glenn Miller Story*. (He chose this on both of his appearances.)

Tom Stoppard (1985): André Previn's *Every Good Boy Deserves Favour*, which was composed for Stoppard's play of the same title.

David Suchet (2009): Christopher Gunning's theme to *Poirot*, in which he starred as the eponymous hero.

CHOSE A RELATIVE'S MUSIC

Jane Asher (1988): Peter and Gordon's *Woman*. Peter is her brother.

Daniel Barenboim (2006): his late ex-wife Jacqueline du Pré's recording of Elgar's *Cello Concerto in E Minor*.

Nina Bawden (1995): her stepson Rupert Bawden's *Two Studies For Orchestra On Scenes From Beroul's*.

Tony Benn (1989): his son Stephen performing a madrigal.

Betsy Blair (2005): her ex-husband, Gene Kelly, singing *I Got Rhythm*.

Martin Clunes (2011): his daughter Emily singing *Your Song* with 'her friend Daisy'.

Ronnie Corbett (his 2007 appearance): his wife, Ann Hart, singing *Music Maestro Please*.

Elvis Costello (1992): his father, Ross Macmanus, singing *At Last* with The Joe Loss Orchestra.

Bing Crosby (1975): his brother's band – Bob Crosby's Bobcats – performing *South Rampart Street Parade*.

John Dankworth (his 1986 appearance): his wife, Dame Cleo Laine, singing *When That I Was And A Little Tiny Boy* (with him accompanying her).

Sir Bernard Delfont (1991): his wife, Carole Lynne, singing *My Heart And I*.

David Dimbleby: his daughter's band (The Kate Dimbleby Band) performing *Song That You'd Like* (his 2008 appearance). He also chose (in 1974) his father Richard describing 'The Lying In State of HM King George VI'.

Anita Dobson (1988): Queen's *Bohemian Rhapsody*, which featured her husband, Brian May, on guitar.

Sister Frances Dominica (2004): her mother Ruth Lamdin's composition, *Cradle Song*.

Jacqueline du Pré (1977): her husband, Daniel Barenboim, playing Mozart's *Piano Concerto No. 27 in B Flat Major*.

(CHOSE A RELATIVE'S MUSIC – *cont.*)

Iain Duncan Smith (2002): *Blue Song* by Susi and Guy. Susi was Susan, his sister.

James Dyson (1999): his son Sam's band, wax.on wax.off, playing *Slowdown*.

Bob Geldof (1992): his wife, Paula Yates, singing *These Boots Are Made For Walking*.

Sir Hugh Greene (1983): an excerpt of his brother Graham Greene's book *In Search of A Character*.

Robert Hardy (1978): his nephew John Hardy's composition, *De Profundis*.

Max Hastings (1986): a recording of his father, MacDonald Hastings, on *Tonight*.

Thora Hird (her 1968 appearance): her son-in-law Mel Tormé singing *Comin' Home Baby*.

Imogen Holst (1972): her father's suite *The Planets* (*Saturn*).

Sally Ann Howes (1951): *She's My Lovely* by her father, Bobby Howes.

Jack Hulbert (1952): *Things Are Looking Up* and *Laughing Gas* by his wife, Cicely Courtneidge.

John Huston (1973): *September Song* by his father, Walter Huston.

Jeremy Irons (his 1986 appearance): his wife, Sinéad Cusack, performing *Demewer But Dangerous*.

Virginia Ironside (1997): her son, Will Grove-White, singing *Hot Tamales* with The Ukulele Orchestra of Great Britain.

Alan Johnson (2007): *Beneath The Sun* by Halima, which featured his son, Jamie.

Rachel Kempson, Lady Redgrave (1989): her husband, Sir Michael Redgrave, performing *If The Heart of A Man* (from *The Beggar's Opera*).

Charles Kennedy (2003): his father, Ian Kennedy, playing *The March of The Cameron Highlanders* on his fiddle.

Neil Kinnock (1988): his daughter, Rachel, singing *Horace The Horse* when she was a child.

Dame Cleo Laine (her 1997 appearance): Alec Dankworth, John Dankworth and The Generation Big Band performing *Early June* (Alec is her son and John Dankworth her husband). She also chose her daughter Jacqueline Dankworth singing *Don't Look Back*.

Vivien Leigh (1952): her husband, Laurence Olivier, performing *If The Heart of A Man* (from *The Beggar's Opera*).

Ben Lyon (1958): his wife, Bebe Daniels, singing *As Round And Round We Go*.

Bebe Daniels (1956) and Ben Lyon (1958): each chose their daughter, Barbara Lyon, singing *Stowaway*.

Sir Cameron Mackintosh (2001): his father Spike Mackintosh And His All Stars playing *High Time*.

Millicent Martin (1963): her husband Ronnie Carroll singing *I Am*.

Brian May (2002): his wife, Anita Dobson, singing Phil Spector's *To Know Him Is To Love Him* (with Brian May on guitar).

Virginia McKenna (2004): her daughter, Louise, performing *Whispers*.

Hayley Mills (1965): her father, Sir John, performing *I'm On A See-Saw* with Louise Brown.

Sheridan Morley (1974): his father, Robert, performing *Jonah And The Whale*, and his grandmother, Dame Gladys Cooper, singing *There Are Those* (with Tommy Steele and Geraldine Page). He also chose his godfather, Noël Coward (*Noël Coward At Las Vegas*).

Randy Newman (2008): his uncle Alfred Newman's composition *Goodbyes* from the film *How Green Was My Valley*.

Yoko Ono (2007): *Beautiful Boy* by her late husband, John Lennon, and *Magic* by their son, Sean.

Sir Peter Pears (his 1983 appearance): six out of his eight choices featured his partner Benjamin Britten – as composer, arranger, conductor or pianist.

André Previn (his 1996 appearance): his wife Anne-Sophie Mutter's recording of Beethoven's *Violin Concerto in D Minor*.

Allan Prior (1979): his daughter Maddy Prior's songs *Canals (Just The Two of Us)* and *Never Been Kissed In The Same Place Twice*.

(CHOSE A RELATIVE'S MUSIC – *cont.*)

Bernice Rubens (1981): her brother, Harold Rubens, playing Franz Liszt's *Piano Sonata In B Minor*.

Maurice Saatchi (1995): his father, Nathan, singing an unidentified song in synagogue.

Peggy Seeger (2001): *Joy of Living* by her husband, Ewan MacColl. She also chose the song *Boatman*, which featured her brother, Mike Seeger.

Phyllis Sellick (2002): in addition to the record she chose of the two of them, she also selected her husband, Cyril Smith, performing the solo in Rachmaninov's *Rhapsody on a Theme of Paganini*.

Ruskin Spear (1973): The Bonzo Dog Doo Dah Band's *The Intro And The Outro*, which featured his son Roger; and his son performing *Dr Rock*.

Imelda Staunton (2005): her mother, Bridie Staunton, performing *Reels And Jigs* with Maria Sonia.

Ralph Steadman (1998): his son, Theo, singing *Wish You Were Here*.

John Thaw (1990): his wife, Sheila Hancock, singing *Little Girls* (from *Annie*).

Emma Thompson (2010): *Florence, It's A Lovely Morning*, from the film version of *The Magic Roundabout*, which was created by her father, Eric Thompson.

Ron Todd (1991): his mother, Emmy Todd, playing *Black And White Rag*.

Stan Tracey (1999): his son Clark's band, the Clark Tracey Sextet, playing *Sherman At The Copthorne*.

Susana Walton (2002): three of her husband Sir William Walton's compositions, *Troilus And Cressida*, *Charge And Battle* (from the film music for *Henry V*) and *Polka* (from *Façade*).

Fay Weldon (2010): her husband Nick Fox's composition *Worst Fears*. She also chose her son, Nick Weldon, performing *People We Once Knew* with Andra Sparks.

Dr Ruth Westheimer (1990): her son, Joel, singing *There Was A Time*.

Paul Whitehouse (2003): his mother, Anita, singing *Unwaith Etto (To See You Again)*.

POPULAR MUSIC

THE MOST POPULAR ARTISTS
CHOSEN BY CASTAWAYS

The Beatles – chosen 252 times

Frank Sinatra – 240

Bing Crosby – 166

Louis Armstrong – 136 (he and Ella Fitzgerald are chosen together 14 times)

Noël Coward – 131

Ella Fitzgerald – 128

Edith Piaf – 109

Bob Dylan – 91

Paul Robeson – 89

Judy Garland – 77

Duke Ellington – 76

Elvis Presley – 73

Nat King Cole – 71

Fats Waller – 67

Fred Astaire – 66

Billie Holiday – 64

The Rolling Stones – 54

Glenn Miller – 54

Dame Gracie Fields – 47

Miles Davis – 44

Bud Flanagan – 43 (34 with Chesney Allen)

Peggy Lee – 43

Benny Goodman – 42

John McCormack – 40

Mantovani – 39

(THE MOST POPULAR ARTISTS CHOSEN BY CASTAWAYS – *cont.*)

Van Morrison – 38

Simon And Garfunkel – 38

John Lennon (without Paul McCartney) – 37

Bob Marley/Bob Marley And The Wailers – 36

Peter Sellers – 36

Count Basie – 35

Ethel Merman – 35

Barbra Streisand – 35

Chesney Allen – 34 (all with Bud Flanagan)

Stevie Wonder – 34

Julie Andrews – 33

Maurice Chevalier – 33

Elton John – 33

Charles Trénet – 35

David Bowie – 32

Kathleen Ferrier – 32

Gertrude Lawrence – 32

Dame Vera Lynn – 31

Glasgow Orpheus Choir – 30

Lena Horne – 31

Dave Brubeck – 29

Peter Dawson – 29

Marlene Dietrich – 29

Kenneth McKellar – 29

Ray Charles – 28

Danny Kaye – 27

Jean Sablon – 27

Richard Tauber – 27

Joan Baez – 26

Shirley Bassey – 26

Erroll Garner – 26

Nina Simone – 26

Leonard Bernstein – 25

Flanders And Swann – 25

Lotte Lenya – 25

Pink Floyd – 24

Hutch (Leslie Hutchinson) – 23

Gene Kelly – 23

The Beach Boys – 22

Eric Clapton/Derek And The Dominos – 22

Sammy Davis Jr – 22

Marvin Gaye – 22

Stanley Holloway – 22

André Kostelanetz Orchestra – 22

Tom Lehrer – 22

Vangelis – 22

Dame Cleo Laine – 21

CHOSEN 20 TIMES

Harry Belafonte, Aretha Franklin, Beniamino Gigli, Eartha Kitt, Joni Mitchell, Artie Shaw, Bessie Smith, Bruce Springsteen

CHOSEN 19 TIMES

Leonard Cohen, Perry Como, Tommy Dorsey, Rex Harrison, Charlie Parker, Oscar Peterson, Paul Simon, Rod Stewart, Paul Whiteman

CHOSEN 18 TIMES

Webster Booth (4 with Anne Ziegler), Buddy Holly

CHOSEN 17 TIMES

Abba, Tony Hancock, Yves Montand

CHOSEN 16 TIMES

Doris Day, Neil Diamond, Dire Straits, Carroll Gibbons, Walter Huston (14 of them *September Song*), Sir Harry Lauder, Bob Newhart, Yvonne Printemps, Art Tatum, Tina Turner (4 with Ike Turner), Sarah Vaughan, John Williams (guitarist)

CHOSEN 15 TIMES

Hoagy Carmichael, Enrico Caruso, Jimmy Durante, The Goons, Al Jolson, Sir Andrew Lloyd Webber, Django Reinhardt, Sir Harry Secombe, Ravi Shankar, Dionne Warwick

CHOSEN 14 TIMES

Louis Armstrong and Ella Fitzgerald (performing together), Johnny Cash, Victoria de los Ángeles, The Eagles, Frank Chacksfield And His Orchestra, James Galway, Jimmy Shand And His Band, Mary Martin, Bette Midler, Thelonious Monk, Queen, Elisabeth Schwarzkopf, Tom Waits

CHOSEN 13 TIMES

Charles Aznavour, Tony Bennett, The Chieftains, George Formby, Stan Getz, Mario Lanza, Little Richard, Miriam Makeba, Dean Martin, The Melachrino Strings And Orchestra, Morriston Orpheus Choir, Elaine Paige, Stephen Sondheim, Tommy Steele, Sarah Vaughan, Dinah Washington

CHOSEN 12 TIMES

Bix Beiderbecke, Acker Bilk, Alfred Drake (4 with Joan Roberts), Percy Grainger, Bill Haley And His Comets, Jimi Hendrix, Bob Hope (9 with Shirley Ross), Vladimir Horowitz, Burl Ives, Mahalia Jackson, Anton Karas, Layton And Johnstone, Joe Loss, The Modern Jazz Quartet, Harry Nilsson, The Regimental Band of The Coldstream Guards, The Royal Scots Dragoon Guards, Mel Tormé, J. Turner Layton

CHOSEN 11 TIMES

Jacques Brel, Max Bygraves, The Clash, Eric Coates, Peter Cook (9 with Dudley Moore), Roberta Flack, Maurice Jarre, Billy Joel, Howard Keel, Frankie Laine, Humphrey Lyttelton, Max Miller, Jelly Roll Morton, Luciano Pavarotti (including 2 as part of The Three Tenors), Diana Ross/The Supremes, Shirley Ross (9 with Bob Hope), Pete Seeger, The Seekers, George Shearing, Sophie Tucker

CHOSEN 10 TIMES

Lale Andersen (all *Lilli Marlene*), The Andrews Sisters, George Butterworth, Judy Collins, Elvis Costello, Frank Crumit, The Kinks, Gordon Macrae, Henry Mancini, Johnny Mathis, Paul McCartney/ Wings (without John Lennon), Liza Minnelli, Dudley Moore (9 with Peter Cook), André Previn, Otis Redding, Cliff Richard, Spike Jones And His City Slickers, The Treorchy Male (Voice) Choir, Kenneth Williams

CHOSEN 9 TIMES

Ambrose And His Orchestra, John Barry, Chuck Berry, Sir John
Betjeman, Victor Borge, Richard Burton, Clara Butt, Feodor Chaliapin,
Phil Collins, David Rose and His Orchestra, Ian Dury, The Everly
Brothers, Ted Heath, The Ink Spots, Tom Jones, Janis Joplin, Stan
Kenton, Monty Python, Willie Nelson, Anthony Newley, The Pogues
(4 times with Kirsty MacColl), Anne Shelton, 'Whispering' Jack Smith,
Mikis Theodorakis, U2, Neil Young

CHOSEN 8 TIMES

Chris Barber, Bunny Berigan, Black Dyke Mills Band, Lucienne Boyer,
Jack Buchanan, Kate Bush (3 with Peter Gabriel singing *Don't Give
Up*), Petula Clark, Ry Cooder, Julie Covington, Lonnie Donegan, The
Dubliners, Percy Faith, Peter Gabriel (3 with Kate Bush singing *Don't
Give Up*), Gerry And The Pacemakers, Astrud Gilberto, Hermione
Gingold (5 of them with Maurice Chevalier singing *I Remember It
Well*), Stéphane Grappelli, Jerry Lee Lewis, Josef Locke, Don Mclean,
Randy Newman, Sir Laurence Olivier, Dory Previn, Radiohead, Stewart
Robertson, Roxy Music, Dinah Shore, Carly Simon (8 different songs),
The Smiths, Sting, Jack Teagarden, The Who

CHOSEN 7 TIMES

Herb Alpert, Pearl Bailey, Chet Baker, The Band
of The Grenadier Guards, Cilla Black, Al Bowlly,
Douglas Byng, John Coltrane, Barbara Cook, Val
Doonican, Billy Eckstine, Bryan Ferry, Reri Grist,
Kenneth Horne/*Round The Horne*, Marilyn Horne, Michael Jackson,
The Jam, Keith Jarrett, Stan Kenton, Albert Ketelby, Frank Loesser, Los
Paraguayos, Ewan MacColl, Jeanette Macdonald, John Martyn, Meat
Loaf, Marilyn Monroe, Mormon Tabernacle Choir, Doretta Morrow
(all *And This Is My Beloved*), Ezio Pinza (6 of them *Some Enchanted
Evening*), Tino Rossi, Sidney Torch And His Orchestra, Simply Red,
Dusty Springfield, Cat Stevens, James Taylor, The Temptations, Topol,
Frankie Vaughan, Ethel Waters, Muddy Waters, Elisabeth Welch, Josh
White, Andy Williams

CHOSEN 6 TIMES

Carmen Amaya, Josephine Baker, Sidney Bechet, Marc Bolan/T. Rex, Glen Campbell, José Collins, Billy Cotton Band, Bobby Darin, John Denver, Barbara Dickson, Nelson Eddy, Enya, Sid Field, Fleetwood Mac, Robert Goulet, Guy Lombardo And His Royal Canadians, Binnie Hale, Tim Hardin, Richard Harris, George Harrison, Coleman Hawkins, Audrey Hepburn, Bobby Howes, Peter Jackson (all *Waltzing Matilda*), Aled Jones, Shirley Jones, Bert Kaempfert, Charlie Kunz, Huddie Ledbetter/Lead Belly, Lew Stone And His Band (4 with Al Bowlly), Kirsty MacColl (4 times with The Pogues), The Mills Brothers, Ray Noble And His Orchestra, Nana Mouskouri, Sinéad O'Connor, The Platters, The Police, Robert Preston, The Proclaimers, Procol Harum, Johnnie Ray, Jim Reeves, Lionel Richie, Andrés Segovia, Victor Silvester (And His Orchestra), Muriel Smith, Jo Stafford, Steeleye Span, Lawrence Tibbett, The Velvet Underground, Dooley Wilson (all *As Time Goes By*)

CHOSEN 5 TIMES

Bryan Adams, Larry Adler, Boney M, June Bronhill (3 with Keith Michell), Big Bill Broonzy, James Brown, Owen Brannigan, Georges Brassens, Eddie Calvert, Nick Cave, The Clancy Brothers And Tommy Makem, John Cleese (3 with Michael Palin), Coldplay, Ray Conniff, Bernard Cribbins, Chris de Burgh, Blossom Dearie, The Doobie Brothers, The Eurythmics, Eddie Fisher, Florrie Forde, Jacqueline François, The Fron Male Voice Choir, Gloria Gaynor, Al Green (one with Lyle Lovett), Emmylou Harris, John Lee Hooker, Engelbert Humperdinck, Harry James, Glynis Johns (all *Send In The Clowns*), Robert Johnson, Jack Jones, Joy Division, Kate And Anna McGarrigle, Stubby Kaye, Gladys Knight (4 with The Pips), Led Zeppelin, Annie Lennox, Les Troubadours Du Roi Baudouin, Marie Lloyd, MGM Studio Orchestra, Guy Mitchell, Matt Monro, Ennio Morricone, Gerry Mulligan, Nusrat Fateh Ali Khan, Seán Ó Riada, Roy Orbison, Les Paul, Jan Peerce, Charles Penrose (all *The Laughing Policeman*), Alan Price, Leontyne Price, Prince, Pulp, Gerry Rafferty/Stealers Wheel, John Raitt, The Red Army Ensemble: Moscow Military District, Lou Reed (all *Walk On The Wild Side*), Joshua Rifkin, John Roberts (4 with Alfred Drake), Kenny Rogers, Tito Schipa, The Shadows, Andy Stewart, Maxine Sullivan, Yma Sumac, Donna Summer, Ted Lewis And His Band, Bryn Terfel, Ben Webster, Wham!, John Williams (composer)

CHOSEN 4 TIMES

Moira Anderson, The Animals, Anne Ziegler (all with Webster Booth), Joan Armatrading, Michael Ball, Shelley Berman, Ernest Bloch, Blondie/ Debbie Harry, Jussi Björling, Pat Boone, Eve Boswell, Jackson Browne, Jeff Buckley, Buena Vista Social Club, Carroll Gibbons and His Boy Friends, Pablo (Pau) Casals, Harry Champion, The Choir of Temple Church, Joe Cocker, Russ Conway, Cicely Courtneidge, Michael Crawford, John Dankworth, Alfred Deller, Dame Judi Dench, Charles Dibdin (all *Tom Bowling*), Sacha Distel, Dr Hook, Earth Wind And Fire, Eminem, Tennessee Ernie Ford, Connie Francis, Reginald Gardiner (all *Trains*), Genesis, Dizzy Gillespie, Ron Goodwin, The Grateful Dead, Macy Gray, Grimethorpe Colliery Band, Marvin Hamlisch, Rolf Harris, Isaac Hayes, Woody Herman, Whitney Houston, Jacques Ibert, Julio Iglesias, Ike Turner (all with Tina Turner), The Jacksons/The Jackson 5, B. B. King, Carole King, Diana Krall, Alison Krauss, Gene Krupa, Laurel And Hardy, Lester Flatt And Earl Scruggs, Meade 'Lux' Lewis, Beatrice Lillie, Julie London, Los Fronterizos, Nellie Lutcher, Madness, The Mamas And The Papas, Lata Mangeshkar, Groucho Marx, Massed Bands, Massive Attack, Keith Michell (3 with June Bronhill), Mighty Sparrow, Charles Mingus, Morecambe And Wise, Oasis, Brendan O'Dowda, Esther Ofarim, Tony Orlando And Dawn, Pet Shop Boys, Quintette Du Hot Club De France, R.E.M., Chita Rivera, Smokey Robinson (all *The Tracks of My Tears*), The Roger Wagner Chorale, Sonny Rollins, Linda Ronstadt, Santana, Bob Seger, The Sex Pistols, Sandie Shaw, Peter Skellern, Steely Dan, Supertramp, Joan Sutherland, Talking Heads, Lionel Tertis, Bonnie Tyler, The Undertones, Rufus Wainwright, The Weather Girls, Weather Report, Robbie Williams, Sir Henry Wood, Narciso Yepes, Lester Young

CHOSEN 3 TIMES

AC/DC, Marian Anderson, Arthur Askey, Winifred Atwell, Dame Janet Baker, The Band, Band Aid, Jeff Beck, George Benjamin, Alan Bennett, George Benson, Bill Evans Trio, Henry Blair (2 with Ray

(CHOSEN THREE TIMES – *cont.*)

Turner), Howard Blake, Blood Sweat And Tears, The Bonzo Dog Doo Dah Band, Booker T. And The MGs, Billy Bragg, Sam Browne, The Byrds, J. J. Cale, Maria Callas, Leslie Caron, José Carreras (including 2 as part of The Three Tenors), The Cars, Jack Cassidy, Carol Channing, Clannad, Jimmy Cliff, Patsy Cline, Rosemary Clooney, Charles Coborn, Eddie Cochran, Alma Cogan, Ornette Coleman, Sam Cooke, Crosby Stills Nash (And Young), The Cyril Stapleton Orchestra, Netania Devrath, Georges Delerue, The Deller Consort, Dion/Dion And The Belmonts, Ken Dodd, Placido Domingo (including 2 as part of The Three Tenors), Nick Drake, Deanna Durbin, Eastman Wind Ensemble, Cliff Edwards, Edwin Hawkins Singers, Ruth Etting, Adam Faith, The Fall, José Feliciano, The Fodens Motor Works Band, Pete Fountain, Stan Freberg, Free, The Fureys, Bobbie Gentry, The Gipsy Kings, Ron Grainer, Georges Guétary, Juanita Hall, Keith Hamshere, Steve Harley And Cockney Rebel, Don Henley, Earl 'Fatha' Hines, Johnny Hodges, Hot Chocolate, Frankie Howerd, Barry Humphries/Dame Edna Everage, Betty Hutton, Frank Ifield, Inti-Illimani, Allan Jones, George Jones, Grace Jones, Norah Jones, Quincy Jones, Kaiser Chiefs, Kid Ory's Creole Jazz Band, Ladysmith Black Mambazo, Danny La Rue, Cyndi Lauper, John Laurie, Little Feat, Trini Lopez, The Luton Girls Choir, Benjamin Luxon, Arthur Marshall, Martha And The Vandellas, Tony Martin, Ralph McTell, George Melly, Johnny Mercer, Mabel Mercer, Pat Metheny, Mike Nichols and Elaine May, Carmen Miranda, Mitch Miller And His Orchestra, Germaine Montéro, The Moody Blues, Christy Moore, Jeanne Moreau, The New Seekers, Ivor Novello, Cavan O'Connor, Mike Oldfield, The Orphans, Michael Palin (all with John Cleese), Dolly Parton, Paul Weston And His Orchestra, Donald Peers, Peter, Paul And Mary, Perez Prado, Planxty, The Ray Ellington Quartet, The Revellers, Debbie Reynolds, Buddy Rich, Rita Williams Singers, Robert Shaw Chorale, Roberto Inglez And His Orchestra, Amália Rodrigues, Rosalind Russell, Buffy Sainte-Marie, Peter Sarstedt, Elizabeth Seal, Neil Sedaka, Semprini, Helen Shapiro, Bobby Short, Keely Smith, Sons of The Pioneers, Jeri Southern, The Specials, Squeeze, Dorothy Squires, Johnny Standley, Kay Starr, The Stranglers, Randolph Sutton, Taj Mahal, Kiri Te Kanawa, Shirley Temple, Jake Thackray, B. J. Thomas, Toto, Traffic, The Verve, Loudon Wainwright III, Jimmy Webb, Barry White,

Margaret Whiting, Slim Whitman, Billy Williams, Hank Williams, Joe Williams, Jackie Wilson, Teddy Wilson, Robb Wilton, Barbara Windsor, Gheorghe Zamfir, Warren Zevon

CHOSEN TWICE (A SELECTION)

John Adams, Robert Alda, Woody Allen, Laurindo Almeida, Pete Atkin, Gene Austin, Gene Autry, The Bachelors, Kenny Ball, Mike Batt, Gilbert Becaud, Derek Bell, Brook Benton, Berlin, The Beverley Sisters, Big Brother And The Holding Company, Björk, The Blue Nile, James Blunt, Earl Bostic, Max Boyce, Paul Brady, Johnny Brandon, Teresa Brewer, Sarah Brightman, Elkie Brooks, Garth Brooks, Georgia Brown, Joe Brown, Burning Spear, Cab Calloway, Eddie Cantor, Captain Beefheart, Cornelius Cardew, Len Cariou, Carl Reiner and Mel Brooks, Elsie Carlisle, The Carpenters, Ronnie Carroll, Carson Robison And His Pioneers, Carmen Cavallaro, Tracy Chapman (chosen twice in one episode by Gok Wan), Ian Charleson, The Charleston Chasers, Chubby Checker, Cher, Chicago, Chicane, The Chipmunks, George Chisholm, The Clerkes of Oxenford, Peggy Cochrane, Comedian Harmonists, The Commodores, Arthur Conley, Harry Connick Jr, Steve Conway, The Crash Test Dummies, Gemma Craven, Randy Crawford, Robert Cray, Creedence Clearwater Revival, Jim Croce, Xavier Cugat, Dorothy Dandridge, Bebe Daniels, Jacqueline Dankworth, Danny And The Juniors, Shaun Davey, Manitas De Plata, Deacon Blue, Johnny Desmond, Dexy's Midnight Runners, Dido, Dr. John, Eileen Donaghy, Donovan, The Doors, Jimmy Dorsey, The Drifters, Irene Dunne, Jonathan And Darlene Edwards, Elbow, Electric Light Orchestra, Gus Elen, Mary Ellis, Lorraine Ellison, Eric Winstone And His Orchestra, Donald Fagen, Marianne Faithfull, Georgie Fame, George Fenton, Léo Ferré, Firehouse Five Plus Two, Stephen Foster, Billy Fury, Jan Garbarek, Carlos Gardel, Dick Gaughan, Geraldo And His Orchestra, Gary Glitter, Tito Gobbi, Nat Gonella, Henry Goodman, Eydie Gormé, Kathryn Grayson, Bobby Hackett, Harry Roy And His Band, Heatwave, Herbie Hancock, The Happy Mondays, Françoise Hardy, The Harry Simeone Chorale, Rita Hayworth, Jennifer Holliday, Judy Holliday,

(CHOSEN TWICE – *cont.*)

Lightnin' Hopkins, Shirley Horn (chosen both times by
Richard Rodney Bennett), Howlin' Wolf, Abdullah Ibrahim,
Jack Payne And His Orchestra, Max Jaffa, Mick Jagger
(both with David Bowie singing *Dancing In The
Street*), Jamiroquai, Janis Ian, Jimmie Lunceford
And His Orchestra, Barb Jungr, Kathie Kay,
Ronan Keating, Greta Keller, Larry Kert,
Bismillah Khan, The Killers, Albert King, Ben
E. King, Dave King, Freddie King, Morgana
King, Emma Kirkby, Lord Kitchener, Beverley
Knight, Mark Knopfler, Sonja Kristina, Kris
Kristofferson, k.d. lang, John Langstaff, Angela Lansbury, The La's,
Le Mystère Des Voix Bulgares, Jerry Lewis, Gordon Lightfoot, Little
Eva, Julian Lloyd Webber, LL Cool J, Dorothy Love Coates, Lyle
Lovett (one with Al Green), Luis Russell And His Orchestra, Patti
LuPone, Frankie Lymon, Father Sydney MacEwan, Madonna, Lena
Martell, George Martin, Millicent Martin, Al Martino, Lee Marvin,
Hugh Masekela, John Mayer, Billy Mayerl, Susannah McCorkle,
Julia McKenzie, Carmen McRae, Sergio Mendes, Freddie Mercury
and Montserrat Caballé, Michel LeGrand And His Orchestra, The
Mike Sammes Singers, Roger Miller, Kylie Minogue, Vaughn Monroe,
Marion Montgomery, Carlos Montoya, Ron Moody, Jerome Moross,
Mouloudji, Mott The Hoople, Anne Murray, Muse, Youssou N'Dour,
Phyllis Nelson, The New York Pro Musica Antiqua, Wayne Newton,
Thomas Newman, Nickelback, Nirvana, Marni Nixon, Jessye Norman,
Laura Nyro, Abi Ofarim (both with Esther Ofarim), Liam O'Flynn,
King Oliver, Tessie O'Shea, Patti Page, Gram Parsons, Harry Partch,
Ann Peebles, Penguin Cafe Orchestra, Esther Phillips, Alfred Piccaver,
Shelley Plimpton, Iggy Pop (including one as Iggy And The Stooges),
The Pretenders, Louis Prima, Primal Scream, Primo Scala And His
Accordion Band, Maddy Prior, The Ramones, Ray Martin And His
Orchestra, Chris Rea, Red Hot Chili Peppers, Steve Reich, Markus
Reinhardt, Niño Ricardo, Robert McFerrin And Adele Addison, Sir
George Robey, Robin Hall And Jimmy MacGregor, Jimmie Rodgers,
Mickey Rooney (once with Judy Garland), Annie Ross, Nino Rota,
Jennifer Rush, Jimmy Rushing, Connie Russell, Nitin Sawhney, The
Scaffold, The Searchers, Peggy Seeger, Del Shannon, Sid Phillips And
His Band, Nancy Sinatra (one with Lee Hazlewood and one with Frank
Sinatra), The Singers Unlimited, Slade, The Small Faces, Soft Cell,

Mercedes Sosa, The Squadronaires, The Steve Miller Band, Al Stewart, John Stewart, The Stone Roses, Wally Stott And His Orchestra And Chorus, Teresa Stratas, The Stylistics, Kay Thompson, Johnny Tillotson, Tony Osborne And His Orchestra, Toots And The Maytals, Arthur Tracy, Travis, Ray Turner (both with Henry Blair), Ritchie Valens, Rudy Vallee, Luther Vandross, Stevie Ray Vaughan, Bobby Vee, Gene Vincent, The Walker Brothers (chosen twice in one episode by Joe Bugner), Jack Warner, Jennifer Warnes, Norma Waterson, Marti Webb, Gillian Welch, Mae West, Roger Whittaker, Lee Wiley, Don Williams, Harold Williams, Brian Wilson (in addition to The Beach Boys), Amy Winehouse, Bill Withers, Arthur Wood, Tammy Wynette, Jimmy Yancey, The Yardbirds (once accompanying Sonny Boy Williamson)

CHOSEN ONCE (A SELECTION)

10cc, ABC, David Ackles, Adam And The Ants, Adele, Christina Aguilera, The Alan Parsons Project, All Saints, Paul Anka, The Archies, Ashton, Gardner And Dyke, Aswad, Corinne Bailey Rae, Anita Baker, The Beautiful South, Beck, Daniel Bedingfield, Belle And Sebastian, Richard Beymer, Big Country, Billy J. Kramer And The Dakotas, Vivian Blaine, Bobby Bloom, Blue Mink, Blur, Bob And Earl, Bob And Marcia, Eric Bogle, Michael Bolton, Bon Jovi, Gary US Bonds, The Boomtown Rats, Boy George/Culture Club, Bread, Brian And Michael, Bucks Fizz, The Bushwackers, David Byrne, James Cagney, Captain Sensible, Eric Carmen, Barbara Cartland, Eva Cassidy, Gene Chandler, Chas And Dave, The Chemical Brothers, Neneh Cherry, Tony Christie, Charlotte Church, Richard Clayderman, The Coasters, The Cocteau Twins, Russ Columbo, Billy Connolly, Chick Corea, Bill Cosby, Country Joe And The Fish, The Cranberries, Cream, Christopher Cross, Sheryl Crow, The Cure, D:ream, The Damned, Dan Ackroyd and John Belushi, Dave And Ansel Collins, Mac Davis, Delaney And Bonnie, Desmond Dekker, Depeche Mode, Destiny's Child, Dr Dre, Fats Domino, Lee Dorsey, Duran Duran, East of Eden, The Easybeats, Duane Eddy, Randy Edelman, Roy Eldridge, Missy Elliott, Brian Eno, David Essex, Gloria Estefan, Everything But The Girl, Ezio, Andy Fairweather-Low, Family, Chris Farlowe, Michael Feinstein, Julie Felix, W. C. Fields, The

(CHOSEN ONCE – *cont.*)

Fine Young Cannibals, Focus, Foreigner, Frankie Goes To Hollywood, Franz Ferdinand, Glenn Frey, The Full Tilt Boogie Band, The Fun Lovin' Criminals, Serge Gainsbourg, Lesley Garrett, Crystal Gayle, Mitzi Gaynor, Barry Gibb (with Barbra Streisand), Goldfrapp, Bobby Goldsboro, Gorillaz, Eddy Grant, Juliette Greco, Green Day, Groove Armada, Dave Grusin, Sacha Guitry, Woody Guthrie, Merle Haggard, Johnny Hallyday, Noel Harrison, P. J. Harvey, Donny Hathaway, Chesney Hawkes, Lee Hazlewood (with Nancy Sinatra), Jim Henson, Herman's Hermits, Hildegarde, Benny Hill, Dan Hill, Faith Hill, Vince Hill, Ronnie Hilton, Patricia Hodge, Michael Holliday, Mary Hopkin, The Housemartins, Huey Lewis & The News, The Human League, The Incredible String Band, Instant Sunshine, Chris Isaak, Eddie Izzard, Hugh Jackman, Janet Jackson, James, Al Jarreau, Jefferson Airplane, Jethro Tull, Jack Johnson, Rickie Lee Jones, Terry Jones, Louis Jordan, Jr. Walker & The All Stars, John Julius Norwich, Katrina And The Waves, The Keynotes, Alicia Keys, Chaka Khan, King Crimson, Kathy Kirby, Kraftwerk, Lenny Kravitz, Patti Labelle, Lady Gaga, Dorothy Lamour, Hugh Laurie, Jackie Leven, Leona Lewis, Liberace, The Libertines, Lieutenant Pigeon, The Lightning Seeds, Bob Lind, Lindisfarne, Little River Band, Long John Baldry, Los Lobos, Arthur Lowe, Lulu, Kenny Lynch, Loretta Lynn, M People, Melissa Manchester, Manhattan Transfer, Barry Manilow, Manos Tacticos And His Bouzoukis, Laura Marling, Wynton Marsalis, Marshall Hain, Steve Martin, Jessie Matthews, Curtis Mayfield, Susan Maughan, John Mayall, George McCrae, McFadden And Whitehead, McFly, Rod McKuen, Melanie, Katie Melua, Men At Work, The Merseys, George Michael, Middle of The Road, Mike + The Mechanics, Bernard Miles, Gary Miller, Mrs Mills, Tim Minchin, Moby, The Mock Turtles, The Monkees, Zero Mostel, The Mothers of Invention, Motörhead, The Move, Alison Moyet, Maria Muldaur, Mungo Jerry, Musical Youth, Johnny Nash, Nena, Michael Nesmith, New Order, The New York Dolls, Juice Newton, Stevie Nicks, Nico, The Nitty Gritty Dirt Band, Klaus Nomi, Paolo Nutini, Michael Nyman, Des O'Connor, The O'Jays, Gilbert O'Sullivan, Peter O'Toole, Billy Ocean, Yoko Ono (with John Lennon), Orchestral Manoeuvres In The Dark, Robert Palmer, Van Dyke Parks, Mandy Patinkin, Billy Paul, The Paul Butterfield Blues Band, Tom Paxton, Freda Payne, Bernadette Peters, Gretchen Peters, Peters & Lee, Madeleine Peyroux, Wilson Pickett, Pink, Gene Pitney, Su Pollard, Portishead, Billy Preston, P. J. Proby,

Puff Daddy and Faith Evans, Steve Race, Rainbow, Lou Rawls, Helen Reddy, The Rezillos, Charlie Rich, The Righteous Brothers, Rihanna, Minnie Riperton, Tom Robinson, The Ronettes, Rose Marie, Demis Roussos, Run-D. M. C., Runrig, Sade, The Sandpipers, Mike Sarne, Boz Scaggs, Seal, Seals & Crofts, The Sensational Alex Harvey Band, Shakira, Tupac Shakur (2Pac), The Shangri-Las, Wayne Shorter, John Shuttleworth, Labi Siffre, Siouxsie And The Banshees, Percy Sledge, Sister Sledge, Heather Small, Hurricane Smith, Soul II Soul, Spandau Ballet, Spooky Tooth, Stan Tracey Quintet, The Staple Singers, Freddie Starr, Ringo Starr, Candi Staton, Status Quo, Steel Pulse, Shakin' Stevens (with Bonnie Tyler), Stiff Little Fingers, Curtis Stigers, The Strawbs, Elaine Stritch, Super Furry Animals, Sweet, The Swingle Sisters, Take That, Tears For Fears, The Temperance Seven, Them, Third World, The Three Degrees, Three Dog Night, Toploader, Tom Petty And The Heartbreakers, The Tourists, The Traveling Wilburys, Ultravox, U.S.A. for Africa, Ricky Valance, Frankie Valli, Ben Vereen, Sid Vicious, Bobby Vinton, Scott Walker, Ian Wallace, Clifford T. Ward, Jeff Wayne, Kanye West, Willard White, The White Stripes, Kim Wilde, Sonny Boy Williamson, Wingy Manone's Dixieland Band, Steve Winwood, Bobby Womack, Robert Wyatt, Wynonna, Jimmy Young, Paul Young, Frank Zappa, Benjamin Zephaniah

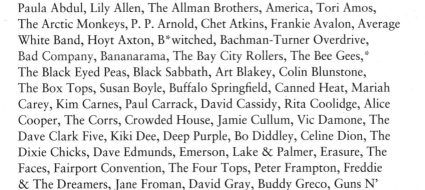

NONE OF THEIR RECORDS EVER CHOSEN (A SELECTION)

Paula Abdul, Lily Allen, The Allman Brothers, America, Tori Amos, The Arctic Monkeys, P. P. Arnold, Chet Atkins, Frankie Avalon, Average White Band, Hoyt Axton, B*witched, Bachman-Turner Overdrive, Bad Company, Bananarama, The Bay City Rollers, The Bee Gees,* The Black Eyed Peas, Black Sabbath, Art Blakey, Colin Blunstone, The Box Tops, Susan Boyle, Buffalo Springfield, Canned Heat, Mariah Carey, Kim Carnes, Paul Carrack, David Cassidy, Rita Coolidge, Alice Cooper, The Corrs, Crowded House, Jamie Cullum, Vic Damone, The Dave Clark Five, Kiki Dee, Deep Purple, Bo Diddley, Celine Dion, The Dixie Chicks, Dave Edmunds, Emerson, Lake & Palmer, Erasure, The Faces, Fairport Convention, The Four Tops, Peter Frampton, Freddie & The Dreamers, Jane Froman, David Gray, Buddy Greco, Guns N' Roses, Arlo Guthrie, Buddy Guy, Screamin' Jay Hawkins, Hawkwind, The Herd, The Hollies, Humble Pie, Billy Idol, Iron Maiden, The Isley Brothers, Joe Jackson, Jean-Michel Jarre, Nick Lowe, Lynyrd Skynyrd,

(NONE OF THEIR RECORDS EVER CHOSEN – *cont.*)

Manfred Mann, The Manic Street Preachers, Marillion, Marmalade, Buddy Miles, Ann Miller, Samantha Mumba, Ricky Nelson, Olivia Newton-John, Donny Osmond (or *any* of the Osmonds), Carl Perkins, Mark Ronson, Leo Sayer, Simple Minds, Sly & The Family Stone, Patti Smith, Snow Patrol, Soft Machine, Sonic Youth, Britney Spears, Lisa Stansfield, Edwin Starr, The Stereophonics, Joss Stone, The Style Council, Supergrass, The Swinging Blue Jeans, Ten Years After, Thin Lizzy, The Thompson Twins, Justin Timberlake, The Troggs, K. T. Tunstall, The Turtles, Shania Twain, UB40, Suzanne Vega, The Village People, Wet Wet Wet, Marty Wilde, Edgar Winter, Johnny Winter, ZZ Top

* However, on 19 February 2012 – after the cut-off date for this book (the seventieth anniversary programme on 29 January) – Lord Prescott chose the Bee Gees' *Stayin' Alive*.

THE MOST POPULAR SONGS CHOSEN
BY CASTAWAYS

This list excludes The Beatles – see page 106.

Non, Je Ne Regrette Rien – chosen 42 times

Underneath The Arches – 34

La Vie En Rose – 32

My Way – 29

Summertime – 27

Night And Day – 26

September Song – 26

Mad Dogs And Englishmen – 24

Over The Rainbow – 24

These Foolish Things – 24

I'll See You Again – 22

As Time Goes By – 21

Ev'ry Time We Say Goodbye – 21

What A Wonderful World – 21

Lilli Marlene – 20

Chariots of Fire – 19

Danny Boy – 19

Imagine – 19

Let's Do It – 19

Begin The Beguine – 18

Blow The Wind Southerly – 18

Some Enchanted Evening – 18

Music

Amazing Grace – 17

Bess, You Is My Woman Now – 17

La Mer – 17

Mack The Knife – 17

Moonlight Serenade – 17

Ol' Man River – 17

Stardust – 17

Manhattan – 16

My Very Good Friend The Milkman –16

Singin' In The Rain – 16

Somewhere My Love (Lara's Theme) – 16

Georgia On My Mind – 15

St Louis Blues – 15

Smoke Gets In Your Eyes – 15

White Christmas – 15

A Foggy Day – 14

Just One of Those Things – 14

The Way You Look Tonight – 14

You'll Never Walk Alone – 14

A Nightingale Sang In Berkeley Square – 13

If You Were The Only Girl In The World – 13

In The Mood – 13

Memory – 13

My Funny Valentine – 13

Oh, What A Beautiful Mornin' – 13

On The Sunny Side of The Street – 13

The Eton Boating Song – 13

Blowin' In The Wind – 12

Cheek To Cheek – 12

Skye Boat Song – 12

Somewhere – 12

Tea For Two – 12

The Harry Lime Theme (from the film *The Third Man*) – 12

Autumn Leaves – 11

Bridge Over Troubled Water – 11

Heartbreak Hotel – 11

I Just Called To Say I Love You – 11

If I Loved You – 11

Moon River – 11

People – 11

Sailing – 11

The Girl From Ipanema – 11

Well Did You Evah? – 11

When I Fall In Love – 11

You're The Tops – 11

You Make Me Feel So Young – 11

CHOSEN 10 TIMES

Alabama Song, America, I Could Have Danced All Night, Miss Otis Regrets, O Sole Mio, Roses of Picardy, Skylark, Stormy Weather, The Birth of The Blues, The Floral Dance, Tiger Rag, When The Saints Go Marching In

CHOSEN 9 TIMES

Come Rain Or Come Shine, I'm Gonna Sit Right Down And Write Myself A Letter, I've Grown Accustomed To Her Face, Layla, Mood Indigo, New York, New York, One For My Baby, Our Love Is Here To Stay, Send In The Clowns, Strange Fruit, Surabaya Johnny, Thanks For The Memory, There's No Business Like Show Business, Wind Beneath My Wings

CHOSEN 8 TIMES

And This Is My Beloved, Candle In The Wind, Falling In Love Again, Honeysuckle Rose, I Get A Kick Out of You, I've Got You Under My Skin, Is That All There Is?, Lullaby of Broadway, Mr Tambourine Man, My Love Is Like A Red, Red Rose, Rock Around The Clock, Rockin' Chair, Take Five, Take The A Train, The Best, Top Hat, White Tie And Tails, Unforgettable, We Shall Overcome, We'll Meet Again, Wouldn't It Be Loverly?, You Can't Always Get What You Want

CHOSEN 7 TIMES

April In Paris, Cabaret, Climb Every Mountain, Colonel Bogey, Deep Purple, I Feel Pretty, I Heard It Through The Grapevine, I'll Be Seeing You, Just An Old Fashioned Girl, Keep Right On To The End of The Road, Laura, London Pride, Milord, My Blue Heaven, No Woman No Cry, Now You Has Jazz, Oh, Lady Be Good, People Will Say We're In Love, Redemption Song, Scarborough Fair, A Shropshire Lad, Swing Low Sweet Chariot, Thank Heaven For Little Girls, The Very Thought of You, They Can't Take That Away From Me, Wish You Were Here, Your Feet's Too Big

CHOSEN 6 TIMES

A Case of You, A String of Pearls, Basin Street Blues, Beautiful Dreamer, Don't Be Cruel, Don't Cry For Me, Argentina, Don't Fence Me In, Embraceable You, Fly Me To The Moon, For All We Know, Gone Fishin', Have You Met Miss Jones?, How High The Moon, (I Can't Get No) Satisfaction, I Can't Give You Anything But Love, I Remember It Well, In The Wee Small Hours of The Morning, Let's Face The Music And Dance, Joe Hill, Like A Rolling Stone, Louise, Misty, My Favourite Things, On Ilkla' Moor Baht 'At, One Love, Raindrops Keep Fallin' On My Head, Sally, Strangers In The Night, Sympathy For The Devil, The Kid From Red Bank, The Lady Is A Tramp, The Sound of Music, The Surrey With The Fringe On Top, Teddy Bears' Picnic, The Times They Are A-Changin', The Trolley Song, Three Coins In The Fountain, What's Going On?, Where Have All The Flowers Gone?, You Made Me Love You, Zorba's Dance (from *Zorba The Greek*)

CHOSEN 5 TIMES

A Whiter Shade of Pale, Ain't Misbehavin', All The Way, Always Look On The Bright Side of Life, Always On My Mind, Age of Aquarius, And The Angels Sing, Another Brick In The Wall, Are You Lonesome Tonight?, Bali Ha'I, Bat Out of Hell, Brown Eyed Girl, Canoe Song, Chattanooga Choo Choo, Common People, The Dam Busters March, Dancing In The Street, Dancing Queen, God Bless The Child, Hello Dolly, (I Dream of) Jeannie With The Light Brown Hair, I Got Plenty of Nuttin', I Got Rhythm, I've Got The World On A String, It Ain't Necessarily So, Jailhouse Rock, Leaning On A Lamp Post, Li'l Darlin', Love Walked In, Makin Whoopee, Maybe It's Because I'm A Londoner, Mull of Kintyre, My Yiddishe Momma, Peggy Sue, Pennies From Heaven, Round Midnight, Simple Twist of Fate, Some of These Days, Someone To Watch Over Me, Space Oddity, The Best Is Yet To Come, The Man That Got Away, The Sound of Silence, The Stately Homes of England, There Is Nothin' Like A Dame, the title theme from *Schindler's List, Tonight, True Love, Tutti Frutti, Voodoo Chile, Walk On The Wild Side, Without You, You Are The Sunshine Of My Life, Your Song*

CHOSE BING CROSBY SINGING *WHITE CHRISTMAS*

Charlie Drake, Bob Hope, Kenneth Horne, Mantovani, Jan Morris, Johnny Speight, Fred Trueman, William Whitelaw, Mike Yarwood

CHOSE FRANK SINATRA'S *MY WAY**

John and Roy Boulting, Geoffrey Boycott, David Broome, Sir Michael Caine, Fay Compton, Gareth Edwards, Sir David Frost, Stewart Granger, Russell Harty, Jimmy Jewel, Barry John, Alan Minter, Des O'Connor, Antoinette Sibley, Wilbur Smith, Johnny Speight, Doris Stokes, Jimmy Tarbuck, Lord Tebbit, Sir Peregrine Worsthorne

* According to a BBC spokesperson: '*My Way* is not banned, but in the past guests have been gently encouraged to think of something else to prevent the song becoming a cliché.' Sir Michael Caine was the most recent castaway to choose it, in December 2009.

CHOSE *TEDDY BEARS' PICNIC*

J. G. Ballard, Michael Heseltine, Willy Russell, Nigel Slater

CHOSE GLORIA GAYNOR'S *I WILL SURVIVE*

Jasper Conran, Lesley Garrett, Donald Pleasence, Pauline Quirke

CHOSE BILLIE HOLIDAY'S *STRANGE FRUIT*

Tallulah Bankhead, John Freeman, Fran Landesman, Ann Leslie, Alan Yentob

Gillian Anderson and Debbie Harry chose Nina Simone's version.

CHOSE CHARLES PENROSE'S *THE LAUGHING POLICEMAN*

Ray Cooney, Cicely Courtneidge, Hugh Grant, Patricia Routledge

CHOSE *COLONEL BOGEY*

Patrick Cargill, Lord Denning, Sir Bernard Ingham, Henry Longhurst, Humphrey Lyttelton, Leslie Welch

CHOSE *ALWAYS LOOK ON THE BRIGHT SIDE OF LIFE*

Tony Adams, Sanjeev Bhaskar, Gary Lineker, Piers Morgan

CHOSE *THE ETON BOATING SONG*

Henry Blofeld, T. E. B. Clarke, Graham Hill, Brian Johnston, Lord Killanin, Margaret Lockwood (twice), Lord Longford, Jean Rook, R. C. Sherriff, John Snagge

CHOSE *FORTY YEARS ON* (HARROW'S SCHOOL SONG)

Barbara Cartland, R. F. Delderfield, Sir Terence Rattigan

Lord Deedes chose 'one of the lesser-known Harrow songs', *Here Sir*.

CHOSE *THE STRIPPER*

Julie Andrews, Stubby Kaye, Ernie Wise

CHOSE *ON ILKLA' MOOR BAHT 'AT*

Roy Castle, Sir Leonard Hutton, Jean Rook, Harvey Smith

CHOSE *LILLI MARLENE*

Lord Ashley, Sir Douglas Bader, Brian Inglis, Jim Laker, Sir Fitzroy MacLean (twice), Norman Mailer, V. S. Naipaul, Yoko Ono, Taki, Professor Heinz Wolff

CHOSE *VICTORY TEST MATCH CALYPSO* (ENGLAND V. WEST INDIES, LORD'S, 1950) BY LORD BEGINNER AND THE CALYPSO RHYTHM KINGS

Denis Compton and Bill Edrich, Cecil Parker

Jim Laker chose Lord Beginner And The Calypso Rhythm Kings, *The Cricket Champions*; Sir Learie Constantine chose Lord Beginner And The Calypso Rhythm Kings, *Australia v. West Indies Calypso*; Rev. David Sheppard chose Lord Beginner And The Calypso Rhythm Kings, *Cricket, Lovely Cricket*; Alec Bedser and Sir Alec Douglas-Home chose Lord Kitchener And St Vincent St Six, *Alec Bedser Calypso*.

CHOSE A FOOTBALL SONG

Nick Clegg: *Waka Waka* – the theme to the 2010 World Cup – by Shakira

Hugh Grant: *Viva El Fulham* by Tony Rees And The Cottagers

Andy Hamilton: *Blue Is The Colour* by Chelsea FC

Frank Skinner: *Back Home* by 1970 World Cup Squad

Tony Adams: *Good Old Arsenal* by Arsenal 1971 Squad

Margaret Forster: *Ossie's Dream (Spurs Are On Their Way To Wembley)* by Chas 'n' Dave

Jack Rosenthal: *Manchester United Calypso* by Ken Jones And His Music

Bill Kenwright: *Call To Arms* by Blueknowz: the song of Everton FC (and the *Z Cars* theme tune)

John Cole: *I'm Forever Blowing Bubbles* by the players of West Ham United

INTERESTING CHOICES

Kingsley Amis – *Shim-Me-Sha-Wabble* by Bud Freeman And His Famous Chicagoans

Anthony Andrews – *Mercedes Benz* by Janis Joplin

Jeffrey Archer – *It's Hard To Be Humble* by Mac Davis

Dame Beryl Bainbridge – *Kiss Me Goodnight Sergeant Major* by Dame Vera Lynn

Sebastian Coe – *History of A Boy Scout* by The Dave Brubeck Quartet (on both occasions that he was on the show)

Joan Collins – *Hava Nagila* by Harry Belafonte

Robin Cousins – *Thunderbirds* theme tune by Barry Gray

Noël Coward – *The Hole In The Ground* by Bernard Cribbins*

Chris Evans – *Rubber Duckie* by Sesame Street

Dame Edith Evans – *Rawhide* by Frankie Laine

Richard Gordon – *A Small Town In Germany* by Jock Strapp Ensemble*

Germaine Greer – *Neway Debebe* (an Ethiopian pop song)

Kathleen Harrison – street barrel organ selection

Edward Heath – *If I Were A Rich Man* by Topol

Susan Hill – *One More Step Along The World I Go* by The Children of Botley Primary School, Oxford

Frankie Howerd – *Knees Up Mother Brown*

Sir Leonard Hutton – *Waltzing Matilda***

Lord Killanin – *Where The Streets Have No Name* by U2

Freddie Mills – the fanfare used at White City before big fights

Helen Mirren – *Pass The Dutchie* by Musical Youth*

Naomi Mitchison – *African Tribal Song* by The Botswana Tribe

(INTERESTING CHOICES – *cont.*)

Dr Desmond Morris – *Drum Battle* by Gene Krupa and Buddy Rich

Derek Nimmo – *Gumboot Dance* by the original London cast of *King Kong*

Jenny Pitman – *A Four-Legged Friend* by Roy Rogers*

Donald Pleasence – *Scouse The Mouse* by Ringo Starr

Eric Porter – *Vito* by Madrid Bullfight Band

Vanessa Redgrave – *Voice of The Stars* by Shirley Temple, Will Hay and Grace Moore

Peter Scott – *Isa Lei* by Fijian Girls

Jean Simmons – *A Cat Named Sloopy* by Rod McKuen

Dennis Skinner – *Daddy, What Did You Do In The Strike?* by Peggy Seeger*

Fay Weldon – *Never Let Your Braces Dangle* by Harry Champion

Jacqueline Wilson – *Nellie The Elephant* by Mandy Miller

* In each case, the castaway's favourite record.

** Many castaways have chosen this Aussie anthem but Sir Len is the only England cricket captain to have done so. Derek Randall chose the 1972 Australian Cricket Team performing *Here Come The Aussies*.

THE ONLY CASTAWAY
TO CHOOSE . . .

ABC – chosen by Loyd Grossman

Adam And The Ants – Frank Oz

Adele – Tony Robinson

Christina Aguilera – Tony Robinson

The Alan Parsons Project – Sir John Harvey-Jones

The Archies – Nigella Lawson

Aswad – Courtney Pine

Anita Baker – Courtney Pine

The Beautiful South – Johnny Vegas

Beck – Colin Firth

Bobby Bloom – Pauline Quirke

Blue Mink – David Niven

Blur – Greg Dyke

Bob And Earl – Julie Walters

Bob And Marcia – Meera Syal

Michael Bolton – Tessa Sanderson

The Boomtown Rats – Marco Pierre White

Bon Jovi – Lynda La Plante

Bucks Fizz – Gerry Cottle

David Byrne – Mo Mowlam

James Cagney – John Osborne

Captain Sensible – Britt Ekland

Barbara Cartland – A. N. Wilson

Eva Cassidy – Ruthie Henshall

(THE ONLY CASTAWAY TO CHOOSE ... – *cont.*)

Gene Chandler – Brian Eno

The Chemical Brothers – Nigella Lawson

Tony Christie – Jenny Pitman

Charlotte Church – Barbara Taylor Bradford

Billy Connolly – Jane Lapotaire

The Coasters – Paul McCartney

Bill Cosby – Jane Asher

Country Joe And The Fish – Salman Rushdie

Cream – Michael Portillo

The Cure – Mary Portas

D:ream – Diane Abbott

The Damned – Jo Brand

Dan Aykroyd and John Belushi – Ian Hislop

Depeche Mode – Tanni Grey Thompson

Destiny's Child – Dame Kelly Holmes

Dr. Dre – John Malkovich

Duran Duran – Professor Brian Cox

The Easybeats – Alan Johnson

Duane Eddy – Michael Nyman

Missy Elliott – Kathy Burke

Brian Eno – Christopher Reeve

Gloria Estefan – Tessa Sanderson

Ezio – Tony Blair

Chris Farlowe – A. A. Gill

Foreigner – Ben Kingsley

The Four Tops – Bob Champion

The Fun Lovin' Criminals – Martin Clunes

Serge Gainsbourg – Viscount Linley

Crystal Gayle – Graham Norton

Goldfrapp – George Michael

Gorillaz – Kathy Burke

Eddy Grant – Lawrence Dallaglio

Juliette Greco – John Simpson

Green Day – Sir Matthew Pinsent

Groove Armada – Martha Lane Fox

Chesney Hawkes – Duncan Bannatyne

Jim Henson – David Mitchell

Herman's Hermits – Rev. David Sheppard

The Housemartins – David Tennant

Huey Lewis & The News – Eve Pollard

The Human League – Duncan Bannatyne

The Incredible String Band – Dr Rowan Williams

Eddie Izzard – David Tennant

Hugh Jackman – Sir Cameron Mackintosh

Janet Jackson – Tessa Sanderson

(THE ONLY CASTAWAY TO CHOOSE ... – *cont.*)

Junior Walker & The All Stars – Trevor Brooking

Katrina And The Waves – David Mitchell

Alicia Keys – Dame Kelly Holmes

Chaka Khan – Martha Lane Fox

King Crimson – Alice Cooper

Kraftwerk – Frank Skinner

Lenny Kravitz – Karren Brady

Lady Gaga – Kathy Burke

Jack Johnson – Rob Brydon

Rickie Lee Jones – Lenny Henry

Leona Lewis – Ruthie Henshall

The Libertines – Monty Don

Lieutenant Pigeon – Jarvis Cocker

Lindisfarne – Kevin Whately

Lulu – Peter Alliss

Barry Manilow – Roger Moore

Jessie Matthews – Quintin Hogg (Lord Hailsham)

Curtis Mayfield – Colin Firth

George McRae – David Niven

Melanie – Lynda La Plante

Men At Work – Simon Weston

The Merseys – Jimmy McGovern

George Michael – Gordon Ramsay

Middle of The Road – Tracey Emin

Mike + The Mechanics – Ralph Steadman

Tim Minchin – David Tennant

The Monkees – Bear Grylls

Motörhead – Grayson Perry

The Move – Harry Enfield

Alison Moyet – Clive James

Maria Muldaur – Jancis Robinson

Mungo Jerry – Mary Portas

Johnny Nash – Imran Khan

Nena – A. A. Gill

Michael Nesmith – Willie Rushton

New Order – Nigella Lawson

Juice Newton – Christopher Hampton

The New York Dolls – Morrissey

Paolo Nutini – Len Goodman

Des O'Connor – Sammy Cahn

The O'Jays – Paul Whitehouse

Gilbert O'Sullivan – Joe Bugner

Peter O'Toole – General H. Norman Schwarzkopf

Orchestral Manoeuvres In The Dark – Professor Brian Cox

Robert Palmer – Sir Clive Woodward

Billy Paul – Jeremy Clarkson

(THE ONLY CASTAWAY TO CHOOSE ... – *cont.*)

Freda Payne – Anita Dobson

Gretchen Peters – Sir Terry Wogan

Peters And Lee – Tony Greig

Madeleine Peyroux – Jeremy Irons

Pink – David Davis

Gene Pitney – Marco Pierre White

Su Pollard – Mark Gatiss

Iggy Pop – Bob Geldof

Billy Preston – Jools Holland

Rainbow – Brian May

Helen Reddy – Marti Caine

The Righteous Brothers – Simon Cowell

Rihanna – Stephen King

Tom Robinson – Boy George

The Ronettes – Anita Dobson

Runrig – Gordon Brown

Sade – Geraldine James

Boz Scaggs – Sebastian Faulks

Seal – Evelyn Glennie

Tupac Shakur (2Pac) – Michael Johnson

The Shangri-Las – Sandie Shaw

Siouxsie And The Banshees – Steve Coogan

Sister Sledge – Paul McKenna

Hurricane Smith – Gene Wilder

Soul II Soul – Gok Wan

The Spice Girls – Peter Blake

Stan Tracey Quintet – Kenneth Clarke

Spandau Ballet – Dame Ellen MacArthur

Freddie Starr – Doris Stokes

Status Quo – Jenny Pitman

Curtis Stigers – Pauline Quirke

Super Furry Animals – Alan Johnson

Sweet – Colin Welland

Take That – Sir Clive Woodward

Them – Imran Khan

Toploader – Charles Kennedy

The Travelling Wilburys – Chris Patten

Ultravox – Richard Dunwoody

U.S.A. for Africa – Archbishop Desmond Tutu

Ricky Valance – Frank Bruno

Sid Vicious – Mario Testino

Bobby Vinton – Nicky Haslam

Scott Walker – Jarvis Cocker

Kanye West – George Michael

Kim Wilde – Gordon Ramsay

Steve Winwood – Will Carling

Wynonna – Celia Imrie

Frank Zappa – Martin Clunes

Benjamin Zephaniah – Michael Mansfield

THE BEATLES

The Beatles are the most popular act on *Desert Island Discs*. Their nearest 'rivals' are Frank Sinatra (chosen 240 times) and Bing Crosby (166). The next most popular pop or rock group is The Rolling Stones, who were chosen 54 times.

BEATLES RECORDS CHOSEN

A Day In The Life – chosen 13 times

A Hard Day's Night – 4

Across The Universe – 1 (but Billy Connolly chose this on both of his appearances)

All My Loving – 4

All You Need Is Love – 6

And I Love Her – 3

And Your Bird Can Sing – 3

Because – 1

Being For The Benefit of Mr Kite – 1

Blackbird – 2

Can't Buy Me Love – 2

Come Together – 3

Dear Prudence – 1

Do You Want To Know A Secret? – 1

Drive My Car – 1

Eleanor Rigby – 11

Golden Slumbers/Carry That Weight – 2

Good Day Sunshine – 1

Happiness Is A Warm Gun – 1

Hello Goodbye – 1

Help! – 10

Here Comes The Sun – 6

Here, There And Everywhere – 3

Hey Jude – 16

I Am The Walrus – 1

I Saw Her Standing There – 1

I Want To Hold Your Hand – 6

I'm A Loser – 1

I'm Looking Through You – 1

I'm Only Sleeping – 1

If I Fell – 3

In My Life – 8

Let It Be – 7

Love Me Do – 9

Lovely Rita – 1

Lucy In The Sky With Diamonds – 5

Martha My Dear – 1

Maxwell's Silver Hammer – 1

Michelle – 2

Octopus's Garden – 1

Paperback Writer – 2

Penny Lane – 12

Please Please Me – 4

Rock And Roll Music – 1

Sgt Pepper's Lonely Hearts Club Band – 5

She Loves You – 10

She Said, She Said – 1

She's A Woman – 1

She's Leaving Home – 3

Something – 3

Strawberry Fields Forever – 6

Taxman – 1

The Ballad of John And Yoko – 1

The End – 1

The Fool On The Hill – 5

The Long And Winding Road – 7

Things We Said Today – 4

This Boy – 1

Till There Was You – 1

Tomorrow Never Knows – 1

Twist And Shout – 4

We Can Work It Out – 1

When I'm Sixty-Four – 8

While My Guitar Gently Weeps – 1

Why Don't We Do It In The Road? – 1

With A Little Help From My Friends – 3

Within You, Without You – 1

Yellow Submarine – 3

Yesterday – 18

You Can't Do That – 1

You Really Got A Hold On Me – 1

You've Got To Hide Your Love Away – 4

WHO CHOSE WHICH BEATLES SONG

YESTERDAY – 18

Arthur Askey

Ian Botham

Geoff Boycott

Antonio Carluccio

Sir Peter Maxwell Davies

Stewart Granger

Sir Bernard Ingham

Margaret Kelly – Miss Bluebell

Sir David King

Jimmy Knapp

Jacques Loussier

Dr Desmond Morris

Spike Milligan

Morecambe and Wise

Cardinal Cormac Murphy O'Connor

Renata Scotto

Twiggy

Franco Zeffirelli

Piers Morgan chose Chris Potter's version, Richard Lester chose Ray Charles's version and Tommy Simpson chose Matt Monro's version.

HEY JUDE – 16

Kenneth Allsop

Gordon Brown

Carmen Callil

Lord Cobbold*

Keith Floyd

Brendan Foster

Rolf Harris

Rachael Heyhoe

John Hurt

Sue Lawley

Ismail Merchant

Richard Noble

Alan Pascoe

Martin Pipe

Professor Raymond Tallis

John Updike

* Chose Paul McCartney's, not The Beatles', version.

A DAY IN THE LIFE – 13

Sanjeev Bhaskar

Alfie Boe

John Conteh

Sir Hugh Greene

Paul Merton

Alan Parker

Donald Pleasence

Charlotte Rampling

David Storey

Chris Tarrant

Frank Warren

Ruby Wax

Tennessee Williams

PENNY LANE– 12

Dick Clement and Ian La Frenais

Engelbert Humperdinck

Graham Hill

Terry Jones

Annie Lennox

Olivia Manning

Derek Nimmo

Sir Trevor Nunn

Lynn Redgrave

Leslie Thomas

Bruce Tulloh

Frances Wood

ELEANOR RIGBY – 11

Charles Aznavour

Dame Beryl Bainbridge

Cathy Berberian

Hermione Gingold

Patricia Hayes

Anthony Horowitz

Sir Geoffrey Howe

Mollie Lee

Jan Pienkowski

Lynn Seymour

Sir Arnold Wesker

HELP! – 10

Jeffrey Archer

Robert Carrier

Gerry Cottle

Henry Cooper

Derek Jameson

David Jason

Gorden Kaye

Adele Leigh

Leo McKern

Rita Tushingham

SHE LOVES YOU – 10

Bill Cullen

David Jacobs

Stephen King

Robin Knox-Johnston

Robert Maxwell

Dennis Taylor

Neil Tennant

Pete Waterman

Simon Weston

Lavinia Young

LOVE ME DO – 9

Cilla Black

Derek Brown

Darcey Bussell

Barbara Castle

Sir Nicholas Grimshaw

Susan Hill

Roger McGough

Tom Stoppard

Jimmy Tarbuck

IN MY LIFE – 8

Tony Blair

Alan Bleasdale

David Essex

Bob Geldof

Len Goodman

George Martin

Jimmy Mulville

Willy Russell

WHEN I'M SIXTY FOUR – 8

Alan Alda

Dr Christiaan Barnard

George Carman QC

Richard Condon

Shirley Conran

Eric Newby

Barry Norman

Mary Wesley

LET IT BE – 7

Rowan Atkinson

Trevor Brooking

Professor Dame Kay Davies

Chris de Burgh

Piers Morgan

Frank Muir

Peter Scudamore

~~~~~~

Jeremy Irons chose Dolores Keane's version.

THE LONG AND WINDING ROAD – 7

Cilla Black

Joe Bugner

Paulo Coelho

Colin Dexter

Sir David Frost

Shirley Hughes

Peggy Lee

ALL YOU NEED IS LOVE – 6

George Foreman

Michael Howard

Penelope Keith

Robin Knox-Johnston

Wayne Sleep

Jackie Stewart

HERE COMES THE SUN – 6

Dame Joan Bakewell

Boris Johnson

Michael Morpurgo

Elaine Paige

Sandie Shaw

Jerry Springer

I WANT TO HOLD YOUR HAND – 6

Mary Archer

Kaffe Fassett

Felicity Green

Sir Andrew Lloyd Webber

George Martin

Jerry Springer

~~~~~~

Dick Francis chose The Boston Pops Orchestra's version.

STRAWBERRY FIELDS FOREVER – 6

Greg Dyke

David Edgar

Kenny Everett

Douglas Fairbanks Jr

Zandra Rhodes

Tim Smit

THE FOOL ON THE HILL – 5

Rosalinde Fuller

Deborah Kerr

Michael Quinn

John Ridgway

Sir Martin Sorrell

~~~~~~

Harvey Smith chose Shirley Bassey's version, and Leonard Slatkin chose The Singers Unlimited's version.

LUCY IN THE SKY WITH DIAMONDS – 5

Nicholas Hytner

Dr Steve Jones

John Ogdon

Dr David Owen

Alan Pascoe

~~~~~~~

George Clooney chose William Shatner's version.

SGT PEPPER'S LONELY HEARTS CLUB BAND – 5

Peter Blake

Kenny Everett

Nicolai Gedda

George Melly

Jackie Stewart

A HARD DAY'S NIGHT – 4

James Clavell

Lawrence Dallaglio

Monty Don

Sir Stuart Rose

~~~~~~~

David Hicks chose Keely Smith's version.

ALL MY LOVING – 4

Arthur Askey

Phil Collins

G. O. Nickalls

David Puttnam

~~~~~~

Brian Epstein chose The George Martin Orchestra's version.

PLEASE PLEASE ME – 4

Kim Cattrall

Anita Dobson

Richard Griffiths

Professor Stephen Hawking

THINGS WE SAID TODAY – 4

Diane Abbott

Professor Jim Al-Khalili

Harry Enfield

Michael Palin

TWIST AND SHOUT – 4

Frank Bough

Sue Johnston

Ann Mallalieu

Jack Vettriano

YOU'VE GOT TO HIDE YOUR LOVE AWAY – 4

Tina Brown

Susan George

John Harle

Terence Stamp

AND I LOVE HER – 3

Richard Curtis

Dick Emery

Mark McCormack

AND YOUR BIRD CAN SING – 3

Ben Elton

Paul Gambaccini

Alan Johnson

COME TOGETHER – 3

Professor Colin Blakemore

Fyfe Robertson

J. K. Rowling

HERE, THERE AND EVERYWHERE – 3

Julian Bream

Chris Evans

George Martin

~~~~~~

Sammy Cahn chose Petula Clark's version.

IF I FELL – 3

Phil Collins

Barbara Murray

James Nesbitt

SHE'S LEAVING HOME – 3

Anthony Grey

Chris Haskins

Lord King

SOMETHING – 3

Lord Donoughue

Clive Dunn

Ed McBain

WITH A LITTLE HELP FROM MY FRIENDS – 3

Margaret Drabble

Sir Lew Grade

Nicolette Milnes-Walker

~~~~~

Emma Thompson chose Joe Cocker's version.

YELLOW SUBMARINE – 3

Baroness Afshar

John Huston

Margaret Kelly – Miss Bluebell

BLACKBIRD – 2

Jenny Agutter

Margaret Forster

CAN'T BUY ME LOVE – 2

Ivy Benson

Sebastian Faulks

GOLDEN SLUMBERS/CARRY THAT WEIGHT – 2

Jimmy Mulville

Andrew Neil

MICHELLE – 2

Mirella Freni

Terry Hands

~~~~~~

Lieutenant Colonel C. H. Jaeger chose The Band of The Irish Guards' version.

PAPERBACK WRITER – 2

Gareth Edwards

Jimmy Savile

ACROSS THE UNIVERSE – 1

Billy Connolly – on two occasions

BECAUSE – 1

Paulo Coelho

BEING FOR THE BENEFIT OF MR KITE – 1

Dodie Smith

DEAR PRUDENCE – 1

Maureen O'Sullivan

DO YOU WANT TO KNOW A SECRET? – 1

George Davies

DRIVE MY CAR – 1

Douglas Adams

GOOD DAY SUNSHINE – 1

Ken Follett

HAPPINESS IS A WARM GUN – 1

Antony Gormley

HELLO GOODBYE – 1

Tristan Jones

I AM THE WALRUS – 1

Hanif Kureishi

～～～～

Lynn Seymour chose Spooky Tooth's version.

I SAW HER STANDING THERE – 1

David Wynne

I'M A LOSER – 1

Robert Lindsay

I'M LOOKING THROUGH YOU – 1

Itzhak Perlman

I'M ONLY SLEEPING – 1

Steven Isserlis

LOVELY RITA – 1
Nina Campbell

MARTHA MY DEAR – 1
Clodagh Rodgers

MAXWELL'S SILVER HAMMER – 1
The Duchess of Kent

OCTOPUS'S GARDEN – 1
James Galway

ROCK AND ROLL MUSIC – 1
Betty Jackson

SHE SAID, SHE SAID – 1
John Cale

SHE'S A WOMAN – 1
Brian Epstein

TAXMAN – 1
Terry Gilliam

THE BALLAD OF JOHN AND YOKO – 1
Donald Sutherland

THE END – 1

Paul McKenna

THIS BOY – 1

Jimmy Tarbuck

TILL THERE WAS YOU – 1

Dame Vera Lynn (performed by The Beatles, but written by Meredith Wilson for *The Music Man*)

TOMORROW NEVER KNOWS – 1

Joanna MacGregor

WE CAN WORK IT OUT – 1

Howard Goodall

WHILE MY GUITAR GENTLY WEEPS – 1

Roger Vadim

WHY DON'T WE DO IT IN THE ROAD? – 1

Richard Dreyfuss

WITHIN YOU, WITHOUT YOU – 1

Richard Briers

YOU CAN'T DO THAT – 1

Ian Stewart

YOU REALLY GOT A HOLD ON ME – 1

Elvis Costello

Edward Heath is the only (non-Beatle) castaway to have been mentioned in a Beatles song. The song was *Taxman*.

ALL THE PEOPLE WHO CHOSE
TWO BEATLES SONGS

Margaret Kelly – Miss Bluebell: *Yesterday* and *Yellow Submarine*

Paulo Coelho: *The Long And Winding Road* and *Because*

Phil Collins: *All My Loving* and *If I Fell*

Kenny Everett: *Strawberry Fields* and *Sgt Pepper's Lonely Hearts Club Band*

George Martin: *Here, There And Everywhere* and *In My Life**

Jimmy Mulville: *Golden Slumbers/Carry That Weight* and *In My Life*

Alan Pascoe: *Hey Jude* and *Lucy In The Sky With Diamonds*

Jerry Springer: *I Want To Hold Your Hand* and *Here Comes The Sun*

Jackie Stewart: *Sgt Pepper's Lonely Hearts Club Band* and *All You Need Is Love*

* Typically fair, Martin chose one song by Paul and one song by John.

PEOPLE WHO CHOSE
ROLLING STONES RECORDS

YOU CAN'T ALWAYS GET WHAT YOU WANT – 8

Gillian Anderson

Sinéad Cusack

Keith Floyd

Katharine Hamnett

Imran Khan

Jimmy Mulville

Ian Rankin

Simon Schama

(I CAN'T GET NO) SATISFACTION – 6

Karan Bilimoria

Raymond Blanc

Bob Champion

Sir Nicholas Grimshaw

Elia Kazan

Sir Andrew Lloyd Webber

SYMPATHY FOR THE DEVIL – 6

Christopher Bruce

Alison Richard

Salman Rushdie

Paul Smith

Sam Taylor-Wood

Zoe Wanamaker

GET OFF OF MY CLOUD – 4

Eileen Atkins

Ian Botham

Timothy Clifford

Jack Straw

GIMME SHELTER – 4

Dr Gwen Adshead

Marianne Faithfull

Bill Nighy*

John Sessions

BROWN SUGAR – 3

Frances Edmonds

Dr Susan Greenfield

Alan Pascoe

LITTLE RED ROOSTER – 2

Cath Kidston

Redmond O'Hanlon

START ME UP – 2
Boris Johnson
Piers Morgan

THE LAST TIME – 2
Lynn Barber
Sir Tim Rice

TUMBLING DICE – 2
Hugh Laurie
Paul Whitehouse

CHOSEN ONCE EACH
Come On – John Bird (editor of *The Big Issue*)
Continental Drift – Marco Pierre White
Honky Tonk Women – Bob Hoskins
Hot Stuff – David Wilkie
It's Not Easy – Dr Desmond Morris
Let It Rock – Elton John
Melody – Viscount Linley
Miss You – Michael McIntyre
Paint It Black – Peter Melchett
Route 66 – Chris Patten
Salt of The Earth – Professor Colin Pillinger
Street Fighting Man – Dame Elizabeth Manningham-Buller
The Rocky Road To Dublin – Frank McCourt
Waiting On A Friend – Charles Kennedy
Winter – Bill Nighy*
You Gotta Move – Tim Smit

*Bill Nighy chose two Rolling Stones songs when he appeared in 2004.

GILBERT AND SULLIVAN

Gilbert And Sullivan have featured in 98* episodes. Here are the most popular shows:

The Mikado – excerpts from this opera have featured on 24 programmes

The Gondoliers – 14

Iolanthe – 13

HMS Pinafore – 12

The Yeoman of The Guard – 12

The Pirates of Penzance – 8

Ruddigore – 8

Patience – 4

Trial By Jury – 3

Princess Ida – 1

* The total adds up to more than 98 because some people chose more than one Gilbert And Sullivan song.

CLASSICAL MUSIC

THE MOST POPULAR CLASSICAL COMPOSERS

Wolfgang Amadeus Mozart – chosen in 792 episodes

Ludwig van Beethoven – 719

Johann Sebastian Bach – 652

Franz Schubert – 362

Giuseppe Verdi – 332

Edward Elgar – 328

Pyotr Ilyich Tchaikovsky – 318

Giacomo Puccini – 297

George Frideric Handel – 283

Richard Wagner – 264

Johannes Brahms – 244

Frédéric Chopin – 235

Richard Strauss – 218

Claude Debussy – 179

Sergey Vasilevich Rachmaninov – 164

Benjamin Britten – 154

Maurice Ravel – 154

Felix Mendelssohn – 152

Jean Sibelius – 151

Ralph Vaughan Williams – 150

Gustav Mahler – 133

Johann Strauss – 127

Igor Stravinsky – 121

Antonín Dvořák – 111

Joseph Haydn – 100

Robert Schumann – 93

Sergei Prokofiev – 85

Frederick Delius – 84

Henry Purcell – 80

Edvard Grieg – 79

Georges Bizet – 76

Gioacchino Rossini – 72

Gabriel Fauré – 71

Antonio Vivaldi – 71

Hector Berlioz – 66

William Walton – 62

César Franck – 57

Camille Saint-Saens – 54

Charles-François Gounod – 51

Hubert Parry – 51

George Gershwin – 50 (and 27 songs)

Gustav Holst – 50

Modest Mussorgsky – 50

Vincenzo Bellini – 49

Dmitri Shostakovich – 49

Nikolai Andreyevich Rimsky-Korsakov – 49

Franz Liszt – 49

Béla Bartók – 48

Thomas Tallis – 47

Claudio Monteverdi – 45

Christoph Willibald Gluck – 43

Jacques Offenbach – 42

Max Bruch – 41

Franz Lehár – 39

Gaetano Donizetti – 37

Leos Janácek – 34

Jules Massenet – 33

Alexander Borodin – 29

Francis Poulenc – 28

Pietro Mascagni – 26

Enrique Granados – 26

Fritz Kreisler – 24*

Aram Khachaturian – 23

Oscar Straus – 22

Heitor Villa-Lobos – 22

Carl Orff – 21

Ruggiero Leoncavallo – 21

Ottorino Respighi – 21

Érik Satié – 20

Léo Delibes – 19

Joaquín Rodrigo – 18

Domenico Scarlatti – 18

Arnold Schoenberg – 18

Michael Tippett – 18

Anton Bruckner – 17

Jeremiah Clarke – 17

Aaron Copland – 16

Kurt Weill – 16**

Tomaso Albinoni and Remo Giazotto – 16

Samuel Barber – 15

Bedrich Smetana – 15

Johann Pachelbel – 14

Richard Addinsell – 13

Eric Coates – 13

Manuel de Falla – 13

Nicolò Paganini – 13

John Dowland – 12

Olivier Messiaen – 12

William Byrd – 11

Charles-Marie Widor – 11

* Some of these are transcriptions or arrangements of traditional songs or other composers' works.

** Not including vocal recordings of *Mack The Knife*.

CHOSEN 10 TIMES

George Butterworth, Joseph Canteloube, Engelbert Humperdinck, Giovanni Pierluigi da Palestrina

CHOSEN 9 TIMES

Gregorio Allegri, Sir Arthur Bliss, Paul Dukas, Manos Hadjidakis, Peter Warlock

CHOSEN 8 TIMES

Arnold Bax, Alban Berg, Erno Dohnanyi, Henry Charles Litolff

CHOSEN 7 TIMES

Samuel Coleridge-Taylor, Alexander Konstantinovich Glazunov, Herbert Howells, Albert Ketelby, Giacomo Meyerbeer, Ariel Ramirez, Claude-Joseph Rouget de l'Isle, Alexander Nikolayevich Scriabin, Franz von Suppé

CHOSEN 6 TIMES

Giovanni Battista Pergolesi, John Gay, Philip Glass, Richard Heuberger, Constant Lambert, Darius Milhaud

CHOSEN 5 TIMES

François Couperin, Georges Enescu, Gerald Finzi, Édouard Lalo, John Tavener, Charles Villiers Stanford, John Williams

CHOSEN 4 TIMES

Thomas Arne, Emmanuel Chabrier, Ernesto de Curtis, Charles Dibdin, Patrick Doyle, Hamilton Harty, Jacques Ibert, Carl Nielsen, Amilcare Ponchielli, John Rutter, Gaspare Spontini, Karlheinz Stockhausen, Georg Philipp Telemann

CHOSEN 3 TIMES

Adolphe Adam, Isaac Albéniz, George Benjamin, Cristóbal de Morales, Vincent d'Indy, Johann Hummel, Roberto Murolo, Anton Rubinstein, Émile Waldteufel, Anton Webern, Haydn Wood

CHOSEN TWICE (A SELECTION)

Carl Philipp Emanuel Bach, Mily Alexeyevich Balakirev, Ronald Binge, Boris Blacher, William Bolcom, William Boyce, Cornelius Cardew, Mario Castelnuovo-Tedesco, Domenico Cimarosa, George Crumb, Tomás Luis de Victoria, Umberto Giordano, Henryk Górecki, Hans Werner Henze, Paul Hindemith, Karl Jenkins (chose himself), Imre Kálmán, Erich Wolfgang Korngold, Alessandro Marcello, Gian Carlo Menotti, Ludwig Minkus, Moritz Moszkowski, Ignacy Paderewski, Arvo Pärt, Jean-Philippe Rameau, Sir Henry Rowley Bishop, Alan Rawsthorne, Henri Sauguet, Alessandro Scarlatti, Sir Arthur Sullivan (apart from his work with W. S. Gilbert), John Tavener, Emil Nikolaus von Rezníček, Jan Dismas Zelenka

CHOSEN ONCE (A SELECTION)

Thomas Adès, Vladimir Davidovich Ashkenazy, Kéler Béla, Herbert Brewer, Elliott Carter, Ernest Chausson, Maurice Duruflé, Robert Fayrfax, Herman Finck, Baldassare Galuppi, Orlando Gibbons, Reinhold Glière, Alexander Goehr, Karel Komzák II, Paul Lincke, George Lloyd (two works both chosen by himself), Antonio Lotti, Nikolai Karlovich Medtner, Joaquín Nin, Pierre Phalese, Tobias Picker, David Popper, Saint-Preux, Noam Sheriff, Robert Simpson, Ambroise Thomas, Jacob van Eyck, Guy Woolfenden, Iannis Xenakis, Carl Michael Ziehrer

~~~~~~

MOST POPULAR CLASSICAL WORKS CHOSEN

Where castaways have chosen different excerpts from a work, I have listed them all under the same work.

Wolfgang Amadeus Mozart, *The Marriage of Figaro* – chosen 109 times
George Frideric Handel, *Messiah* – 109

Ludwig van Beethoven, *Symphony No. 9 in D Minor 'Choral'* – 97

Wolfgang Amadeus Mozart, *The Magic Flute* – 89
Richard Strauss, *Der Rosenkavalier* – 85

Wolfgang Amadeus Mozart, *Don Giovanni* – 84
Giacomo Puccini, *Tosca* – 84

Sergey Rachmaninov, *Piano Concerto No. 2 in C Minor* – 82

Johann Sebastian Bach, *St Matthew Passion* – 80

Giacomo Puccini, *La Bohème* – 79

Richard Wagner, *Tristan und Isolde* – 73 (including 44 people who chose *Liebestod*)

Giuseppe Verdi, *Requiem* – 71

Edward Elgar, *Enigma Variations* – 70
Franz Schubert, *String Quintet in C Major* – 70

Music

Giacomo Puccini, *Turandot* – 64 (including 34 people who chose *Nessun Dorma*)

Ludwig van Beethoven, *Symphony No. 6 in F Major 'Pastoral'* – 62

Giuseppe Verdi, *La Traviata* – 58

Johann Sebastian Bach, *Mass in B Minor* – 57
Edward Elgar, *Pomp and Circumstance March No. 1 in D Major; 'Land of Hope And Glory'* – 57

Ludwig van Beethoven, *Piano Concerto No. 5 in E Flat Major 'Emperor'* – 56
Richard Wagner, *Die Walküre* – 56 (including 28 people who chose *Ride of The Valkyries*)

Ludwig van Beethoven, *Symphony No. 7 in A Major* – 54

Johann Sebastian Bach, *Concerto For Two Violins in D Minor* – 53

Wolfgang Amadeus Mozart, *Così fan Tutte* – 52
Giacomo Puccini, *Madame Butterfly* – 52
Pyotr Ilyich Tchaikovsky, *Swan Lake* – 52

Edward Elgar, *Cello Concerto in E Minor* – 51

Gabriel Fauré, *Requiem* – 49
Richard Strauss, *Four Last Songs* – 49

Ludwig van Beethoven, *Violin Concerto in D Major* – 47
Richard Wagner, *Die Meistersinger von Nürnberg* – 47

(MOST POPULAR CLASSICAL WORKS CHOSEN – *cont.*)

Claude Debussy, *Claire de Lune* from *Suite Bergamasque* – 46

Ludwig van Beethoven, *Symphony No. 5 in C Minor* – 44

Wolfgang Amadeus Mozart, *Clarinet Concerto in A Major* – 42
Ludwig van Beethoven, *Fidelio* – 42
Richard Wagner, *Götterdämmerung* – 42

Antonín Dvořák, *Symphony No. 9 in E Minor, 'From The New World'* – 41
George Gershwin, *Rhapsody In Blue* – 41

Felix Mendelssohn, *A Midsummer Night's Dream* – 40
Hubert Parry, *Jerusalem* – 40
Igor Stravinsky, *The Rite of Spring* – 40

Christoph Willibald Gluck, *Orpheus And Euridice* – 39
Gustav Holst, *The Planets* – 39

Johannes Brahms, *Violin Concerto in D Major* – 38
Maurice Ravel, *Daphnis And Chloe* – 38
Johann Strauss II, *Die Fledermaus* – 38
Pyotr Ilyich Tchaikovsky, *Romeo And Juliet: Fantasy Overture* – 38
Giuseppe Verdi, *Otello* – 38

Antonio Vivaldi, *The Four Seasons* – 36

Johann Sebastian Bach, *Toccata And Fugue in D Minor* – 35
Johann Sebastian Bach, *Goldberg Variations* – 35

Gustav Mahler, *Symphony No. 5 in C Sharp Minor* – 34

Ludwig van Beethoven, *String Quartet No. 13 in B Flat Major* – 33
Ludwig van Beethoven, *Symphony No. 3 in E Flat Major 'Eroica'* – 33
Georges Bizet, *Carmen* – 33
Edvard Grieg, *Piano Concerto in A Minor* – 33
Wolfgang Amadeus Mozart, *Piano Concerto No. 21 in C Major* – 33
Pyotr Ilyich Tchaikovsky, *Piano Concerto No. 1 in B Flat Minor* – 33

Sergey Rachmaninov, *Rhapsody On A Theme of Paganini* – 32
Giuseppe Verdi, *Rigoletto* – 32

Edward Elgar, *The Dream of Gerontius* – 31
Gustav Mahler, *Das Lied Von Der Erde* – 31
Wolfgang Amadeus Mozart, *Symphony No. 40 in G Minor* – 31
Sergei Sergeyevich Prokofiev, *Romeo And Juliet* – 31
Nikolai Andreyevich Rimsky-Korsakov, *Scheherazade* – 31
Johann Strauss II, *Blue Danube Waltz* – 31
Giuseppe Verdi, *Aida* – 31

Johann Sebastian Bach, *The Well-Tempered Clavier* – 30
Max Bruch, *Violin Concerto No. 1 in G Minor* – 30
Claude Debussy, *Prélude À L'Après Midi D'Un Faune* – 30
Edward Elgar, *Violin Concerto in B Minor* – 30
Wolfgang Amadeus Mozart, *Requiem in D Minor* – 30
Jean Sibelius, *Symphony No. 2 in D Major* – 30
Pyotr Ilyich Tchaikovsky, *Sleeping Beauty* – 30

(MOST POPULAR CLASSICAL WORKS CHOSEN – *cont.*)

Vincenzo Bellini, *Norma* – 29

Giuseppe Verdi, *Va Pensiero Sull'ali Dorate* (*Chorus of The Hebrew Slaves* from *Nabucco*) – 29

Modest Petrovich Mussorgsky, *Boris Godunov* – 28

Gioachino Rossini, *The Barber of Seville* – 28

Ralph Vaughan Williams, *Fantasia On Greensleeves* – 28

Benjamin Britten, *Peter Grimes* – 27

George Frideric Handel, *Water Music* – 27

Ludwig van Beethoven, *String Quartet* No. 15 in A Minor – 27

Ralph Vaughan Williams, *Fantasia On A Theme By Thomas Tallis* – 27

Giuseppe Verdi, *Falstaff* – 27

Pietro Mascagni, *Cavalleria Rusticana* – 26

Claude Debussy, *La Danse de Puck* (from *Préludes*) – 26

Henry Purcell, *When I Am Laid In Earth (Dido's Lament)* (from *Dido and Aeneas*) – 26

Edvard Grieg, *Peer Gynt* – 25

Wolfgang Amadeus Mozart, *Serenade No. 13 in G Major 'Eine Kleine Nachtmusik'* – 25

Pyotr Ilyich Tchaikovsky, *1812 Overture* – 25

Giuseppe Verdi, *Don Carlos* – 25

Johannes Brahms, *Symphony No. 4 in E Minor* – 24

Charles-François Gounod, *Ave Maria* – 24

Felix Mendelssohn, *Hear My Prayer* – 24 (including 14 people who chose *O For The Wings of A Dove*)

Johann Sebastian Bach, *Brandenburg Concerto No. 5 in D Major* – 23

Franz Lehár, *The Merry Widow* – 23

Wolfgang Amadeus Mozart, *String Quintet No. 4 in G Minor* – 23

Franz Schubert, *Piano Quintet in A Major 'Trout'* – 23

Franz Schubert, *Winterreise* – 23

Igor Stravinsky, *Petrushka* – 23

Ludwig van Beethoven, *Piano Sonata No. 14 in C Sharp Minor 'Moonlight Sonata'* – 23

Pyotr Ilyich Tchaikovsky, *Nutcracker Suite* – 23

Ralph Vaughan Williams, *The Lark Ascending* – 23

Johann Sebastian Bach, *Orchestral Suite No. 3 in D Major* – 22 (including seven people who chose the 2nd movement, *Air On A G String*)

Johannes Brahms, *Piano Concerto No. 2 in B Flat Major* – 22

Johannes Brahms, *Symphony No. 1 in C Minor* – 22

Franz Schubert, *Symphony No. 8 in B Minor 'Unfinished'* – 22

Johann Sebastian Bach, *Jesu, Joy of Man's Desiring* (from *Cantata No. 147*) – 21

Gaetano Donizetti, *Lucia di Lammermoor* – 21

Antonín Dvořák, *Cello Concerto in B Minor* – 21

Carl Orff, *Carmina Burana* – 21

Felix Mendelssohn, *Violin Concerto in E Minor* – 21

Jean Sibelius, *The Swan of Tuonela* – 21

Pyotr Ilyich Tchaikovsky, *Eugene Onegin* – 21

Ludwig van Beethoven, *String Quartet No. 14 in C Sharp Minor* – 21

CHOSEN 20 TIMES

Georges Bizet, *Au Fond Du Temple Saint* (from *The Pearl Fishers*)

Alexander Borodin, *Prince Igor*

Wolfgang Amadeus Mozart, *Piano Concerto No. 23 in A Major*

Maurice Ravel, *Bolero*

Érik Satie, *Trois Gymnopédies*

Jean Sibelius, *Finlandia*

Pyotr Ilyich Tchaikovsky, *Symphony No. 6 in B Minor 'Pathétique'*

CHOSEN 19 TIMES

Hector Berlioz, *Symphonie Fantastique*

Frederick Delius, *On Hearing The First Cuckoo In Spring*

Frederick Delius, *The Walk To The Paradise Garden* (from *A Village Romeo And Juliet*)

Wolfgang Amadeus Mozart, *Symphony No. 41 in C Major 'Jupiter'*

Maurice Ravel, *Pavane Pour Une Infante Défunte*

CHOSEN 18 TIMES

Johann Sebastian Bach, *Brandenburg Concerto No. 3 in G Major*

Johannes Brahms, *Symphony No. 2 in D Major*

Benjamin Britten, *Serenade For Tenor, Horn And Strings*

Frédéric Chopin, *Étude in E Major*

Frédéric Chopin, *Étude in F Major*

Claude Debussy, *La Mer*

George Frideric Handel, *Ombra Mai Fu (Largo)* from *Xerxes*

Joseph Haydn, *The Creation*

Felix Mendelssohn, *The Hebrides Overture (Fingal's Cave)*

Sergey Rachmaninov, *Piano Concerto No. 3 in D Minor*

Franz Schubert, *Symphony No. 9 in C Major 'Great'*

CHOSEN 17 TIMES

Benjamin Britten, *War Requiem*

Jeremiah Clarke, *Trumpet Voluntary*

Ruggero Leoncavallo, *I Pagliacci*

CHOSEN 16 TIMES

Johann Sebastian Bach, *Suite For Solo Cello No. 1 in G Major*

Frédéric Chopin, *Nocturne in E Flat Major*

César Franck, *Panis Angelicus*

Wolfgang Amadeus Mozart, *Horn Concerto No. 4 in E Flat Major*

Wolfgang Amadeus Mozart, *Piano Concerto No. 20 in D Minor*

Giacomo Puccini, O *Mio Babbino Caro* from *Gianni Schicchi*

Camille Saint–Saens, *Carnival of The Animals*

Franz Schubert, *String Quartet No. 14 in D Minor, 'Death And The Maiden'*

Robert Schumann, *Piano Concerto in A Minor*

Jean Sibelius, *Violin Concerto in D Minor*

Thomas Tallis, *Spem In Alium*

Richard Wagner, *Lohengrin*

CHOSEN 15 TIMES

Tomaso Albinoni and Remo Giazotto, *Adagio for Organ and Strings In G Minor*

Johann Sebastian Bach, *Brandenburg Concerto No. 1 in F Major*

Johann Sebastian Bach, *Brandenburg Concerto No. 2 in F Major*

Johann Sebastian Bach, *Brandenburg Concerto No. 6 in B Flat Major*

César Franck, *Symphonic Variations*

Charles-François Gounod, *Faust*

Igor Stravinsky, *The Firebird*

Pyotr Ilyich Tchaikovsky, *Symphony No. 5 in E Minor*

Pyotr Ilyich Tchaikovsky, *Violin Concerto in D Major*

Heitor Villa–Lobos, *Bachianas Brasileiras No. 5*

William Walton, *Façade*

CHOSEN 14 TIMES

Edward Elgar, *Symphony No. 1 in A Flat Major*

George Frideric Handel, *Arrival of The Queen of Sheba* from *Solomon*

George Frideric Handel, *Zadok The Priest*

Jules Massenet, *Thaïs*

Jacques Offenbach, *Orpheus In The Underworld*

Johann Pachelbel, *Canon in D Major*

Joaquín Rodrigo, *Concierto De Aranjuez*

Franz Schubert, *Piano Sonata No. 21 in B Flat Major*

Dmitri Shostakovich, *Symphony No. 5*

Jean Sibelius, *Symphony No. 1 in E Minor*

Jean Sibelius, *Symphony No. 5 in E Flat Major*

Giuseppe Verdi, *Il Trovatore*

CHOSEN 13 TIMES

Johannes Brahms, *Symphony No. 3 in F Major*

Frédéric Chopin, *Les Sylphides*

Frédéric Chopin, *Fantaisie-impromptu in C Sharp Minor*

Gustav Mahler, *Symphony No. 2 in C Minor 'Resurrection'*

Felix Mendelssohn, *Elijah*

Wolfgang Amadeus Mozart, *Ave Verum Corpus*

Maurice Ravel, *La Valse*

Robert Schumann, *Scenes From Childhood* (including nine people who chose *Träumerei*)

Johann Strauss II, *Tales From The Vienna Woods*

Ludwig Van Beethoven, *Piano Concerto No. 4 in G Major*

Ludwig Van Beethoven, *Piano Sonata No. 8 in C Minor*

CHOSEN 12 TIMES

Richard Addinsell, *Warsaw Concerto*

Johann Sebastian Bach, *Sheep May Safely Graze* (from *Cantata No. 208*)

Hector Berlioz, *Les Nuits D'Été*

Johannes Brahms, *Piano Concerto No. 1 in D Minor*

Edward Elgar, *Cockaigne Overture*

Claudio Monteverdi, *Vespers 1610*

Richard Strauss, *Also Sprach Zarathustra*

Ludwig Van Beethoven, *String Quartet No. 16 in F Major*

CHOSEN 11 TIMES

Johann Sebastian Bach, *Brandenburg Concerto No. 4 in G Major*

Léo Delibes, *Lakmé*

Edward Elgar, *Sea Pictures*

César Franck, *Symphony in D Minor*

Enrique Granados, *Danzas*

Gustav Mahler, *Symphony No. 9 in D Major*

Claudio Monteverdi, *The Coronation of Poppea*

Giacomo Puccini, *Manon Lescaut*

Maurice Ravel, *Piano Concerto in G Major*

Camille Saint-Saens, *Samson And Delilah*

Bedrich Smetana, *Má Vlast*

Oscar Straus, *Mariette*

Igor Stravinsky, *Symphony of Psalms*

Charles-Marie Widor, *Organ Symphony No. 5 in F Minor*

CHOSEN 10 TIMES

Johann Sebastian Bach, *St John Passion*

Samuel Barber, *Adagio For Strings*

Joseph Canteloube, *Songs of The Auvergne*

Joseph Haydn, *Trumpet Concerto in E Flat Major*

Engelbert Humperdinck, *Hansel And Gretel*

Leos Janacek, *Sinfonietta*

Gustav Mahler, *Rückert-Lieder*

Camille Saint–Saens, *Symphony No. 3*

Franz Schubert, *Schwanengesang*

Pyotr Ilyich Tchaikovsky, *Symphony No. 4 in F Minor*

Richard Wagner, *Parsifal*

Ralph Vaughan Williams, *Serenade To Music*

AFICIONADOS

Three or more selections from the same composer in a single programme:

JOHANN SEBASTIAN BACH

Sir Roger Penrose and Sir Richard Woolley chose four works.

Douglas Adams, Dame Peggy Ashcroft, Reginald Goodall, Joyce Grenfell, Pamela Hansford Johnson, Robert Henriques, Wally Herbert, Dr Reginald Jacques, Erich Leinsdorf, Anthony Minghella, Harold Pinter, Don Thompson, Dame Sybil Thorndike, Mitsuko Uchida, Jon Vickers and Helen Watts chose three works.

JOSEPH HAYDN

Geoffrey Grigson chose three works.

WOLFGANG AMADEUS MOZART

Sybille Bedford, Oliver Messel, Harford Montgomery Hyde, Sir Nicholas Sekers and Baroness Maria von Trapp chose four works.

Dannie Abse, Alan Bullock, Sir Frederick Gibberd, Sir John Gielgud, Jane Glover, James Lovelock, André Previn, Robert Robinson, Lord Roll, Sir Magdi Yacoub and Donald Zec chose three works.

GIACOMO PUCCINI

Barbara Taylor Bradford chose three of Puccini's works in 2003 and two in her 1985 appearance.

FRANZ SCHUBERT

Claudio Arrau, Jacqueline du Pré, Artur Rubinstein and Baroness Maria von Trapp chose three works.

PYOTR ILYICH TCHAIKOVSKY

Dame Ninette de Valois chose three works.

LUDWIG VAN BEETHOVEN

James Ellroy chose five works. No one has chosen four works.

The Beaux Arts Trio, Sir Colin Davis, Malcolm Muggeridge (two on his second appearance), Enoch Powell and Bill Sowerbutts chose three works.

GIUSEPPE VERDI

Tito Gobbi and Dennis Noble chose three works.

RICHARD WAGNER

Rita Hunter and Enoch Powell chose four works.

Lord Boothby, T. C. Fairbairn, Linda Esther Gray and John Tomlinson chose three works.

***

CHOSE WAGNER'S *RIDE OF THE VALKYRIES* FROM *DIE WALKÜRE*

A selection: Sir Menzies Campbell, George Cole, R. F. Delderfield, Richard Dimbleby, Charlie Drake, Wing Commander Guy Gibson, Irene Handl, Robertson Hare, David Hicks, Michael Holroyd, Margaret Lockwood, Vic Oliver, John Ridgway, Richard Todd

***

CHOSE JOHN WILLIAMS PLAYING *CAVATINA* FROM *THE DEER HUNTER*

A selection: John Cleese, Michael Crawford, Michael Deeley, Chris Tarrant.

PEOPLE WHO CHOSE A PLANET FROM GUSTAV HOLST'S *THE PLANETS*

MARS, THE BRINGER OF WAR
Sir Alan Cobham

Barry Cryer

Jimmy Edwards

Ann Haydon-Jones

James Herbert

David Jason

Judith Kerr

Quentin Poole

Dickie Valentine

Henry Williamson

VENUS, THE BRINGER OF PEACE
Lord Robens

Edward Woodward

JUPITER, THE BRINGER OF JOLLITY
Sir Arthur Bryant

Gordon Beningfield

Most Rev. Dr George Carey

Will Carling

Andrew Davis

Lieutenant-Colonel Sir Vivian Dunn

David Essex

Christopher Hopper

(PEOPLE WHO CHOSE A PLANET – *cont.*)

Elspeth Huxley

Tamara Karsavina

Lord Lichfield

Sir Peter Mansfield

Les Murray

James Prior

Angela Rippon

Patricia Routledge

Lord John Stevens

Lord Tebbit

SATURN, THE BRINGER OF OLD AGE

Brian Aldiss

Imogen Holst

Brian May

URANUS, THE MAGICIAN

Wayne Marshall

NEPTUNE, THE MYSTIC

Antonio

Maurice Jacobson

Sheila Scott

MERCURY, THE WINGED MESSENGER

None

PEOPLE WHO CHOSE A SEASON FROM VIVALDI'S *FOUR SEASONS*

WINTER

Richard Chamberlain

Ray Cooney

Antal Dorati

Paul Eddington

Martin Gilbert

Sir Nicholas Henderson

Thomas Keneally

Annie Lennox

Sir Ian McKellen

Ismail Merchant

Bill Morris

SPRING

Isabel Allende

Raymond Blanc

Michael Elkins

Linton Kwesi Johnson

Rachel Kempson, Lady Redgrave

Roy MacGregor-Hastie

George Melly

Nina and Frederik

Lynn Redgrave

Marisa Robles

Albert and Michel Roux

Martin Sheen

Sir John Wolfenden

SUMMER

Don Black

Lionel Hale

Lucy Irvine

Miriam Karlin

Carla Lane

Frank Muir

AUTUMN

Alan Bullock

Giuseppe di Stefano

Thelma Holt

THE MOST POPULAR
HYMNS CHOSEN

Ave Maria – 42

Hallelujah Chorus from Handel's *Messiah* – 41

Jerusalem – 40

The Twenty-Third Psalm – 32 (Alan Clark and
Gordon Brown chose it sung in Gaelic)

Abide With Me – 18

Amazing Grace – 17

Guide Me O Thou Great Redeemer/Jehovah – 11

Battle Hymn of The Republic – 10

The Holy City – 8

Dear Lord And Father of Mankind – 7

Eternal Father, Strong To Save – 6

God Be In My Head – 5
He Who Would Valiant Be – 5
How Great Thou Art – 5
Onward, Christian Soldiers – 5

For All The Saints – 4
Praise My Soul, The King of Heaven – 4

Now Thank We All Our God – 3

Immortal, Invisible, God Only Wise – 2
Jerusalem of Gold – 2
The Old Rugged Cross – 2
Rock of Ages – 2

Be Thou My Vision – 1
For The Beauty of The Earth – 1
Holy, Holy, Holy – 1
I Vow To Thee My Country – 1
O Praise The Lord From Heaven – 1
What A Friend We Have In Jesus – 1

The following hymns have never been chosen: *All Things Bright And Beautiful, Fight The Good Fight, Nearer My God To Thee, We Plough The Fields And Scatter* or *There Is A Green Hill.*

The Lord's Prayer was chosen by 13 castaways – including Tallulah Bankhead, Dame Gladys Cooper, Ruthie Henshall, Danny La Rue, Beatrice Lillie, Hugh Lloyd, Al Read and Sir Alec Rose.

CHOSE *JERUSALEM*

A selection: Gordon Brown, Noel Edmonds, Rocco Forte, Martin Gilbert, Katherine Hamnett, Mike Harding, Roy Hattersley, Graham Hill, Valerie Hobson, Frankie Howerd, Sir Digby Jones, Nicole Kidman, Miriam Margolyes, Barbara Mullen, Lord Oaksey, Wendy Richard, Sir Alec Rose, Jack Rosenthal, Zena Skinner, Barbara Taylor Bradford, Ron Todd, Ted Willis

CHOSE *KOL NIDREI* (A JEWISH PRAYER SUNG AT THE BEGINNING OF YOM KIPPUR)

A selection: Ben Helfgott, Sir Stanley Kalms, Joe Loss, Miriam Margolyes, Dame Shirley Porter

THE MOST POPULAR CHRISTMAS CAROLS CHOSEN

In The Bleak Midwinter – 13

Once In Royal David's City – 13

Silent Night – 13

O Come All Ye Faithful – 8

God Rest Ye Merry, Gentlemen – 5

The Holly And The Ivy – 5

Hark! The Herald Angels Sing – 3

The First Noel – 3*

Ding Dong Merrily On High – 2

O Little Town of Bethlehem – 2

The Twelve Days of Christmas – 2

Away In A Manger – 1

I Saw Three Ships – 1

The Little Drummer Boy – 1

While Shepherds Watched Their Flocks – 1

* Includes Sir Laurens van der Post, who chose the St Andrew's College Choir, East Africa, singing *The First Nowell* in Swahili.

～～～～～

None of the following has ever been chosen: *Good King Wenceslas*, *We Wish You A Merry Christmas* or *We Three Kings of Orient Are*.

ANTHEMS CHOSEN

Land of My Fathers (Wales) – 17

Waltzing Matilda (Australia) – 14

Scotland The Brave (Scotland) – 12

La Marseillaise (France) – 7

God Save The Queen (Great Britain) – 3

Ayah (Kenya) – 1

Deutschlandlied (Germany) – 1

Frantisek Skroup (Czechoslovakia) – 1

The Hatikvah (Israel) – 1

Colin Montgomerie chose *Flower of Scotland* as sung by the crowd at the Scotland *v.* England Rugby Union match on 17 March 1990.

Rule Britannia has been chosen seven times by castaways including Sir Alan P. Herbert (twice), Sir Michael Hordern (twice) and Princess Margaret.

PEOPLE WHO BROUGHT PRIVATE TAPES OR RECORDINGS

Paul Abbott,* Sir John Betjeman, Prince Chula Chakrabongse of Thailand, Martin Clunes,* James Dyson,* Robertson Hare,* Lord Killanin, Ben Kingsley,* Neil Kinnock,* Fran Landesman, Tasmin Little, Sir Cameron Mackintosh,* Fay Maschler (two), Selina Scott, Peter West, Dr Ruth Westheimer,* Paul Whitehouse*

* Featuring themselves or a member of their family.

CHOSE WORDS INSTEAD OF MUSIC

POETS CHOSEN (excluding Shakespeare, see pages 160–2)

Dylan Thomas – 45

T. S. Eliot – 17

Sir John Betjeman – 9

W. H. Auden – 5

Philip Larkin – 4

W. B. Yeats – 4

William Blake – 3

Rudyard Kipling – 3

Walter de la Mare – 2

Gerard Manley Hopkins – 2

John Keats – 2

Samuel Taylor Coleridge – 2

Hilaire Belloc – 1

Robert Browning – 1

Robert Burns – 1

e. e. cummings – 1

Robert Frost – 1

A. E. Housman – 1

John Milton – 1

Percy Bysshe Shelley – 1

Edith Sitwell – 1

Wallace Stevens – 1

William Wordsworth – 1

Benjamin Zephaniah – 1

CHOSE A READING FROM DYLAN THOMAS

A selection: John Arlott (who had nurtured Dylan Thomas's career at the BBC), Dame Peggy Ashcroft, Henry Cecil, Richard Chamberlain, Roald Dahl, Monica Dickens, Roy Dotrice, Geraint Evans, James Fox, John Freeman, Hugh Griffith, Miriam Margolyes, Millicent Martin, Roger McGough, Virginia McKenna, Yehudi Menuhin, Princess Michael of Kent, Andrea Newman, Alan Plater, Anthony Quayle, Gerald Scarfe, Sir Harry Secombe, Virginia Wade, Emlyn Williams

CHOSE A W. H. AUDEN READING

Roy Hattersley, Richard Hoggart, Alexander McCall Smith, Sir Stephen Spender, Julian Symons

CHOSE A T. S. ELIOT READING

A selection: Terry Hands, Susan Hill, Harold Hobson, Sue Lawley, Raymond Postgate, Vincent Price, Robert Robinson, A. L. Rowse, Wilfred Thesiger, P. L. Travers

CHOSE A SIR JOHN BETJEMAN READING

A selection: David Bailey, Wendy Craig, Lord Healey, Jeremy Lloyd, Warren Mitchell, Frank Muir, Suggs

CHOSE A READING FROM JAMES JOYCE

Peter Blake – Molly Bloom's soliloquy from *Ulysses*

Tom Driberg, Tyrone Guthrie, Raymond Postgate and Robert Robinson – the 'Anna Livia Plurabelle' chapter from *Finnegans Wake*

CHOSE READINGS FROM DICKENS

Ursula Bloom – *Dombey and Son*

Max Miller – *Captain Cuttle* (from *Dombey and Son*)

Tyrone Power – *Mr Pickwick's Christmas*

CHOSE AN EXCERPT FROM OSCAR WILDE'S *THE IMPORTANCE OF BEING EARNEST*

Dame Peggy Ashcroft, Leslie Phillips, Sheila Sim, Dame Veronica Wedgwood

CHOSE A TONY HANCOCK RECORDING

Patrick Cargill, Graham Hill, Hugh Lloyd, Matt Munro, Ray Reardon and Antoinette Sibley – *The Blood Donor* (in which Patrick Cargill and Hugh Lloyd featured)

Sebastian Coe, Sheila Hancock and Sidney James – *Sunday Afternoon At Home* (in which Sidney James featured)

Marti Caine and June Whitfield – *Test Pilot*

Charlie Watts – *The Reunion Party*

Barbara Windsor – extract from *The Secret Life of Anthony Hancock*

CHOSE A BOB NEWHART RECORDING

Cilla Black, Sir James Callaghan, Des Lynam, Trevor Philpott and Margaret Thatcher – *Introducing Tobacco To Civilization*

Michael Bond, Dr George Carey, Ian Hendry, Graham Hill and Sandy Powell – *The Driving Instructor*

Roger Moore and Sir Ralph Richardson – *The Cruise of The USS Codfish*

James Herriot – *A Friend With A Dog*

Robert Morley – *Abe Lincoln v. Madison Avenue*

CHOSE A SKETCH BY MIKE NICHOLS AND ELAINE MAY

Richard Curtis – *Nichols And May At Work*

Michael Powell and Emeric Pressburger – *Disc Jockey*

Terry Scott – *Improvisations To Music (Rachmaninov's Piano Concerto No. 2)*

CHOSE A TOM LEHRER SKETCH

Brian Aldiss and Patrick Stewart – *So Long, Mom (A Song For World War III)*; Brian Aldiss also chose *The Vatican Rag*

Tariq Ali – *Send The Marines*

Sir Arthur Bliss and Harry Carpenter – *The Elements*

Dr Jacob Bronowski – *The Wild West*

Bill Bryson – *Poisoning Pigeons In The Park*

Andy Hamilton and Mo Mowlam – *National Brotherhood Week*

Anthony Howard – *When You Are Old And Grey*

Roger Moore – *I Hold Your Hand In Mine*

Erich Segal – *Fight Fiercely, Harvard*

CHOSE A JOYCE GRENFELL SKETCH

Stephanie Beacham – *Story Time*

Rachael Heyhoe – *Nursery School*

Dame Celia Johnson – *I'm Going To See You Today*

Maureen Lipman – *First Flight*

June Whitfield – *Old Tyme Dancing*

CHOSE GERARD HOFFNUNG'S 1958 SPEECH AT THE OXFORD UNION

James Bolam, Jim Clark, Winston Graham, Sir Peter Hall, Beryl Reid, Donald Sinden

CHOSE AN ALAN BENNETT RECORDING

Carol Channing – *Civil War*

Sir David Frost – *Aftermyth of War*

Robin Ray – *Take A Pew*

CHOSE A RECORDING BY THE GOONS

Raymond Baxter, Bryan Forbes and Michael Palin – *Tales of Men's Shirts*

Richard Briers – *The White Box of Greatbardfield*

Bernard Cribbins – *Dishonoured*

Bruce Fogle and Julia Foster – *The Ying Tong Song*

Mike Harding and Marti Webb – *The Dreaded Batter Pudding Hurler of Bexhill-on-Sea*

David Jason – *The International Christmas Pudding*

Michael Mansfield – *What's The Time, Eccles?*

CHOSE A PETER COOK AND DUDLEY MOORE SKETCH (OR SONG)

Rob Brydon and Petula Clark – *Lengths*

John Fortune – *The Frog And The Peach*

Richard Ingrams – *Goodbyee*

Barry John and Gerald Scarfe – *Art Gallery Sketch*

George Martin – *Bollard*
Dudley Moore – *Little Miss Britten*
Sheridan Morley – *The Ravens*

CHOSE AN EXCERPT FROM NOËL COWARD'S *PRIVATE LIVES*

Prince Chula Chakrabongse of Thailand, Noël Coward, Dame Cleo Laine, Sir Osbert Lancaster, Miriam Margolyes, Alec Waugh, Dorian Williams

CHOSE A CRICKET COMMENTARY

Henry Blofeld, Rory Bremner, Leon Brittan, Robert Dougall, John Major, Sir Matthew Pinsent, Jimmy Tarbuck, Charlie Watts

CHOSE A FOOTBALL COMMENTARY

Richard Attenborough, Stephen Frears, Tommy Steele

CHOSE A COMMENTARY ON THE DERBY

Scobie Breasley, T. E. B. Clarke, Wilfrid Hyde-White

THE SOUND OF SHAKESPEARE

HAMLET – chosen by 26 castaways

Nine chose the *To Be Or Not To Be* soliloquy.

Four chose *Now I Am Alone, O, What A Rogue.*

Three chose *The Queen's Closet* scene.

HENRY V – 13

Seven chose the St Crispin's Day speech.

Four chose *Once More Unto The Breach.*

THE TEMPEST – 12

Six chose Prospero's speech *Our Revels Now Are Ended.*

AS YOU LIKE IT – 9

Six chose *All The World's A Stage.*

RICHARD II – 9

Three chose John O'Gaunt's speech.

CYMBELINE – 6

All six chose *Fear No More The Heat O' The Sun.*

RICHARD III – 5

All five chose *Now Is The Winter of Our Discontent.*

TWELFTH NIGHT – 5

Four chose *When That I Was And A Little Tiny Boy.*

OTHELLO – 3

THE MERCHANT OF VENICE – 2

CHOSEN ONCE

A Midsummer Night's Dream, Julius Caesar ('Friends, Romans, countrymen'), *Love's Labours Lost, Much Ado About Nothing, Romeo And Juliet, The Taming of The Shrew, Venus and Adonis*

SONNETS

Shakespeare's sonnets were chosen 19 times.

Ten chose *Shall I Compare Thee To A Summer's Day.*

Two chose *My Mistress' Eyes Are Nothing Like The Sun.*

Two chose *Let Me Not To The Marriage of True Minds.*

CASTAWAYS WHO CHOSE . . .

SHAKESPEARE

Include: Harold Abrahams, Richard Attenborough, Lauren Bacall, Dame Janet Baker, Dame Joan Bakewell, Sir John Betjeman, Gyles Brandreth, Mike Brearley, Richard Briers, Leon Brittan, Tony Britton, Coral Browne, A. S. Byatt, Noël Coward, Sir Robin Day, Dame Judi Dench (on two occasions), Dame Edith Evans, Cyril Fletcher, Michael Gambon, Princess Grace of Monaco, Gerald Harper, Dame Wendy Hiller, Sir Michael Hordern (on two occasions), Derek Jacobi, Molly Keane, Herbert Lom, Dame Ngaio Marsh (two selections), Virginia McKenna, Sir John Mortimer, Anne-Sophie Mutter, Dandy Nichols, David Niven, Barry Norman, Nigel Patrick, Vincent Price, Claire Rayner, Sir Michael Redgrave, Sir Ralph Richardson, Prunella Scales, Donald Sinden, Maggie Smith, C. P. Snow, Dame Sybil Thorndike, David Tomlinson, P. L. Travers, Rita Tushingham, Des Wilson, Michael York, Franco Zeffirelli

MARTIN LUTHER KING'S 1963 'I HAVE A DREAM' SPEECH

Barbara Castle, David Edgar, Sir David Frost, Trevor McDonald, Jessye Norman, Ron Pickering, Anna Scher

A SPEECH BY SIR WINSTON CHURCHILL

This Was Their Finest Hour (18 June 1940)

Robbie Brightwell

Sir Robin Day (chosen on both occasions he was on the show)

Robert Fisk

Michael Heseltine

Robert Maxwell

Benno Moiseiwitsch

Redmond O'Hanlon

Quentin Reynolds

A. L. Rowse

Gladys Young

We Shall Fight Them On The Beaches (4 June 1940)

Colin Cowdrey

Evelyn Laye

OTHER CHURCHILL SPEECHES CHOSEN – ONCE EACH

Blood, Toil, Tears And Sweat (13 May 1940) – Georg Solti

Every Man To His Post (11 September 1940) – Cyril Mills

Meeting With Roosevelt (24 August 1941) – Sir David Frost

Speech on 14 August 1946 – Sir Anton Dolin

Speech on the bombing of London (11 September 1940) – Richard Briers

These Are Great Days (Speech To Boys of Harrow School, 29 October 1941) – Edward Fox

The War of The Unknown Warriors (14 July 1940) – Victor Borge

V E Day (8 May 1945) – Des O'Connor

Westward Look The Land Is Bright (27 April 1941) – Lord Longford

JOHN F. KENNEDY'S INAUGURAL ADDRESS

Sir Robin Day, Des Wilson

SOUNDS OR SOUND EFFECTS . . .

Paddy Ashdown – birdsong on Kung mountain

Sir David Attenborough – birdsong from the lyrebird (which imitates other sounds)

Rev. W. Awdry – sound effects from the West Highland train line near Tyndrum and sound effects of trains in the hills

David Bellamy – recording of small children playing nursery games

Alan Bennett – 'West of Exeter' (railway sounds)

Sir John Betjeman – sound effects of country and town railway, a recording of the bells of Thaxted Church, Essex and the Padstow townspeople performing their May Day ceremony (Padstow 'Obby 'Oss)

Terence Cuneo – recording of a French locomotive

Frances Day – recording of the bark of the Rhodesian Lion Dog

Victoria de los Ángeles – sound effects of birds, animals, crowds, traffic

Fred Dibnah – sound of a locomotive steam engine

Jimmy Edwards – sound of a USAF jet plane

Rod Hull – recording of the song of a skylark

Herbert Lom – a prolonged standing ovation

Sandy MacPherson – recording of Sparkie Williams, a 1958 champion talking budgerigar

Roger McGough – sound of foghorns on the Mersey

Sarah Miles – sound of a bull elephant trumpeting

Frances Perry – sound of Galapagos Sea Lions

Jonathon Porritt – humpback whale music

Eric Porter – montage of noises he would be glad to have left behind

James Robertson Justice – recording of the call of a flock of pink-footed geese

Vikram Seth – nightingales and Lancaster Bombers recorded in a Surrey Wood in 1942

David Shepherd – stereo recordings of a steam locomotive

Anthony Steel – recording of the sounds of Piccadilly Circus

Noel Streatfeild – recording of the bells of St Paul's Cathedral

Alan Titchmarsh – the evening song of a blackbird

Fred Trueman – Yorkshire County Cricket Club's tables and chairs

Mary Wesley – the dawn chorus

Ann Widdecombe – sounds of the hippo

Brigadier Peter Young – recording of a Hoolock gibbon, London Zoo

UNIQUE SOUND CHOICES

Rev. W. Awdry – Mabel Constanduros and Michael Hogan performing *The Bugginses Prepare For A Party*

John Biffen – Stanley Baldwin's speech on *The English Character*

Conrad Black – General Douglas MacArthur's Report to Congress, 19 April 1951

Sir Adrian Boult – King George V's Silver Jubilee message to the Empire (6 May 1935) (chosen by Sir Adrian on both of his appearances)

Marti Caine – Andrew Timothy reading the Shipping Forecast

Jackie Charlton – World Cup Final 1966 (last minute of extra time)

Les Dawson – W. C. Fields, *The Day I Drank A Glass of Water*

David Dimbleby – Richard Dimbleby's commentary on the Lying In State of HM King George VI

Dame Edith Evans – Peter Ustinov's *The Grand Prix of Gibraltar*

(UNIQUE SOUND CHOICES – *cont.*)

Sir John Gielgud – Sir Ralph Richardson's recital of William Blake's *The Chimney Sweeper And The Sick Rose*

Joan Greenwood – Sarah Bernhardt performing *Phèdre*

Susan Hampshire – Greta Garbo and Melvyn Douglas in a scene from the film *Ninotchka*

Sir Cedric Hardwicke – extract from the talk given by George Bernard Shaw on his ninetieth birthday, 24 July 1946

Ben Helfgott – the opening of the 1956 Olympic Games in Melbourne

Anthony Howard – Nye Bevan speaking at the anti-Suez rally at Trafalgar Square, November 1956

Richard Ingrams – Harold Macmillan's 'She Didn't Say Yes, She Didn't Say No' – from the Prime Minister's speech to the 1962 Conservative Party Conference where he mocked the Labour Party

Hammond Innes – John Laurie reciting Robert Burns' *Helen of Kirconnell*

Kenneth McKellar – John Laurie reciting William McGonagall's *The Tay Bridge Disaster*

Vincent Price – Franklin D. Roosevelt's Human Rights speech

John Sessions – William Faulkner's acceptance speech for the Nobel Prize for Literature 1950

Elisabeth Söderström – Finnish Language Course: *Starting Finnish*

Ralph Steadman – William S. Burroughs' Thanksgiving prayer

Ben Travers – Tom Walls talking about the 1932 Derby for which Walls (who was also an actor who had starred in many of Travers's plays) had trained the winner – April The Fifth

Peter Ustinov – H. H. Asquith's speech on the budget, 1909

Ann Widdecombe – Richard Dimbleby's report from Belsen concentration camp, 1945

STORIES BEHIND CHOICES

David Suchet chose Frankie Vaughan's *You'll Never Walk Alone* because he and his brother would sing this when they were forced to swim in the freezing sea every Sunday while at boarding school. 'We used to walk down from the school, the headmaster would be in front of us boys, and he would walk into the sea, and no one was allowed to pause. We used to hold hands and sing *You'll Never Walk Alone* as we walked into the icy sea.'

Maureen O'Sullivan chose *Dear Prudence*, which The Beatles wrote about her daughter Prudence who was with them in India.

David Cameron chose Benny Hill's *Ernie (The Fastest Milkman In The West)*, which he said was the only song whose words he could remember.

Sir Hugh Greene, who had been a reporter in Berlin right up to the start of World War II, chose *Die Fahne Hoch (Raise The Banner)* by the Nazi Storm Troopers.

Tony Blair chose Bruce Springsteen's *4th of July Asbury Park (Sandy)* because it was the song that reminded him of the early days of his relationship with Cherie Booth.

Gloria Hunniford dedicated many of her eight choices to her daughter Caron, who'd died two years earlier. One was Van Morrison's *Have I Told You Lately* which Caron and Russ Lindsay danced to at their wedding. Another was Cliff Richard's *Miss You Nights*, which Cliff sang to Caron as she battled cancer.

Chili Bouchier chose Fred Hartley singing *I Love My Chili Bom-Bom* – because she got her name from the song (from an admirer) while working at Harrods. She was born Dorothy.

Timothy Spall chose Jimmy Nail's *Cowboy Dreams*. Jimmy Nail was his co-star in the TV series that brought them both fame: *Auf Wiedersehen, Pet*.

Alan Coren chose Instant Sunshine playing *Tittle Tattle Rag*. Instant Sunshine featured Miles Kington, who was a columnist in *Punch*, the magazine Coren edited.

John Conteh chose Paul McCartney and Wings's *Band On The Run*. Conteh was one of the celebrities featured on the cover of the album of the same name.

Jimmy Savile chose Lee Dorsey's *Working In The Coal Mine*. As a Bevin Boy, conscripted during World War II, Savile had worked as a coal miner in the South Kirby Colliery, West Yorkshire.

Lord Killanin chose the Olympic Hymn. He was the sixth president of the International Olympic Committee.

David Croft chose Arthur Lowe performing *I Couldn't Do A Thing Like That*. David Croft co-wrote and produced *Dad's Army*, the TV series that made Lowe famous.

Frank Bruno chose a song to remind him of his wife, Laura, Ricky Valance's romantic song *Tell Laura I Love Her*.

Kaye Webb, who chose *Puffin Song* by Doug Turner, was editor of Puffin Books for nearly 20 years.

Ernie Wise chose David Rose And His Orchestra's *The Stripper* and Gene Kelly *Singin' In The Rain* – both of which he had performed a routine to in *Morecambe And Wise* shows.

Martin Bell chose True Tones singing *Foreign Journalist's Calypso*. It was a calypso 'sung against' him in St Lucia in 1979 which mentions him by name (in an uncomplimentary way).

Jessica Mitford chose the Centenary Choir's rendition of *The Red Flag*. She was a lifelong communist (by contrast with her sisters Diana and Unity, who were fascists).

Sebastian Coe (in his 1981 appearance on the programme) chose the 1980 Olympic Hymn. It was at these Olympics in Moscow that he won his first gold medal.

CHOSE AN APPROPRIATE SONG FOR A DESERT ISLAND

Sir Jack Brabham – *We Never Talk Much (We Just Sit Around)* by Danielle Darrieux and Fernando Lamas

Kenneth Connor – *A Life On The Ocean Wave* by Royal Yacht Band

Len Goodman – *Island In The Sun* by Harry Belafonte

Valerie Hobson – *Time Is On My Hands* by Denny Dennis

Dame Celia Johnson – *Sail Away* by Noël Coward

Derek Randall – *Happy To Be On An Island In The Sun* by Demis Roussos

Twiggy – *On My Own* from *Les Misérables*

17 castaways chose Charles Trénet's *La Mer*.

PRESENTERS' CHOICES

ROY PLOMLEY (1942–1985)
1942 – interviewed by Leslie Perowne

1. Wolfgang Amadeus Mozart – *Il Seraglio Overture*

2. George Gershwin – *Bess, You Is My Woman Now* (from *Porgy And Bess*)

3. Fred Elizalde – *Harmonising*

4. Alexander Borodin – *Polovtsian Dances* (from *Prince Igor*)

5. Jean Sablon – *Pour Vous, J'Avais Fait Cette Chanson*

6. Alexander Borodin – *String Quartet No. 2 in D Major* – 3rd movement

7. Duke Ellington And His Orchestra – *Creole Rhapsody*

8. Johann Strauss II – *Die Fledermaus* Act 2 (finale)

ROY PLOMLEY
1958 – interviewed by Eamonn Andrews

1. Annabelle Hill – *Another Op'nin, Another Show*

2. Fred Elizalde – *Harmonising*

3. Covent Garden Opera Company – *Oh What A Feast, What A Wonderous Night* (from *Die Fledermaus*)

4. Tou Tsin-Fan – *Chou Ting-Tai Au Tombeau De Liang Chan-Po*

5. Bob Hope and Shirley Ross – *Thanks For The Memory*

6. Aleksandr Andreyevich Arkhangelsky – *Eucharist Canon*

7. Oscar Straus – *Mariette* Act 2 (finale)

8. Ludwig van Beethoven – *Piano Concerto No. 5 in E Flat Major 'Emperor'*

Book choice: *Who's Who In The Theatre*

Luxury item: Desk with a typewriter and paper

MICHAEL PARKINSON (1985–1988)
1972 – interviewed by Roy Plomley

1. Gene Kelly – *Singin' In The Rain* (castaway's favourite)

2. George Frideric Handel – *Messiah*

3. The Stan Getz Quartet – *Here's That Rainy Day*

4. Frank Sinatra – *I Wish I Were In Love Again*

5. Blossom Dearie – *Mad About The Boy*

6. Stan Kenton And His Orchestra – *How High The Moon*

7. Robert Goulet – *If Ever I Would Leave You*

8. Billie Holiday With Teddy Wilson And His Orchestra – *As Time Goes By*

Book choice: Death In The Afternoon by Ernest Hemingway

Luxury item: Typewriter and paper

SUE LAWLEY (1988–2006)
1987 – interviewed by Michael Parkinson

1. Sergey Vasilievich Rachmaninov – *Rhapsody On A Theme of Paganini* (castaway's favourite)

2. Giacomo Puccini – *Madame Butterfly*

3. The Beatles – *Hey Jude*

4. Henry Purcell – *Sound The Trumpet* (from *Birthday Ode 'Come Ye Sons of Art Away'*)

5. Gustav Holst and Christina Rossetti – *In The Bleak Midwinter*

6. T. S. Eliot – lines from T. S. Eliot's *Four Seasons* read by Sir John Gielgud

7. Dory Previn – *Lady With The Braid*

8. Ella Fitzgerald – *Ev'ry Time We Say Goodbye*

Book choice: *French Provincial Cooking* by Elizabeth David

Luxury item: Iron and ironing board

KIRSTY YOUNG (2006–PRESENT)

Kirsty Young has never been a castaway herself. However, in an interview, she revealed that her choices would include ELO's *Mr Blue Sky* – 'because I remember one of the happiest moments of my childhood was singing that, running through a school playing field with my friends' – and Neil Diamond's *I Am, I Said*, 'because it reminds me of my mother coming to kiss me goodnight smelling of Chanel No. 5, wearing a fringe dress and looking beyond glamorous'.

LUXURIES

THE LUXURY

The rules state that the chosen luxury item must not be anything animate or indeed anything that enables the castaway to escape from the island, for instance a radio set, sailing yacht or aeroplane. In Roy Plomley's own words, the luxury had to be 'an inanimate object purely for the senses, which is not going to help you live'.

As we shall see, there were plenty of exceptions to this rule . . .

CASTAWAYS WHO CHOSE FAMILY PHOTOGRAPHS OR A PHOTOGRAPH ALBUM

Count Basie, Stephanie Beacham (a photograph of her children), Maeve Binchy, Henry Blofeld, Frank Bruno, Jackie Collins, Cicely Courtneidge, Josephine Cox, Bear Grylls, Sir Peter Hall, Marvin Hamlisch (a picture of his mother when she was 17), Gloria Hunniford, Frank Ifield, Hattie Jacques (and a recording of her family), Hugh Laurie, Anna Massey, Paul McKenna, David Nixon, Sir Trevor Nunn, Al Read, James Stewart, Doris Stokes, Barbara Taylor Bradford, Margaret Thatcher, Paul Tortelier (a photo of his wife), Alfred Wainwright*, Kaye Webb (a very big photograph album on a wheeling table), Elisabeth Welch (a photo of her mother), Marco Pierre White (a picture of his daughter)

*Alfred Wainwright chose a photograph of his wife (and one of the 1928 Blackburn Rovers FC team) as his book choice.

... SOMETHING ELSE TO REMIND THEM OF THEIR FAMILY

Gillian Anderson – recordings of her daughter and her 'love' reading their own stories and poetry

Bernard Braden – a pair of his wife's earrings

Dora Bryan – a stereoscope with slides of her family

Sir Lewis Casson – the 1912 portrait of his wife, Dame Sybil Thorndike (plus a tape recorder)

Barry Cryer – a tape recorder with a cassette of recordings from home

Stephen Frears – a painting by his wife

Martin Gilbert – drawings of his two children

Sir Alec Guinness – a leather wallet containing photos of his family and dog

Trevor Howard – one of his wife's cakes

Joanna Lumley – a specially commissioned John Ward painting of family and friends

Roger Moore – a video player and films of his family

Mary Portas – 'a set of different fragrances, from the people I love'

Sir Stephen Spender – a painting or sculpture and a photograph of his daughter

Anthony Steel – a portrait of his wife by Annigoni

... A FAMILY MEMBER'S POSSESSION

William Douglas-Home – his daughter's two teddy bears

A. A. Gill – his children's pillows

Michael Rosen – the didgeridoo belonging to his late son Eddie

Bernice Rubens – a painting by her daughter

Barbara Woodhouse – her mother's ormolu clock

... A PERSONAL POSSESSION

Tallulah Bankhead – her portrait by Augustus John

Raymond Blanc – a good-luck stone (from his wife)

Marlene Dietrich – her mementoes box

Christina Foyle – her commonplace book

Sir Edmund Hillary – a painting he had of the Kathmandu valley

Frankie Howerd – the cross given to him by his mother

Gorden Kaye – a clock given to him for turning on the Oxford lights

Dame Ellen MacArthur – a fluffy purple worm (which has been with her on all her sailing voyages)

Sir Peter Pears – a painting from his own collection

Anne Shelton – the little cross that hangs over her bed

Dame Sybil Thorndike – a blue vase, which had been an engagement present

~~~~~~~~~~~~~~~~~~~~~~~~

Acrobat Philippe Petit chose an object found by his father that, as yet, no one can identify.

... A LUCKY CHARM

Webster Booth (an ivory pig), Donald Sinden, Chris Tarrant (his lucky sixpence)

CASTAWAYS WHO CHOSE PRACTICAL LUXURIES

Some of the following may well be considered rule-breakers.

Maria Aitken – Amazonian rain-maker

Edward Allcard – a five-ton block of lead as a keel for a schooner

John Biffen – a rain gauge

Sir Harrison Birtwistle – a chainsaw

Marti Caine – a solar-powered do-it-yourself kit (having chosen a DIY manual as her book)

Joseph Cotten – a boat-building book

Frederick Forsyth – a bow and arrows

Bamber Gascoigne – carpentry tools

Gary Glitter – Elastoplast

Dr Thor Heyerdahl – a wood-carving kit

David Jason – a complete carpenter's toolbox

Stubby Kaye – a hard hat

Tom Keating – a mattock

Herbert Kretzmer – a Zippo lighter

Andy McNab – a golok (a type of machete originating in South-east Asia)

Jamie Oliver – a Leatherman (like a Swiss army knife but more substantial)

Marguerite Patten – a trowel for digging

David Penhaligon – 30 feet of steel

Dame Shirley Porter – a large Swiss army knife

George Shearing – a metal construction set

Rod Steiger – an eternal electric fan

Mel Tormé – an air-conditioner

Sir William Walton – a funicular for hills

Peter West – a set of gardening tools

Vivienne Westwood – a multilingual dictionary

Billy Cotton requested a ticket home.

... A SNORKEL OR DIVING APPARATUS

Dame Peggy Ashcroft ('a frogwoman's outfit'), Pat Barker, Jung Chang, Christopher Chataway, Chris de Burgh, Chris Evans (a pair of swimming goggles with prescription lenses), Hugh Fearnley-Whittingstall, Professor James Fenton (and harpoon), Dame Margot Fonteyn, Antony Gormley, Jeremy Isaacs, Dr Desmond Morris (chose a snorkel mask on his first visit, in 1968, and a snorkel on his second, in 2004), Christopher Reeve, Oliver Sacks, Peter Scott, Peter Scudamore, Peter Sellers, Eric Shipton, Colin Thubron

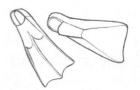

... A FISHING ROD

Ian Botham, Jack Charlton, Loyd Grossman, Geoffrey Palmer (a fly-fishing rod)

... INSECTICIDE/INSECT REPELLENT

Sir Ranulph Fiennes (Antisan for insect bites), Dulcie Gray, Ann Haydon-Jones, Thora Hird, Andrea Levy (mosquito repellent), John Schlesinger

Michael Heseltine chose a mosquito net, while Lucy Irvine chose mosquito coils.

... SUN PRODUCTS

Lauren Bacall (suntan lotion), Joan Bennett (suntan lotion), Joan Collins (large bottle of suntan oil and moisturizer), James Ellroy (sun block), Edward Heath (suntan lotion), Nicholas Hytner (large supply of total-block suncream), Ursula Jeans (sunburn lotion), Nicole Kidman (sun block), Glenys Kinnock (a toilet bag full of skin-barrier creams), Annie Lennox (suncream), Sue MacGregor (unlimited supply of sun block – nicely scented), Mark McCormack (suntan lotion), Alan Parker (suntan lotion), Flora Robson (sunbathing oil), Elisabeth Schwarzkopf (suntan oil), Maggie Smith (sun-barrier cream and a straw hat), June Whitfield (cocoa butter and a hat)

. . . AN UMBRELLA

Jean Carson, Robert Fabian, Raymond Mays, Nyree Dawn Porter, Carrie Tubb (a parasol)

. . . WATERCRAFT

Sir Peter Bonfield – a windsurfer

Chris Brasher – a sailing dinghy

Barry Briggs – a surfboard

Professor Baruch Blumberg – a flat-water kayak suitable for rough water

Sir Adrian Cadbury – a fibreglass sculling boat

Jeremy Clarkson – a jet ski

George Clooney – an anchored yacht

Bernard Cornwell – 'my boat – but not to escape'

Michael Denison and Dulcie Gray – a raft

Katharine Hamnett – an aircraft carrier, to decorate

Lord Montague – a windsurfing board

Rosalind Plowright – a windsurfer

Tim Robbins – a surfboard

John Wain – a canoe

Peter Alliss chose a sand-yacht.

. . . A FIREARM

Jeffrey Bernard – a high-powered hunting rifle and ammunition

Imran Khan – a shotgun and a clay pigeon trap

Fay Weldon – a shotgun (with which to shoot crocodiles)

Artur Rubinstein and David Walliams each chose firearms with which to shoot themselves.

. . . A TELESCOPE

Sir Arthur Bliss, John Boorman, Sir James Callaghan (and a star-gazing book), William Davis, Brian Eno (a radio telescope), Robertson Hare, Bob Hoskins, Sir Fred Hoyle, Peter Jones, Ben Kingsley, Sir Denys Lasdun, Patrick Lichfield (an astronomical telescope), Patrick Moore, Jan Morris (an astronomical telescope with *Catalogue of Nebulae*), Nigel Nicolson, Eric Porter (or a microscope), Sir Tim Rice, Carl Sagan (a reflecting telescope), the Duke of Westminster, Michael York

~~~~~~

Professor Robert Winston requested glass and tools to make a telescope.

. . . BINOCULARS OR FIELD GLASSES

Kenneth Allsop, Eamonn Andrews, Sir David Attenborough, Sir Arthur Bliss, Robert Dougall, Sir Alec Douglas-Home, John Fowles, Sir Alan P. Herbert (twice), Bishop Trevor Huddleston, Penelope Lively, Frank McCourt, Redmond O'Hanlon (a pair of green, insulated Leica binoculars 8 x 20), Nick Park (his own 'amazing pair of binoculars'), Stephen Potter, Steve Race, Sir Stanley Rous, Fred Trueman, Dame Veronica Wedgwood

. . . A WATCH OR CLOCK

Richard Condon (a calendar watch), Michael Foot (an alarm clock encased in Welsh tinplate), Henry Hall (a watch), Otto Preminger (a 'beautiful watch'), Erich Segal (a stop watch), Sheila Sim (a clock)

~~~~~~

Sir Michael Tippett chose an egg timer.

. . . LIGHTING EQUIPMENT

Charlie Drake – a Regency candelabra

Celia Imrie – a cut-glass crystal chandelier with candles

The Duchess of Kent – a lamp with solar batteries

John Laurie – a reading glass with light

Monica Mason – a torch

Frances Perry – a lamp with solar batteries

...FLOWERS, PLANTS OR SEEDS

Lindsay Anderson – mixed flower seeds and a watering can

Baroness Haleh Afshar – a rose bush

Acker Bilk – apple seeds

Ronald Eyre – a supply of flower bulbs

Sir Nicholas Henderson – a box of different seeds

Lucy Irvine – an apple pip

Dame Celia Johnson – a rose cutting and some English soil

Pat Kirkwood – a gardenia bush

C. A. Lejeune – soil and rose bushes

Vic Reeves – potato seeds

June Ritchie – onion plants

James Robertson Justice – mixed flower seeds

Miriam Rothschild – bag of wildflower seeds

Ned Sherrin – seed potatoes

Geoffrey Smith – a bundle of prunings from a good vineyard so he could plant his own vines

Kathleen Turner – roses

Willard White – seeds

Sir Andrew Lloyd Webber chose a herb garden.

Kenneth More chose an English rock garden.

Athene Seyler chose six feet of English hedgerow.

Claire Tomalin chose a garden.

Leonard Rosoman chose a sloping lawn.

.. A TREE

Eleanor Bron – sycamore trees

Michael Crawford – a cherry tree

Bevis Hillier – a bonsai tree

Sir Michael Hordern – an elm tree

Elizabeth, Countess of Longford – an orange tree

~~~~~~

Willy Russell chose an English meadow with an oak tree.

. . . MONEY OR VALUABLES

Stanley Baxter – the Koh-i-Noor diamond

Rupert Davies – a lump of jade

Tito Gobbi – a bar of gold

Ron Grainer – a flame opal

Stephane Grappelli – the Koh-i-Noor diamond

Bob Hope – 'a little money'

Kenneth Horne – a piece of crystal

Marghanita Laski – a gold bracelet called the Lion of Judah

Eric Robinson – £1 million in pound notes

Posy Simmonds – the Crown Jewels

Norman St John Stevas – an emerald

Baroness Trumpington – the Crown Jewels: so someone will look for her

Joy Worth – expensive jewellery

Brigadier Peter Young – a ton of treasure, dated about 1642

. . . A ROBOT

Vladimir Ashkenazy – a well-programmed robot

John Keegan – a French-speaking man robot

CASTAWAYS WHO CHOSE CLOTHES

Tony Bennett – a suit

Coral Browne – a sable coat

Leslie Crowther – a sport suit

René Cutforth – silk vests and pants

Roy Dotrice – an evening dress suit

Harold Evans – silk pyjamas

Howard Jacobson – never-ending supply of pressed shirts and trousers

Margaret Kelly, Miss Bluebell – the first dress she wore on stage

Edgar Lustgarten – a woman's evening gown

Helen Mirren – silk underwear

Molly Parkin – her entire outfit including her Andrew Logan brooch

Beryl Reid – 'a silk garment for floating about in'

Wilfred Pickles – his yellow waistcoat

Janette Scott – a complete 'glamour outfit'

Katharine Whitehorn – a negligee

Hardy Amies chose a dressing case.

Sue Lawley requested an iron and ironing board.

Norris McWhirter chose a roll of cloth.

. . . SHOES

Danny Baker – his blue suede shoes

Keith Floyd – a pair of hand-made blue suede shoes

Seamus Heaney – Doc Marten boots

P. J. Kavanagh – a pair of shoes

Alexander McCall Smith – a pair of hand-made shoes

Ian McEwan – Italian leather hand-stitched hiking boots

Kristin Scott Thomas – a pair of mules by Christian Louboutin

. . . ACCESSORIES

Sir Cecil Beaton – a cashmere shawl

Brian Blessed – a scarf given to him by the Dalai Lama

Sir Adrian Boult – Panama hats stuffed with barley sugar

Sinéad Cusack – a big hat with a lot of muslin

Fenella Fielding – French silk-lined leather gloves

Sidonie Goossens – a handbag 'with contents'

Stubby Kaye – a hard hat

Jack Warner – a blue silk scarf

June Whitfield – a hat (plus cocoa butter)

. . . HANDKERCHIEFS

Hugh Grant, MacDonald Hastings, and Jane Horrocks, who chose an endless supply of tissues

CASTAWAYS WHO CHOSE
A PAINTING

Richard Adams – Leonardo da Vinci's *The Annunciation*

Dave Allen – a painting by Van Hook

Eileen Atkins – an Atkinson Grimshaw painting

Hermione Baddeley – a painting by Renoir

Cilla Black – Leonardo da Vinci's *Mona Lisa*

Dirk Bogarde – *Conversation Piece* by John Singer Sargent – a painting of the Sitwells

Sir Edward Boyle – Sickert's *Drawing of a Lady*

John Braine – Magritte's *The Empire of Light*

Sir Arthur Bryant – Kneller's *Girl in a Golden Gown* and Velázquez's *The Little Princess*

George Carman QC – a painting of the Grand Canal in Venice

Peggy Cummins – a painting of circus horses by Toulouse-Lautrec

Finlay Currie – a 17th-century miniature by Peter Oliver

Dame Judi Dench – Titian's *The Man with a Glove*

Monty Don – Rembrandt's *Hendrickje Bathing*

Margaret Drabble – Cockerill's *Ariadne's Thread*

Francis Durbridge – Matisse's *Still Life with Oriental Rug*

Percy Edwards – Constable's *Willy Lott's Cottage*

Dame Gracie Fields – a reproduction of Renoir's *The Picnic*

Sir John Gielgud – a watercolour of Versailles by Raoul Dufy

Richard Griffiths – Velázquez's *Las Meniñas*

Robert Hardy – *Young Lady in Profile* by Giovanni Ambrogio de Predis

Nicky Haslam – a large 18th-century picture

(CASTAWAYS WHO CHOSE A PAINTING – *cont.*)

Susan Hill – The Barnes Collection (paintings)

Stratford Johns – a painting by Goya

Sir Frank Kermode – Palmer's *Moonlit Landscape*

David Lodge – *Nymph in a Landscape* by Palma Vecchio

Jacques Loussier – Dalí's *The Crucifixion*

Lorin Maazel – Vermeer's *The Piano Lesson*

Sir John Mortimer – Velázquez's *Old Woman Frying Eggs*

John Neville – a landscape painting by Ivon Hitchens

Christopher Ondaatje – Deranyagala's *The Blue Nude*

Dennis Potter – Edward Hopper's *Gas*

Charlotte Rampling – a ballet picture by Degas

Gerald Scarfe – a river painting by Turner

Arthur Scargill – Leonardo da Vinci's *Mona Lisa*

Simon Schama – Rembrandt's *Bathsheba at her Bath*

Donald Sinden – his favourite picture in the Walker Art Gallery

Nigel Slater – Howard Hodgkin's *Learning About Russian Music*

John Snagge – a painting by Rembrandt

Patience Strong – Indian painting showing the Crucifixion

Dr Roy Strong – Vermeer's *View of Delft*

Mary Ure – a painting by Rembrandt in the National Gallery

Jack Vettriano – Bacon's *Triptych, May–June, 1973*

Minette Walters – Van Gogh's *Irises*

Susan Hampshire chose a painting of a 16th-century patch box.

Sir Peter Maxwell Davies chose copperplate engravings of Dürer's *Passion*.

Tyrone Power chose Leonardo da Vinci's notebooks.

Richard Rogers requested his wife, Ruth, 'but if this is disallowed, then a painting'.

Juliet Stevenson selected Masaccio frescos in the Brancacci chapel.

Wendy Toye chose framed Ronald Searle drawings.

Professor Heinz Wolff requested a collection of landscape pictures.

... A SCULPTURE

Dr Christiaan Barnard, Josephine Barstow, Glynis Johns and David Kossoff – Michelangelo's *David*

Gyles Brandreth, Bernard Cribbins and Brian Sewell – Michelangelo's *Pietà*

Raymond Baxter – Rodin's *Danae*

Bob Champion – a bronze statue of the racehorse Aldaniti (on which he had won the Grand National)

Victoria de los Ángeles – the *Nike of Samothrace*

Stewart Granger – a gold statuette of Sir Winston Churchill

Felicity Green – a bronze sculpture by Giles Penny

Robert Hardy – a Greek sculpture of a female head

Sir Nicholas Henderson – a sculpture from The Louvre

David Hicks – a Mexican crystal skull

Graham Hill – David Wynne's *The Dancers*

Sir Osbert Lancaster – *Venus de Milo*

Dame Ngaio Marsh – two Chinese figures of musicians

Paul Robeson – a carved Benin head

Vidal Sassoon – a piece of sculpture by Baracal

Jennifer Saunders – Elisabeth Frink's *Tribute Heads*

Georg Solti – Michelangelo's *The Last Judgement*

Baroness Maria Von Trapp – statue of Madonna and Child from the seventeenth century

Sir William Walton – a small piece of sculpture

Dame Rebecca West – a carved stone head of a Chinese philosopher

Kenneth Williams – Michelangelo's *Apollo*

. . . PAINTING OR DRAWING EQUIPMENT

Sir Ken Adam (a sketchpad and felt pens to design with), Eva Bartok, Tony Bennett, Michael Bentine, Quentin Blake (Arches watercolour paper), Max Boyce, Billy Butlin (drawing board, paper and pencils), Sir Neville Cardus (watercolour painting equipment), Leslie Caron, Richard Chamberlain, Diane Cilento, Alma Cogan (paper, pencils, paints), Pauline Collins (papers, pencils, paints), Shirley Conran, Sir Terence Conran (an endless supply of A4 paper and 4B pencils), Noël Coward, Peter Cushing (and model soldiers), David Dimbleby (a collection of drawing books, pencils and varnish), Sir Anthony Dowell (sketch pad and paints), Iain Duncan Smith (oil paints), Brian Epstein, Peter Finch, Elisabeth Frink (drawing and writing materials), Raymond Glendenning (watercolour paints), Rex Harrison (painting equipment for oils and watercolours), Debbie Harry (paints and paper), Lord Healey, Sir Robert Helpmann (box of paints), David Hemmings (architectural pens and paper), David Hockney (paper, pencils and a battery-operated sharpener), Gerard Hoffnung (his paintbox and tuba), Barry Humphries (painting materials on his first appearance; 'my paints' on a subsequent), Paul Johnson, Dame Vera Lynn (watercolour paints, brushes and paper), Marcel Marceau, Alec McCowen, Trevor McDonald (box of paints, brushes and paper), Geraldine McEwan (box of paints), Julia McKenzie, Keith Michell, Ron Moody (oil painting), Ted Moult (drawing materials), Beverley Nichols (easel and oil painting equipment), Lilli Palmer, Alan Parker (watercolour paintbox plus brush and pad), Grayson Perry ('loads of really good pens and paper'), Dennis Price (painting materials), Frederic Raphael, Zandra Rhodes (sketchbook, pens and pencils), Gerry Robinson (painting kit – easel, oils, brushes), Ginger Rogers, Antony Sher (pens, charcoal, paints), Dodie Smith (sketching materials), Liz Smith (a complete artist's set), Jon Snow (a set of watercolours and an endless supply of paper), Earl of Snowdon, Sir Stephen Spender, Sheila Steafel, Norman Thelwell, Topol, Stanley Unwin, Frankie Vaughan, Virginia Wade (writing and sketching materials), David Wilkie

. . . MATERIALS FOR SCULPTING OR MODELLING CLAY

Quentin Crewe (a potter's wheel), Rolf Harris (a chisel for sculpting), Herbert Lom (modelling clay), Virginia Ironside (a big bag of plaster to make heads of friends with), Jack Rosenthal (clay for making sculpture), Imelda Staunton (modelling clay and tools), Ralph Steadman (chisels), Johnny Vegas (a kiln)

CASTAWAYS WHO CHOSE WRITING MATERIALS

Claudio Abbado, Dawn Addams, Isabel Allende, Rev. W. Awdry, Dame Beryl Bainbridge (on her first appearance she requested an old-fashioned diary with pens; on her second appearance, she chose pens and paper), George Baker, Dame Janet Baker, Dame Joan Bakewell, Peter Barkworth (beautifully bound blank book and ballpoint pens), Julian Barnes, Stan Barstow (twice), Nina Bawden, Rachel Billington, Robert Bolt, Russell Braddon (red ink), Richard Branson, Brenda Bruce, A. S. Byatt (a large filing cabinet full of A4 paper and pens), Ian Carmichael (twice – plus beer on his first appearance), Sir Hugh Casson, Carol Channing, Robbie Coltrane, Jilly Cooper, Patricia Cornwell, Michael Crawford, John Curry, Sinéad Cusack, Dame Ninette de Valois, Monica Dickens, Diana Dors, Jacqueline du Pré, Gerald Durrell, Tracey Emin (a pen which would never run out), Douglas Fairbanks Jr, Marianne Faithfull (pen from Asprey's with attached magnifying glass), Ralph Fiennes (pen and unlimited supplies of ink and paper), Anne Fine, Margaret Forster, Bill Fraser, Sir David Frost, Paul Gallico, Dr Jane Goodall, Winston Graham, Juliette Greco, Joyce Grenfell, Christopher Hampton, Irene Handl, Roy Hattersley ('boy writer's set'), Nigel Hawthorne, Jack Higgins, Patricia Highsmith, Anthony Horowitz, Elizabeth Jane Howard, Kazuo Ishiguro ('big roll of paper'), P. D. James, Terry Jones, M. M. Kaye, Brian Keenan, Robin Knox-Johnston, Jane Lapotaire, Hugh Lloyd, Jonathan Lynn, Shirley Maclaine, Sir Fitzroy MacLean, Dan Maskell, Michael McIntyre (a pen), Sir Ian McKellen, Virginia McKenna, Bernard Miles, Hayley Mills, Naomi Mitchison, Andrew Motion, Malcolm Muggeridge, Anthony Newley, John Julius Norwich,

(CASTAWAYS WHO CHOSE WRITING MATERIALS – *cont.*)

Alan Pascoe (a diary), Siân Phillips, Harold Pinter, Alan Plater, Donald Pleasence, Jonathon Porritt, Dr Magnus Pyke, Anthony Quayle, Dame Marie Rambert, Frederic Raphael (Mont Blanc pen, nibs and spiral squared notebooks), Ian Richardson, J. K. Rowling, Vikram Seth, Rev. David Sheppard, Delia Smith, Paul Smith, C. P. Snow, Andy Stewart, Jackie Stewart, Janet Street-Porter, George Thomas (Viscount Tonypandy), Fay Weldon, Sir Arnold Wesker, Alan Whicker, Dorian Williams, Barbara Windsor (and a Union flag), Sir Terry Wogan (with bottles), Maurice Woodruff, Susannah York

. . . MUSIC MANUSCRIPT PAPER (AND WRITING IMPLEMENTS)

Julian Bream (along with his guitar), Anthony Burgess, Mantovani (and indigestion tablets), Sir Peter Maxwell Davies, George Mitchell, Vic Oliver

. . . A TYPEWRITER (AND PAPER)

Dennis Brain, John Bratby, Sammy Cahn, Barbara Castle, Charlie Chester, John Cole, Russ Conway, Alan Coren, Bebe Daniels, R. F. Delderfield, Margaret Drabble, Ian Fleming, Lady Antonia Fraser, John Freeman, Professor J. K. Galbraith, Sir Hugh Greene, Jane Grigson, Earl of Harewood (twice), Brian Inglis, Neil Jordan, Philip Larkin, George MacDonald Fraser (with spare ribbons), Barry Norman (and a desk with cricket balls in the drawers), Michael Parkinson, Ron Pickering, John Pilger, Jean Plaidy (and a hostess gown), Roy Plomley (with a desk), Robert Powell, Ralph Reader, Eric Sykes, E. P. Thompson, Timothy West, Emlyn Williams, Tennessee Williams, Des Wilson

. . . A WORD PROCESSOR

Malcolm Bradbury, Max Hastings (linked to a Fleet Street newspaper), Derek Jameson, Lucinda Lambton, Sarah Miles, Rose Tremain

CASTAWAYS WHO CHOSE A RADIO

David Blunkett (a radio/cassette machine), Sir Chris Bonington, Rory Bremner, Jim Clark, Arthur C. Clarke (solar powered), Clarissa Dickson Wright,* Sir Anthony Dowell, Boy George, Alan Johnson (digital radio), Betty Kenward, Nigel Lawson, Ken Loach (for football results), Joe Loss, Alan Minter (solar powered), Sheridan Morley, Andrew Neil,* C. Northcote Parkinson, Terry O'Neill,* Rev. Ian Paisley (a high-powered radio), Nicholas Parsons (portable radio with an endless supply of batteries), James Prior, Sir Alec Rose, Leonard Sachs, Alan Sillitoe (a communications receiver – for receiving only), Harvey Smith, Ruskin Spear, Wynford Vaughan-Thomas (a radio and TV receiver)

* Chose a wind-up radio.

. . . A SPECIFIC RADIO STATION OR PROGRAMME

Sir Roger Bannister – solar-powered receiver with which to receive Radio 4

Virginia Bottomley – Radio 4's *Today* programme

Professor Asa Briggs – the BBC archives from 1945 to 1954

Sue Johnston – BBC Radio 5 Live

Neil Kinnock – Radio 4

Gavin Laird – a year's recording of the *Today* programme

Ken Livingstone – the World Service

Raymond Briggs asked for a full-size billiard table with Radio 4 built into each of the legs.

. . . A TELEVISION

Joan Collins, Michael Green (digital TV), Tony Hancock, Jenny Pitman, Keith Waterhouse (with a video and eight films)

Sir Robert Mark chose a sleeping bag and a TV that doesn't work.

. . . CABLE OR SATELLITE TELEVISION

Martin Amis (cable TV), Dickie Bird (a satellite to watch Test matches), Pamela Stephenson (a television set with satellite link-up)

. . . A TELEPHONE

Geoffrey Boycott (a telephone line to a sports newspaper), Elton John (so he could find out the scores of his beloved Watford FC), Jack Higgins (a mobile phone), Lulu, Alfred Marks (one that's out of service), David Mellor (one that's disconnected), Nana Mouskouri, Salman Rushdie (unlisted radio telephone), Gloria Swanson, Julie Walters

. . . A COMPUTER

Al Alvarez (with poker game software), Paddy Ashdown, Sir Chris Bonington (powerbook G3 laptop computer), Dr George Carey (and an empty bottle), Professor Richard Dawkins,* Carl Djerassi (a solar-powered computer with a secret compartment containing a white powder), Umberto Eco, John Julius Norwich, Bernard Levin, Dame Norma Major,* Sarah Miles, Michael Portillo,* Jean Rook, Clive Stafford Smith, Baroness Williams (linked to the internet)

* In each case, a solar-powered laptop.

. . . A FILM PROJECTOR

Dame Judi Dench (plus Basil Brush films), John Ogdon, Edmundo Ros (with films), Dickie Valentine (with films), Frank Worrell (with cricket films)

Shami Chakrabarti chose a private screening room with movies.

Penelope Wilton chose an open-air cinema with a selection of films.

. . . A VIDEO OR DVD PLAYER

Joss Ackland – video player with cassettes of old movies

Tariq Ali – mini DVD player

Placido Domingo – video player and cassettes of his own performances

Sir Denis Forman – satellite dish and TV set

Robin Knox-Johnston – video recorder and tapes of the Queen Mother's parade

David Mitchell – DVDs of sitcoms and DVD player

Matt Munro – video and TV

David Shepherd – wind-up video player

David Tennant – solar DVD player loaded with the seven series of *The West Wing*

Neil Tennant – DVD projector and DVDs

Alan Yentob – video recorder

. . . A TAPE RECORDER

Charles Aznavour, Sir Lewis Casson (plus the 1912 portrait of Dame Sybil Thorndike), Alistair Cooke, Dame Gladys Cooper, Cyril Fletcher, Lionel Hampton, Rolf Harris (asked for *two* tape recorders), Anna Massey (as well as family photographs), Sir Brian Rix, Zena Skinner, Leopold Stokowski, June Whitfield, Sir John Wolfenden

. . . A CAMERA (AND FILM)

Eve Arnold (plus a dark room), Gordon Harker, Benny Hill (a film camera), Elspeth Huxley, Jeremy Irons, Lupino Lane, Joanna Lumley (a video camera)

~~~~~

Valerie Singleton chose a photographic dark room.

. . . A SPECIFIC FILM OR TV PROGRAMME

Carmen Callil: *The Commitments*

David Gower: *Rumpole of the Bailey*

Clive Jenkins: *Citizen Kane*

David Tennant: *The West Wing*

Stan Tracey: *Oh, Mr Porter!*

Irene Worth: The Beatles' new colour television show

Gerald Harper chose a videotape or film of the full five days' play of a Test match.

CASTAWAYS WHO CHOSE
EVEN MORE MUSIC

Thereby challenging the idea of taking just eight records to a desert island . . .

Nick Hornby – an MP3 player or iPod

Geraldine James – an iPod

Charles Kennedy – a CD player

Sir Christopher Meyer – a jukebox

Lynn Redgrave – an excerpt from the BBC recording *Just William*

Peter Rogers – a ninth record: Massenet's *Elégie*

Richard Attenborough chose a set of record catalogues.

Jacques Brunius chose a broken and unplayable pop record.

Montserrat Caballé chose a record box.

Virginia McKenna chose language tapes to learn Italian and Swahili.

Sir Terry Wogan chose a radio-cassette player and language tapes.

. . . A KARAOKE MACHINE

Brenda Blethyn, Clive James, Martha Lane Fox, Sam Taylor-Wood

CASTAWAYS WHO CHOSE BOOKS AS A LUXURY

The choice of a book – in addition to the complete works of Shakespeare and a Bible – made its first appearance on 9 October 1951. Some castaways, however, also chose a book as their luxury item.

Leon Brittan – a collection of large-scale Ordnance Survey maps of England

Dame Gladys Cooper – the complete works of Shakespeare (in 1952, before this was automatically given to every castaway)

Sir Colin Davis – a packing case of books, including a Persian dictionary

Richard Dreyfuss – books delivered to the island on a regular basis

Mike Harding – Ordnance Survey maps and a set of books about the Fells

Lenny Henry – graphic novels

Hammond Innes – *The Guinness Book of Records*

Peggy Mount – an 'enormous cookery book'

Emlyn Williams – an encyclopaedia

John Arlott chose a second-hand bookshop, while Emmylou Harris and Professor W. E. Swinton both requested a library.

CHOSE A NEWSPAPER

Basil Boothroyd (current popular newspaper), Paul Dacre (a subscription to the *Guardian* for one year), Sir David Frost (the Sunday papers), Sir Cedric Hardwicke, Des O'Connor (daily delivery of *The Sporting Life*), Cyril Ray (airmail edition of *The Times*), Griff Rhys Jones, Simon Weston (daily newspapers), Mike Yarwood (a daily newspaper)

CASTAWAYS WHO CHOSE A BED

Diane Abbott (a nice bed with comfortable mattress, sheets and a mosquito net), Dannie Abse, Rex Alston, Richard Baker, Lillian Board, Sir Michael Caine (a large bed with 50 per cent goose down and 50 per cent feather pillows), Nina Campbell, Jarvis Cocker (with a mosquito net), Sebastian Coe, Anita Dobson, Dick Emery, Dick Francis (a waterbed), Susan George,* Rumer Godden,* Tony Greig, Patricia Hayes,* Michael Holroyd (a waterbed – twice), Derek Jacobi (a waterbed), Sidney James (a double bed), Molly Keane ('netted from snakes and flies'), Evelyn Laye, Margaret Leighton (Girl Guide campbed), Ann Mallalieu,* Millicent Martin,* Paul Merton, Morrissey ('a comfy bed with lots of pillows'), Pat Moss, David Niven, Michael Palin, Sir Peter Pears, Oliver Postgate ('a comfortable bed'), Vincent Price (a double bed), Anita Roddick (comfortable bed with pillows and sheets), Lord Sainsbury, Antoinette Sibley, Wilbur Smith (brass bedstead and a feather mattress), Elisabeth Söderström, Joan Sutherland, Joanna Trollope (with white Egyptian sheets), Richard Wattis, Ruby Wax ('a huge bed'), Colin Welland, Mary Wesley (a large double bed with pillows – but only after being told that she couldn't choose Lord Healey), A. N. Wilson (plus blankets), Edward Woodward

* Requested a four-poster bed.

David Bellamy chose linen sheets.

Tony Robinson chose a luxury mattress and pillow.

. . . A PILLOW

Duncan Bannatyne, Karren Brady (her own pillow), Lady Diana Cooper (a bag of pillows, in which she will smuggle in her dog), George Foreman, A. A. Gill (his children's pillows), Princess Grace of Monaco, Lady Mosley (a soft pillow), John Hurt, Lang Lang (two feather pillows), David Puttnam (goose-down pillow), Sue Ryder, Mario Testino (his own pillow)

. . . A DUVET

Helena Kennedy (goose down), Elijah Moshinsky, Cathleen Nesbitt, Terence Stamp

. . . A HAMMOCK

Ronnie Corbett, Stephen King (a water hammock), Janet Suzman (mink-lined hammock), Sir Magdi Yacoub, Franco Zeffirelli (a hammock from Hermès)

. . . A SLEEPING BAG

Cyril Connolly (a foam-rubber sleeping bag), Joy Nichols (a mink sleeping bag)

. . . A HOT WATER BOTTLE

Lady Isobel Barnett, Lord Brabazon of Tara, Cath Kidston, Jan Morris

. . . SOMETHING TO SIT ON

Sir Isaiah Berlin – a large armchair stacked with cushions

Christabel Bielenberg – a comfortable chair

Commissioner Catherine Bramwell-Booth – 'a strong wooden armchair'

Lord Carrington – an armchair

Christopher Fry – a rocking chair

(CASTAWAYS WHO CHOSE SOMETHING TO SIT ON – *cont.*)

Graham Hill – an armchair

Jack Parnell – an armchair

Ruth Prawer Jhabvala – a chaise longue by a window

Sir Bobby Robson – a sun lounger with a canopy to protect him from the sun

Most Rev. Robert Runcie – a rocking chair

Julian Symons – a couch

John Thaw – a large comfortable armchair

Alice Thomas Ellis – 'a very comfortable sofa'

Eddie Waring – a couch

George Weidenfeld – an armchair (plus a coffee machine and a rescue signal)

Paul Weller – a settee

~~~~~

When Morecambe and Wise appeared on the show, Eric chose a deckchair and Ernie chose a deckchair ticket-machine.

Sir Brian Rix chose a proper orthopaedic cushion.

. . . FURNITURE

Les Dawson – a piece of Georgian furniture

Arthur Negus – a Chippendale cabinet

. . . A RUG

Jenny Agutter – an oriental rug

John Fortune – a rug made by the Baluch people from Afghanistan

CASTAWAYS WHO CHOSE FOOD

Shirley Abicair – a case of avocado pears

Joss Ackland – a huge jar of liquorice

Alan Alda – Italian pasta

Lord Ashley – smoked salmon (and wine)

Pam Ayres – a large basket of sugared almonds

Michael Bogdanov – a 50-pound jar of Marmite

Matthew Bourne – spotted dick with Lyle's syrup

Peter Carey – a 'magic' pudding and a drink

Antonio Carluccio – white truffles

Robin Cousins – marzipan

Lawrence Dallaglio – Marmite

Richard Dunwoody – an endless supply of ice cream

Sir David Frost – potato crisps

Whoopi Goldberg – Wise potato chips

Dr Susan Greenfield – an endless supply of curry

(CASTAWAYS WHO CHOSE FOOD – *cont.*)

Geoffrey Grigson – pâté de foie gras

Stephen Hawking – crème brûlée

Ian Hislop – Frosties

Virginia Holgate – a never-ending supply of smoked salmon

Trevor Howard – cake

Thomas Keneally – a can of Beluga caviar, spoon and tin opener

Sir Osbert Lancaster – live sturgeon

Arthur Marshall – nougat

Sir Robert Mayer – seedless grapes

Sherrill Milnes – herrings in sour cream

Jessica Mitford – a supply of Gentleman's Relish

Johnny Morris – yeast

Archie Norman – a jar of Marmite

Hal Prince – bouillabaisse with langouste and wine

Clodagh Rodgers – prawn cocktails

Sir Basil Spence – spaghetti

Terence Stamp – one of his wheat-free loaves

Dennis Taylor – a limitless supply of yoghurt

Wilfred Thesiger – a supply of acid drops

Dr Ruth Westheimer – a large box of marrons glacés

Michael Winner – a big supply of caviar

Malcolm Muggeridge chose a beehive.

Suggs chose a nucleus of bees.

Sir Norman Wisdom – a pot of stew with two dumplings

... CONDIMENTS OR FLAVOURINGS

James Dyson – olive oil

Germaine Greer – hot spices

Ruthie Henshall – a jar of Hellmann's mayonnaise

Renée Houston – parsley

Sally Ann Howes – garlic

Boris Johnson – a large pot of French mustard

Ludovic Kennedy – tartare sauce

Ann Leslie – an enormous amount of garlic with a garlic press

Derek Nimmo – garlic

Gordon Ramsay – a fresh vanilla pod

Rick Stein – Thai fish sauce

... CHOCOLATE

Diana Dors, Evelyn Glennie, Lord Goodman (an enormous box of chocolate gingers), Lord Healey (a very big box of chocolates including nougat), Dame Kelly Holmes, Sir Kenneth MacMillan (Godiva chocolates from Belgium)

... A RESTAURANT

Sybille Bedford – a French restaurant in full working order

Richard Curtis – Notting Hill Pizza Express

Matt Lucas – Oslo Court, his favourite London restaurant

Peter Mayle chose the menu from his favourite Parisian restaurant.

. . . COOKING APPARATUS OR UTENSILS

Betsy Blair – an ice-cream maker

Lionel Blair – an oyster knife

Heston Blumenthal – Japanese knives

Robert Carrier – a tagine

J. P. Donleavy – his own long-handled spoon to make dressings

Anton Edelmann – a wok

Sir Cameron Mackintosh – a solar-powered Magimix

Ismail Merchant – a cooking range

Anton Mosimann – a steamer for cooking

Enoch Powell – a smoking device to smoke fish

John Schlesinger – a battery-powered Magimix

Jerry Springer – a cheeseburger machine

Dame Kiri Te Kanawa – cooking knives

Emma Thompson – a saucepan: heavy-bottomed with a removable handle

Archbishop Desmond Tutu – an ice-cream maker (especially for rum and raisin flavour)

Donald Zec – an ice-cream machine

Garrison Keillor chose a set of china (four place settings).

. . . A REFRIGERATOR

Danny La Rue, Sir Sacheverell Sitwell, Isaac Stern

Archbishop John Sentamu chose a kitchen.

CASTAWAYS WHO CHOSE
TEA AND COFFEE

TEA

Ambrose, Tony Benn (and a kettle), Alan Bennett (an unending supply of afternoon teas), Lord Denning, Ken Dodd, Arthur Edwards (an inexhaustible supply of tea and a kettle), Brendan Foster, Penelope Keith (Lapsang Souchong), Peggy Mount ('in abundance'), Anna Neagle, Anna Raeburn, Patricia Routledge (on her first appearance she chose varieties of tea and a tea-making outfit; on her second appearance she requested a tea service with tea), Jean Simmons, Gene Wilder (Earl Grey)

Irene Thomas chose a teddy bear stuffed with tea bags on her first appearance and a teddy bear stuffed with tea and lily of the valley on her second.

COFFEE

Claire Bloom (an espresso machine), John Cale (an espresso machine with coffee beans), Professor Brian Cox (a coffee machine), Penelope Leach, Tasmin Little (an endless supply), Jimmy Mulville (a solar-powered espresso machine), Sir Simon Rattle (Italian coffee machine and grinder), Vanessa Redgrave (and condensed milk), George Weidenfeld (a coffee machine with an armchair and a rescue signal)

John Malkovich and Francesca Simon each chose a cappuccino maker.

CASTAWAYS WHO CHOSE DRINKS

BEER OR LAGER

Martin Bell (a barrel of Adnam's ale, brewed in Suffolk), Wilfrid Brambell (plus Scotch whisky), Ian Carmichael, Harry Enfield, Alan Jones (Australian lager)

Laurie Lee chose materials for making wine or beer.

Mark Tully chose a modern mini brewery.

BRANDY

Sir Alec Guinness (apricot brandy), Ian Hendry, Sir Peter O'Sullevan (Calvados), Michael Powell, Ken Russell, Terry Thomas

CHAMPAGNE

John Arlott, Sir John Betjeman, Melvyn Bragg, Howard Brenton, Tony Britton (plus Scotch), Jasper Conran (an endless supply of vintage Krug), Sir Robin Day (chose champagne on his first appearance and *magnums* of champagne on his second appearance), Frances Edmonds (Bollinger '69), Britt Ekland (a case of Evian water filled with champagne), Hubert Gregg (chose pink champagne), Hugh Griffith, Douglas Hurd, Dinsdale Landen, Prue Leith (a jeroboam), Andrea Newman, Edna O'Brien (Cristal), Lord Oaksey (cargo of champagne), Siân Phillips (solar-powered refrigerator full of champagne), Christopher Plummer (jeroboam of Taittinger), Sir Terence Rattigan (Dom Perignon), Lady Redgrave, Egon Ronay, Ronald Searle ('the best possible'), Athene Seyler, Moira Shearer, John Smith (a case), Paul Theroux, Sue Townsend ('a swimming pool of champagne'), Sir Ian Trethowan, Angus Wilson, Jeanette Winterson (a case of Krug)

Jane Asher asked for a hot bath with an extra tap for cold champagne.

Dick Bentley requested a champagne-making kit.

RUM

Carlos Acosta (case of Havana rum), Andrew Davies (an endless supply of mojitos), Tyrone Guthrie, Jonathan Pryce (endless supply of rum punch)

VODKA

Howard Goodall (ice-cold vanilla vodka and tonics), Sir Terry Wogan.

WHISKY

Kingsley Amis (on his second appearance; on his first appearance he chose American whiskey), Lieutenant-Colonel John Blashford-Snell (malt whisky), Wilfrid Brambell (plus lager), Tony Britton (plus champagne), David Cameron (a crate of Scotch whisky), Cecil Day-Lewis (bourbon), Basil Dean, Rumer Godden (a widow's cruse* filled with whisky), Dame Daphne du Maurier (plus ginger ale), Robertson Hare, Burl Ives (Tobermory), Madhur Jaffrey, Jimmy Knapp (a case of Talisker), Ed McBain, Eric Newby, R. C. Sherriff, Lord Shinwell, Fred Zinnemann ('a very large self-renewing bottle of Scotch')

* From the widow's cruse in the Old Testament: a jar of oil which never runs out.

~~~~~

Dirk Bogarde chose a distillery.

WINE

Sir Michael Balcon, Michael Ball (Cloudy Bay Sauvignon Blanc), James Bolam (selected cases of French wine), Richard Briers (a huge supply of Chardonnay), David Broome, Robert Carrier (Burgundy), Julian Critchley (a case), David Davis ('A magic wine cellar which never runs out'), Cecil Day-Lewis, Frankie Dettori (a lifetime's supply of Pinot Grigio), John Eliot Gardiner (Sancerre), Julian Fellowes ('two enormous casks of Chateau Margaux'), Ken Follett (entire cellar of a great collector of French wine), General Sir John Hackett (six dozen bottles of Chateau La Tour 1962), Robert Hanbury-Tenison (a cask of claret), Laurence Harvey (a barrel of wine), P. D. James (claret), Roy Jenkins (a case of Bordeaux), Graham Kerr, Sir Andrew Lloyd Webber, Natalia Makarova (Chateau Margaux 1961), Daniel Massey, James Nesbitt (a bottle of chilled Sancerre for every night), Adrian Noble, Edna O'Brien ('vault of a very good white wine'), Gene Pitney (a case of Opus One wine), Anthony Powell, Sir Simon Rattle (German white wine), Jancis Robinson (cellar of wines and a corkscrew), Leonard Rossiter (Moselle), Donald Sutherland ('case of really good vintage wine'), Lord Tebbit (drinking fountain with taps for Sancerre and claret), Alec Waugh

Quentin Crewe requested the cellar from Trinity College, Cambridge.

Tony Iveson chose two established vines and a tin bath to make wine.

Laurie Lee chose materials for making wine or beer.

Arnold Ridley requested a wine-making kit.

Frank Warren chose a Merlot grapevine.

Hugh Williams chose a corkscrew.

A STILL

Roald Dahl (as well as tobacco seeds and grapevine cuttings), Denholm Elliott, Clement Freud, Christopher Gable, Henry Longhurst, Sir Fitzroy MacLean, John Slater

Sir Torquil Norman requested a miniature still with a little ice-making machine attached to it to make dry martinis.

OTHERS

Three castaways chose gin – Mark Lubbock, Frank Swinnterton (plus vermouth) and Raymond Leppard (with dry martini and lemons) – with Freddie Jones choosing a Liebig condenser for distilling gin. Rex Palmer chose 'alcohol', Paul Tortelier chose cider and Mark Elder chose sherry.

NON-ALCOHOLIC DRINKS

Anthony Julius (San Pellegrino water on tap), Jessye Norman (Perrier water), George Chisholm (an engraved glass and supply of bitter lemon)

CASTAWAYS WHO CHOSE SMOKES

CIGARETTES

Donald Campbell, Nick Clegg (a 'stash' of cigarettes), Joan Greenwood, William Hartnell, Jack Hulbert, Sir Trevor Nunn (king-size cigarettes), Bruce Oldfield, Derek Walcott (a carton of cigarettes)

Harry Enfield chose beer and a cigarette machine.

TOBACCO

Roald Dahl (tobacco seeds – plus a still and grapevine cuttings)

William Hardcastle (a tobacco plant)

Sheila Scott (tobacco seeds)

Robert Stephens (a tobacco plant)

Zoe Wanamaker (Samson tobacco and Rizla liquorice papers)

Jeremy Irons requested Rizla liquorice papers.

Tom Sharpe chose 'a ton of snuff'.

A PIPE

Victor Gollancz (a Meerschaum pipe), Sir Compton Mackenzie (pipes and matches), Magnus Magnusson, Sir Michael Redgrave (pipes and matches), Sir Ralph Richardson (pipes and matches on his first appearance; pipes and tobacco on his second), Ben Travers (pipes and tobacco)

CIGARS

Malcolm Arnold (Green Havana), Sir Thomas Beecham,* George Cole,* Sir Bernard Delfont (and matches), David Dimbleby,* Phil Edmonds (Royal Jamaica), Fred Emney, Sir Lew Grade (a crate of Montecristo cigars), John Huston,* Jimmy Savile,* Lady Soames,* Pete Waterman* (and matches)

* Specified Havana cigars.

CASTAWAYS WHO CHOSE MEDICINE

Dame Ninette de Valois – an everlasting bottle of sleeping pills

Adam Faith – cold cure (as well as a pack of cards and writing materials)

Ricky Gervais – 'a vat of Novocaine'

Mantovani – indigestion tablets (as well as music manuscript paper, pencils and a rubber)

Jimmy McGovern – haemorrhoid cream

Sir Frederick Ashton requested 'happy pills'.

Robert McCrum chose St John's wort.

... NARCOTICS

Susan Blackmore – a handful of cannabis seeds

Hanif Kureishi – marijuana seeds

Fran Landesman – cannabis seeds

Norman Mailer – a stick of marijuana

Peregrine Worsthorne – hallucinogenic drugs

.. A METHOD OF SUICIDE

Lynn Barber – a cyanide pill

Sir Clifford Curzon – a pill to put him to sleep for ever

Stephen Fry – a suicide pill

Peter Jonas – cyanide, in a joint, in champagne truffle, in a fridge

Nigella Lawson – liquid Temazepam, 'to give me the possibility of a very pleasant exit . . .'

Peter Nichols – cyanide (if he can't have a tower and telescope or a full-size snooker table)

Artur Rubinstein – a revolver with which to shoot himself, as he was sure he would want to after even just a few days of solitude

David Walliams – a pistol with which to shoot himself if lonely

CASTAWAYS WHO CHOSE SEWING, KNITTING OR TAPESTRY EQUIPMENT

Mary Archer – needles, cotton and material

Richard Rodney Bennett – a 6mm 36-inch circular knitting needle with a point at each end

Julia Foster – a tapestry-making kit

Adelaide Hall – crochet needles and wool

Heather Harper – knitting wool and needles

Dame Sybil Hathaway, Dame of Sark – canvas and tapestry tools

Patricia Hodge – a supply of embroidery

Deborah Kerr – wool and a crochet hook

Elizabeth, Countess of Longford – a tapestry-making kit

Mary Martin – scissors, needles and thread

Wendy Richard – a tapestry 'to make'

Prunella Scales – a huge tapestry kit

Sylvia Syms – tapestry-making materials

CASTWAYS WHO CHOSE SPORTS GEAR

GOLF EQUIPMENT

Clubs and/or balls unless otherwise specified:

Peter Brough and Archie Andrews, Arthur Askey, Sir Douglas Bader, Danny Blanchflower, Lord Boothby, Mike Brearley, Scobie Breasley, Trevor Brooking, David Bryant, Max Bygraves, Sir Menzies Campbell,

Alice Cooper (an indoor golf driving range), Ronnie Corbett, Joe Davis, David Farrar, Bruce Forsyth (on his first appearance he chose clubs and balls; on his second appearance he chose a sand iron), Len Goodman, Dickie Henderson, Sir Leonard Hutton, Christopher Lee, Roger Livesey, Lord Longford, Dan Maskell, Johnny Mathis (golf bag), Richard Murdoch, Ray Reardon, Sir Bobby Robson, Alex Salmond, Martin Sheen, Tommy Simpson, Johnny Speight, Eric Sykes, Jimmy Tarbuck, Leslie Thomas, Sarah Vaughan, Michael Wilding, Kenneth Wolstenholme, Sir Clive Woodward

CRICKET EQUIPMENT

Eric Barker – a bowling machine

Sir Learie Constantine – a bat

David Essex – a set of cricket equipment

Sebastian Faulks – a wicket, bat, net, an endless supply of balls and a bowling machine that can be set to replicate the style of any bowler

David Hare – a bat and a bowling machine

Harold Hobson – a bat

Brian Johnston – an automatic bowling machine and balls

Jim Laker – a ball

Gary Lineker – a bowling machine

Piers Morgan – his bat

Bill Morris – a bat signed by 'the three Ws' (Frank Worrell, Everton Weekes and Clyde Walcott)

Sir Tim Rice – a cricket bag

Sir Martin Sorrell – bat, ball and stumps

~~~~~~

John Major chose an Oval cricket ground replica and a bowling machine.

A FOOTBALL

Tony Adams, Tom Courtenay, Lewis Gilbert, Andy Hamilton, Dave King, John Peel (and a wall to kick it against; he admitted the only time he felt graceful was when he was playing football), Bill Shankly, Tom Stoppard (a plastic football)

~~~~~~

Chef Nico Ladenis chose Cantona's Manchester United football shirt.

TENNIS EQUIPMENT

Baroness Blackstone – a tennis wall, balls and a racket

Gordon Brown – a tennis ball machine and a racket

Charlton Heston – tennis practice equipment

Mary O'Hara – tennis practice equipment

Milton Shulman – a racket and a ball machine

Peter Ustinov – a racket

~~~~~~

Dan Maskell chose tennis balls (along with golf balls, pencil and paper).

A (BOXING) PUNCHBAG

Jack Solomons, Taki

JUGGLING EQUIPMENT

Gerry Cottle – juggling clubs

Tanni Grey Thompson – five juggling balls

David Tomlinson – Eddie Gray's juggling equipment

CASTAWAYS WHO CHOSE A CAR

Rowan Atkinson (a car to clean), Dame Joan Bakewell (a yellow Lamborghini), Chris Barber, Vince Cable (an Aston Martin), Patrick Cargill (his Bentley), Steve Coogan (a fully restored Morris Minor Traveller with wooden detail), Michael Gambon ('a car to listen to music in'), Frank Gardner (a solar-powered buggy), Brian Glover (an MGTD 2952), Woody Herman (a Jaguar XJ6), Jimmy Jewel (a Rolls-Royce), Dame Celia Johnson (a Rolls-Royce), Michael Johnson (McLaren SLR), Roger McGough (a black cab), George Michael (Aston Martin DB9), Gordon Pirie (a motor car), Buddy Rich (a Ferrari, parked underneath the island's palm tree), Ronald Searle (a car fitted with a telescope), Tommy Steele (a sports car), Sir Norman Wisdom, Ernie Wise (a yellow Rolls-Royce)

Iain Banks chose the front seat of a Porsche.

. . . A BICYCLE

George Davies (a Cannondale), Kitty Godfree, Kenneth McKellar, Luciano Pavarotti, Dennis Skinner, Paul Tortelier (and cider), Michael White

J. G. Ballard chose a unicycle.

Ian McMillan chose a tandem bike with wooden models of his family at the front.

CASTAWAYS WHO CHOSE A BATH

Kate Adie (a large Victorian bath with claw feet), Jane Asher (hot bath with extra tap for cold champagne), Marti Caine (bath with solar-heated water and bubble bath), Mark Gatiss (a Victorian bath and hot water), Robert Harris ('a nightly fragrant bath'), Lord Hailsham (plus soap), Nicola Horlick, Glenda Jackson, Sir John Mortimer (on his first appearance he requested a marble bath with constant hot water; on his second appearance he merely asked for a bath), Dr David Owen, Chris Patten, Derek Randall (with warm water), Claire Rayner (with hot water, soap and towels), Lord Sainsbury (a large bath with a constant supply of hot water), Dame Freya Stark (with a hot-water system), Dr David Starkey (hot and cold running water, bath tub and bath oil), Peter Ustinov (with solar-heated water), William Whitelaw (with a hot-water system).

Will Carling chose a flotation tank.

Arthur Hailey chose hot water.

. . . TOILETRIES

Lord Annan (bath essence), Margaret Atwood (a huge vat of Culpeper's Rose Geranium bath salts), Rabbi Lionel Blue (a toilet bag), Kim Cattrall (fragrant body cream), Carl Davis (shampoo), Jack de Manio (scented soap), Ken Dodd (a box of scented soap), Clive Dunn (soap), Elizabeth Esteve-Coll (expensive perfumed hand cream), Edward Fox (Limes toilet water by Floris), Gwen Ffrangcon-Davies (a large bottle of toilet water), Oleg Gordievsky ('good toiletries for my bath'), Thora Hird (cleansing milk), Carla Lane (French shampoo), Paul O'Grady (Skin So Soft by Avon), Pauline Quirke (shampoo), Esther Rantzen (bath salts), Vidal Sassoon (a dozen bottles of Vidal Sassoon hair shampoo), Twiggy (cold cream), Gok Wan (lip balm), Jack Warner (soap)

. . . PERFUME

Jill Balcon (a barrel of Guerlain's Jicky perfume), Jill Bennett, Grace Bumbry, Betty Driver (Eau de Soir perfume by Sisley), Miriam Karlin, Felicity Kendal, Dame Cleo Laine (chosen on both appearances), Dame Alicia Markova (chose perfume on her first appearance and then specified the perfume Knowing by Estée Lauder on her second), Jessie Matthews, Ruby Miller, Barbara Murray, John Osborne, Ravi Shankar, Gillian Shephard (Madame Rochas), Franco Zeffirelli

. . . AFTERSHAVE OR COLOGNE

Lord Deedes – Mister Trumper's aftershave

Albie Sachs – 'a little bottle of aftershave'

Terry Scott – Eau de Cologne

Kenneth Williams – a crate of Cologne

. . . A BATHROOM

Ronald Harwood (his own), Baroness Scotland (a luxurious bathroom), Chad Varah (own bathroom run by solar power with hot and cold water and a video player attached)

Moira Anderson and Kenny Everett each chose a bathroom suite.

. . . A SHOWER

Clare Francis (a fresh-water shower), Michael Howard (plus some soap), James Ivory (with hot water), Sir Stuart Rose (a power shower with white fluffy towels and constant hot water), Ann Widdecombe ('luxury hot shower')

. . . A TOILET

Mike Leigh (plus toilet paper), Miriam Margolyes, Michael Nyman

... TOILET PAPER

John Bird, actor and comedian (2,000 soft loo rolls), Andy Kershaw

... A SHAVING KIT

Alec Bedser, Robbie Brightwell, Sir Anton Dolin (an electric razor), Sir Jonathan Miller, Sir Matthew Pinsent, John Ridgway, Lord Robens (an electric razor with batteries)

Billy Connolly requested an electrical device to heat shaving foam.

... A TOOTHBRUSH

Wendy Craig (toothbrushes), Sir Robert Helpmann (and toothpaste), Patricia Neal (and toothpaste), Tessa Sanderson, Herbert Wilcox (and toothpaste)

CASTAWAYS WHO CHOSE A MIRROR

Simon Cowell

Shirley Anne Field (a large Chippendale mirror)

Dick Francis

Sir Terry Frost (for company – not for vanity)

Terry Gilliam ('At least I can see who I am talking to: my only companion is me')

Hughie Green

Don McCullin

Graham Norton

Marjorie Proops

Alfred Wainwright

Mary Wilson

. . . MAKE-UP

Barbara Cartland,* Hildegarde (face and hand creams), Nora Swinburne,* Barbara Taylor Bradford (a bag of eye make-up, especially mascara), Sophie Tucker, Billie Whitelaw,* Mary Wilson (make-up set, mirror and comb)

* Requested a make-up box.

Annie Ross requested false eyelashes.

. . . A MANICURE SET

Cilla Black (and nail varnish), Gemma Craven, Colin Dexter, Stanley Holloway (and a pedicure set), Mary Peters (with a comb)

Alan Bleasdale chose nail clippers.

. . . LIPSTICK

Shirley Bassey, Hermione Gingold (chose lipstick on her first appearance and a barrel of lipstick on her second), Betty Jackson (red lipstick), Beryl Reid

. . . HAIR RESTORER

Stirling Moss, George Chisholm (and a trumpet)

. . . A COMB

Winifred Atwell (for her hair and for making music), Mary Peters (with a manicure set etc.), Margaret Rutherford (a bejewelled golden comb)

. . . GROOMING PRODUCTS

Darcey Bussell – eyelash curlers

Simon Callow – a nose-hair trimmer

Barbara Dickson – a very large set of solar-powered hair rollers

Dame Vera Lynn – curling tongs

Frank Muir – a navel brush

Arlene Phillips – tweezers

Eve Pollard – tweezers

Ted Ray – a dozen hairnets

Selina Scott – a hairbrush

Barbara Windsor – hair pieces

Duncan Goodhew chose a wig.

CASTAWAYS WHO CHOSE A
MUSICAL INSTRUMENT

BAGPIPES

James Mason, Christy Moore (the uilleann pipes – the national bagpipe of Ireland), Kevin Whateley (Northumbrian pipes)

A BANJO

Brian Aldiss, H. E. Bates, Billy Connolly, Peggy Seeger (a banjo with plastic head and an inexhaustible supply of strings and pegs)

A CELLO

Terry Hands, John Humphrys, Fyfe Robertson, Julian Lloyd Webber

A CLARINET

John Hegarty, Bob Monkhouse, David Suchet (his own clarinet with an unlimited supply of reeds), Don Thompson

DRUMS (OR A DRUM KIT)

Alfie Boe (his own), Des Lynam, Michael Mansfield, Timothy Spall, Eric Thompson

Charlie Watts chose drumsticks.

A FLUTE

Alan Bates, James Galway (a golden flute), John Simpson, Dame Harriet Walter

A GUITAR

Douglas Adams (a Martin D. 28 left-handed guitar), Joan Armatrading, Sir David Attenborough, Tony Blair, Julian Bream, Rob Brydon, James Burke, Harry Carpenter, Eric Clapton, Martin Clunes (an electric guitar), Kenneth Connor, John Conteh (an electric guitar), Bing Crosby, Charles Dance, Sacha Distel, Val Doonican, Greg Dyke (together with a guide to playing it), Colin Firth, David Gilmour (an acoustic Martin D.35 guitar), John Gregson, John Lee Hooker, Maxwell Hutchinson, Eric Idle, Linton Kwesi Johnson (a bass guitar), Bill Kenwright, Viscount Linley, Moira Lister, Jeremy Lloyd, Richard Madeley, James Mason, Brian May (his own guitar: the Red Special), Paul McCartney, Richard Noble, Jon Pertwee, Cliff Richard, Sir Harry Secombe, Pat Smythe, Daley Thompson (together with an instruction book), Max Wall, Ian Wallace, Bert Weedon, Wilson Whineray, Marty Wilde, John Williams

A MOUTH ORGAN/HARMONICA

Michael Eavis,* Geraint Evans, Paul Jones, Lynda La Plante, Ewan McGregor (a chromatic harmonica, i.e. one that can change key), Bill Nighy* (a boxed set of blues harps), Dilys Powell,* Neil Simon (a large harmonica), Tod Slaughter.

* Requested instructions as well.

AN ORGAN

Jo Brand (a church organ), Warren Mitchell (chose the organ from the Royal Albert Hall), David Steel (a cathedral organ), Victoria Wood (a cinema organ)

A PIANO

Anthony Andrews, Julie Andrews (on both of her appearances),
Arthur Askey (on two of his appearances), Michael Aspel, Sir David
Attenborough (on two of his four occasions), Richard Attenborough
(plus a conductor's baton), Daniel Barenboim (with a mattress), John
Barry,** Richard Rodney Bennett, Steven Berkoff, Sanjeev Bhaskar,*
Richard Briers, Dave Brubeck,** Roy Castle, Alan Clark, Petula Clark
(on two of her appearances – the second time she asked for her own
piano), Sebastian Coe (with a guide to playing it), Phil Collins, Tom
Conti, Dame Catherine Cookson, Elvis Costello (an upright piano),
David Croft, Richard Dimbleby, Sacha Distel,* David Edgar, Maria
Ewing, Marty Feldman, Michael Flanders and Donald Swann (two
pianos), Paul Gambaccini, Catherine Gaskin, Harvey Goldsmith,
Marius Goring, Professor A. C. Grayling (a good piano), Sheila
Hancock* (with music scores), Doris Hare, James Herbert,* Earl Hines,
Jools Holland, Anthony Hopkins, Sir Michael Hordern, Alan Howard,
Elizabeth Jane Howard, Richard Ingrams,** David Jacobs (and family
photographs), Jim Laker (plus a cricket ball), Tom Lehrer, Vivien Leigh,
Jack Lemmon, Alan Jay Lerner (with wife's picture attached), Liberace,
John Lill (a solar-powered piano), Margaret Lockwood, Jacques
Loussier, Barry Manilow, Princess Margaret, Sir Robert Mayer, Sir Ian
McKellen,* George Melly, Sir John Mills (on two of his appearances
– the second time he asked for his own piano), Anthony Minghella,
Viscount Montgomery of Alamein, Dudley Moore, Cliff Morgan,
Cardinal Cormac Murphy O'Connor, Randy Newman, John Osborne
(with an instruction book), Elaine Paige, Dame Joan Plowright (on both
of her appearances), André Previn (on both of his appearances), Alan
Price, Suzi Quatro, Robin Ray, Nelson Riddle, Willie Rushton, Clare
Short, Victor Silvester, Stephen Sondheim (on both of his appearances),
Dorothy Squires, James Stewart, Meera Syal, John Tavener (an upright
piano), Michael Tilson Thomas (Yamaha computerized concert grand
piano), Ron Todd, Dorothy Tutin, Sir Laurens van der Post
(on both of his appearances), Elsie and Doris Waters (with
sheet music), Roger Waters,* Marti Webb, Paul Whitehouse,
Dr Rowan Williams, Natalie Wood

* Requested a grand piano (something that Roy Plomley never allowed for
fear it might be used as shelter).

** Requested a piano on the first appearance and a grand piano on the second.

(CASTAWAYS WHO CHOSE A PIANO – *cont.*)

Rod Hull requested a pianola and a supply of piano rolls.

Gordon Jackson requested a dummy piano keyboard – as did Joseph Cooper who, as the presenter of *Face the Music,* used to play one to test the guests' knowledge of classical music.

Clive James requested a karaoke piano.

Humphrey Lyttelton and Hugh Masekela each requested a keyboard, while George Martin requested an electric keyboard.

Sir Roger Penrose requested a 19-note piano.

John Piper requested a pianola.

A SAXOPHONE

Kenneth Clarke, John Dankworth, Richard Eyre, Georgie Fame, Benny Green, David Hempleman Adams, Engelbert Humperdinck, Warren Mitchell, Courtney Pine (a 1939-edition tenor sax), Ronnie Scott, Jack Straw

A TRUMPET

Louis Armstrong, Harry Corbett, Valentine Dyall, Dizzy Gillespie, Humphrey Lyttelton

A UKULELE

George Formby (his first ukulele), Arthur Haynes, Rachael Heyhoe, Tessie O'Shea, Leslie Sarony, Frank Skinner

A VIOLIN

Robert Fisk, James Herriot, Nigel Kennedy, Yehudi Menuhin (plus strings), Frank Muir,* Anne-Sophie Mutter,* Itzhak Perlman (with strings and a case), Sandy Powell, Julian Slade, Jeremy Thorpe, Donald Wolfit (with instructions)

* Chose a Stradivarius.

OTHER INSTRUMENTS

Five castaways chose a clavichord: Sir Thomas Armstrong, George Guest, Igor Kipnis, George Malcolm, George Martin.

Five castaways chose a trombone: Owen Brannigan, George Chisolm, Rt Rev. Gerald Ellison, Lord Soper, Jack Teagarden

Two castaways chose a harp: the duo Nina and Frederick, and Richard Lester

Two castaways chose a harpsichord: Sir Peter Hall and Noel Rawsthorne

Two castaways chose a tin whistle: Paddy Moloney and Jimmy Shand

Two castaways chose a tuba: Ron Goodwin and Gerard Hoffnung

Two castaways chose a viola: John Rutter and The Amadeus String Quartet

One castaway chose an accordion: Bill Cullen

One castaway chose castanets: Dame Eva Turner

One castaway chose a concertina: Ted Willis

One castaway chose a cor anglais: Henry Williamson

One castaway chose a euphonium: Jimmy Edwards

One castaway chose a double bass: Gerald Moore

One castaway chose a horn: Michael Flanders

One castaway chose a hurdy-gurdy: Sir Eduardo Paolozzi

One castaway chose a lute: John Harle

One castaway chose an oboe: Mitch Miller

One castaway chose a penny whistle: Paul Rogers

One castaway chose a synthesizer: Martin Shaw ('to make up my own music')

One castaway chose a vibraphone: Peter Nichols

CASTAWAYS WHO CHOSE PLACES OR LANDMARKS

David Bailey – Nelson's Column

Lionel Bart – Nelson's Column

Sir Christopher Bland – two and a half miles of a Hampshire chalk stream

Ben Elton – the British Museum

Joan Fontaine – the Taj Mahal

Sir Christopher Frayling – the Victoria and Albert Museum

Bob Geldof – the Metropolitan Museum in New York

Valerie Hobson – the Albert Memorial

Martin Pipe – the Cheltenham winning post

Terry Pratchett – New York's Chrysler building

Jocelyn Stevens – a one-mile stretch of the River Test in Hampshire

Bryn Terfel – the Millennium Centre in Cardiff

Rita Tushingham – the Albert Memorial

Kenneth Tynan – the Pleasure Gardens of Barcelona

Frances Wood – the war memorial outside Euston Station

Denis Norden chose a model of the Tower of London.

Sir Harry Secombe chose a replica of Broadcasting House (with plastic announcers).

CASTAWAYS WHO CHOSE
THE UNION FLAG (JACK)

Mollie Harris, Russell Harty (with a flagpole – to claim the island for Britain), Tristan Jones, Barbara Windsor (as well as writing materials)

CASTAWAYS WHO CHOSE
RELIGIOUS LUXURIES

BUDDHIST

V. S. Naipaul (the Enlightened Buddha), Sandie Shaw (Omamori Gohonzon), P. L. Travers (a little marble Buddha), Anton Walbrook (Indo-Chinese Buddha)

CHRISTIAN

Sir John Betjeman – the lower half of the west window of Fairford Church, Gloucestershire

Alfred Brendel – a Bavarian rococo church

Group Captain Leonard Cheshire – photograph of the face on the Holy Shroud at Turin

Anne Shelton – a cross

CASTAWAYS WHO CHOSE ENTERTAINMENTS AND PASTIMES

CHESS

Dr Jacob Bronowski (an antique chess set), Joe Bugner, Robin Cook,* Aaron Copland, Leo Genn (with a problem book), Robert Lindsay,* Lorin Maazel (with a problem book), Robert Maxwell,* Leslie Phillips (with jade pieces), Steve Race, Roger Vadim,* Terry Waite*

*Chose a chess computer.

Sir Geoffrey Howe chose a computer bridge game.

A DOLL'S HOUSE

Dame Janet Baker, Glenda Jackson (Queen Mary's dolls' house)

PLAYING CARDS

Sir Frederick Ashton, Bill Bailey, Adam Faith (as well as cold cure and writing materials), Sir Stanley Kalms, Alvar Liddell, Gavin Lyall, Max Miller, Robert Morley (two packs of cards with photographs of family on the backs), Dandy Nichols, Tex Ritter (and a guitar), Omar Sharif (several decks), Godfrey Winn (for bridge)

Gian Carlo Menotti chose tarot cards.

CROSSWORDS

Thomas Keneally – collection of *Times* crosswords

Birgit Nilsson – Swedish crossword puzzles

Simon Russell Beale – daily Araucaria crossword

Victoria Wood chose a bumper book of Sudoku with blank pages and pen.

SCRABBLE

Eva Burrows, Helene Hanff, June Spencer

A SNOOKER OR BILLIARD TABLE

Don Black, Raymond Briggs (with Radio 4 built into each of the legs), Steve Davis, Rocco Forte, Patrick Stewart (a billiard table and a shed to keep it in)

AN INFLATABLE RUBBER WOMAN

Vincent Brome, Michael Crawford, Oliver Reed

Cornelia Parker chose a solar-powered vibrator.

SUNDRY ENTERTAINMENTS

Anthony Asquith – a seaside pier with slot machines

Tina Brown – a roller-coaster

Bill Bryson – a basketball and hoop with a little hard standing

Frank Cottrell Boyce – a ferris wheel

Kenneth Horne – a mah-jong set

Clive James – a game of *Space Invaders*

Tom Jones – a bucket and spade

Barbara Kelly – a beach ball

Michael Morpurgo – a waterslide

Barbara Mullen – a dartboard and darts of different weights

Richard Murdoch – a test-your-strength fairground machine

Dennis Potter – a train set

Ian Rankin – a traditional American pinball machine

Peter Sallis – a No. 7 Meccano outfit

Malcolm Williamson – a puppet theatre

Jacqueline Wilson – a fairground carousel

VIRTUAL CHOICES

A virtual-reality London Symphony Orchestra so he can conduct it – Professor Igor Aleksander

Virtual-reality sherry trifle – Armando Iannucci

Virtual-reality headset – Maurice Saatchi

Virtual-reality module – Paco Peña

CASTAWAYS WHO CHOSE TO DO SOMETHING HORRIBLE TO . . . MARGARET THATCHER

John Cleese – a life-sized papier-mâché model of Margaret Thatcher and a baseball bat

Roger Fluck and Peter Law – Margaret Thatcher's resignation speech (they appeared on the programme in 1987, three years before Mrs Thatcher resigned)

Ian Stewart – Mrs Thatcher pickled in a Damien Hirst sculpture

Jeffrey Archer chose a plasticine model of Roy Plomley and a pin.

Barry Sheene chose an effigy of Denis Healey and a supply of pins.

Dr Steve Jones chose the stuffed body of the then Minister of Education, Kenneth Clarke.

CASTAWAYS WHO CHOSE PETS

Although the *Desert Island Discs* rules state that luxury items are supposed to be inanimate objects, some castaways ignored this stricture and got away with it. Others didn't.

Fay Compton – her two dogs

Hetty King – a parrot

Princess Michael of Kent – an oriental cat

Leslie Mitchell – a silver box containing a singing bird

Nigel Patrick – his 'useless dog'

Sir Malcolm Sargent – a dog

General Norman Schwarzkopf – his dog, Bear

When told that he couldn't take a real dog, Bruce Fogle asked for a molecular engineering laboratory with which to create a dog.

Dora Bryan asked for a dog but when told by Michael Parkinson that she had to take an inanimate object, she settled for a stuffed dog.

UNIQUE LUXURIES CHOSEN
BY CASTAWAYS

A twelfth-century candlestick in the Victoria and Albert Museum – John Noakes

A 78rpm record of *The Laughing Policeman* (to smash on the rocks) – John Sessions

An accountancy course – Robert Swan

Aladdin's lamp – Julian Herbage

An all-purpose prosthetic arm – Julian Clary

Autographed letters of Lord Nelson – Nicholas Monsarrat

A ballroom and a robotic dance instructor – Rita Dove

A Barclaycard – Spike Milligan; on his second appearance he chose a barometer

A bespoke statue of Archbishop Desmond Tutu – Anna Scher

A box of plastic straws to fiddle with – Stephen Poliakoff

A canvas roll containing a dissecting set – Sir Jonathan Miller

Cat food – Sheila Hancock

Contact lenses – Frank Bough

A Continental railway timetable – Alfred Hitchcock

A crystal ball – Peter Bull

Dice to test the luck of a ship rescuing him – Sir Ralf Dahrendorf

A dog whip – Colonel A. D. Wintle

A dojo (Japanese martial arts school) – William Hague

An endless team of Man Fridays – Lady Tebbit

An expensive ivory back-scratcher – Tito Gobbi

A gilabra (cloak of gold) – Kathleen Hale

Glue – Sir Anthony Caro

A gold rail pass – Sir Peter Parker (head of British Rail)

A gym – Peter Blake

Hans Christian Andersen's mechanical bird and birdcage – Dr Ludwig Koch

A horse saddle – Terry Thomas

Hot lemon flannels (as provided in Chinese restaurants) – Alison Steadman

Hovercraft wheelchair with capuccino machine – Alan Hacker

A junkyard – William Gibson

A large photo of a lot of people at a race meeting – Sir Fred Hoyle

The law of the land (so he could break it) – Benjamin Zephaniah

A life-size laminated photo of James Caan from *Dragon's Den* (on which she planned to bodysurf) – Kathy Burke

A live performance of *A Midsummer Night's Dream* from the Regent's Park open-air theatre – Robert Atkins

A loofah – Adele Leigh

The mace of the House of Commons – Betty Boothroyd (she was Speaker of the House of Commons)

A magic carpet – Doris Lessing

A magic flute – Ralph Kohn

His memory – Oz Clarke

A metal detector – Leslie Grantham

Michael Palin (stuffed) – John Cleese

The microscope used to examine the lineage of the roundworm – Sir John Sulston

A motorway service station – Noel Edmonds

'My life for the next thirty years' – Yoko Ono (which would take her to 2037, by which time she would be 104)

Not paying tax or insurance – Victor Borge

(UNIQUE LUXURIES CHOSEN BY CASTAWAYS – *cont.*)

Olympic gold medal and award – Lord Killanin (he was the sixth President of the International Olympic Committee)

A parking meter and plenty of change – Stanley Holloway

A parking meter and caravan – Maureen Lipman

A parking space – Rabbi Hugo Gryn (Rabbi at the West London Synagogue, where parking spaces were at a premium)

Parquet floor and tap shoes – Anthony Rolfe Johnson

Peanuts and treats to tame animals and birds – Kyra Vayne

Personal pouch with a silver lion in it – Joan Baez

A picture of Charlie Chaplin and a model of a Rolls-Royce – Wilfrid Hyde-White

A picture of Marilyn Monroe – Bob Monkhouse

A pin – Richard Gordon

Premium Bonds – Bud Flanagan

A Roman helmet in the British Museum – Deryck Guyler

Salvation Army crest – General Frederick Coutts

A self-operated nuclear strike force – John Bird (actor and comedian)

A set of bird-ringing tools (including rings, and a book to learn shorthand) – Phil Drabble

A silken tent (for luxury, not survival) – John Updike

A six-inch nail – Pen Hadow

A snowglobe – Roy Hudd

A solar-powered mixing desk – Ian Dury

The sports results – Michael Grade

A steam-roller – Fred Dibnah

A stone from the stomach of a fossilized dinosaur – Captain Jacques Cousteau

Strings and strings of false pearls – Lady Antonia Fraser

A Swedish wooden horse – Dame Beryl Grey

A tightrope – Lesley Garrett

A time machine – Brian Aldiss

To be missed by the people she loves – Luise Rainer

A trap (minus a donkey) – Sir John Harvey-Jones

A trip around my island on Concorde – Paulo Coelho

Twenty tons of pine needles – Elia Kazan

A ventriloquist's dummy – Brian Reece

A very long stainless-steel shaft to encourage pole-dancing mermaids – Felix Dennis

A weekend in Paris – Arthur English

On 1 April 1963, for an April Fool's Day stunt, Roy Plomley interviewed a man masquerading as the 88-year-old theatrical manager Sir Harry Whitlohn, who claimed to be the only man living to have collaborated with Brahms. He chose as a luxury a small mountain.

BOOKS

CASTAWAYS WHO CHOSE AN APPROPRIATE BOOK

Sir David Attenborough – *Shifts and Expedients of Camp Life* by W. B. Lord (on three of his four appearances on the programme, 1979, 1998, and 2012, the seventieth anniversary of the programme)

Pat Barker – a book on tropical fish to identify them with

Gordon Beningfield – a manual on how to swim

Don Black – *14,000 Things To Be Happy About* by Barbara Ann Kipfer

Jackie Charlton – an encyclopaedia of how to survive (on his second appearance, in 1996)

Joseph Cotten – a boat-building book

Michael Crawford – *The Complete Book of Self-Sufficiency* by John Seymour (on the third of his three appearances, in 1999)

Dame Judi Dench – an Ordnance Survey map of the world (on her second appearance, in 1998)

Phil Edmonds – a book on the flora and fauna of the island

Rowland Emett – *The Anatomy of Melancholy* by Robert Burton

Bruce Fogle – a book on canoe craft

Tanni Grey Thompson – a guide to edible foods on a desert island

MacDonald Hastings – a field guide to flora and fauna on the island

Desmond Hawkins – a field guide to the birds of the island

Eric Hosking – a field guide to the island's birds

Leslie Gilbert Illingworth – instructions for making a still

Jeremy Irons – a construction manual (on his first appearance, in 1986) and *The Ashley Book of Knots* by Clifford Ashley (on his second, in 2006)

Clive James – a book about how to build a plane out of palm fronds and coconut fibre by Willy Messerschmitt (on his first appearance, in 1980)

David Jason – the complete boat-builder's book

Jack Jackson – a do-it-yourself boat-building book

Des Lynam – *Encyclopaedia of Natural Medicine*

Dame Vera Lynn – a book on edible fruits and vegetables (on her second appearance, in 1989)

Barry Manilow – *Man vs Wild: Survival Techniques from the Most Dangerous Places on Earth* by Bear Grylls

George Martin – a manual on practical engineering (on his first appearance, in 1982) and a book on how to build a boat (on his second appearance, in 1995)

Maureen O'Sullivan – a book on animal communication

Sir Peter Pears – *Tropical Plants and Their Cultivation* by Louis Bruggeman (on his first appearance, in 1969)

Eve Pollard – *Maritime Intelligence and Publications*

Terry Pratchett – *Edible Plants of the South Seas* by Emile Massal

Leontyne Price – *How To Be Your Own Best Friend* by Mildred Newman and Bernard Berkowitz

Jennifer Saunders – *Traveller's Prelude* by Freya Stark

Neil Simon – *How To Swim*

. . . A DO-IT-YOURSELF BOOK

Marti Caine, Harvey Goldsmith, Virginia Holgate, David Steel, Tommy Steele, June Whitfield

. . . AN SAS SURVIVAL GUIDE OR MANUAL

Dame Ellen MacArthur, J. K. Rowling, Dame Shirley Porter

CASTAWAYS WHO CHOSE THEIR OWN AUTOBIOGRAPHY

Louis Armstrong	Robertson Hare
Jim Clark	Thora Hird
Dame Catherine Cookson	Engelbert Humperdinck
Lady Diana Cooper	Gorden Kaye*
Sir Anton Dolin	Otto Preminger
Diana Dors	

* Gorden Kaye chose his book from *This is Your Life*.

. . . THEIR OWN DIARY

Peter Barkworth, Stubby Kaye, Peter Nichols (his diary, kept since he was 18, in order to relive his life since 1945)

Sir Robert Mayer chose his visitors' book.

Joe Loss chose a selection of personal letters.

. . . A RELATIVE'S BOOK

Martin Bell – *Corduroy* by Adrian Bell (his father)

Joy Beverley – *Book of Soccer* by Billy Wright (her husband)

Sarah Churchill – *Reminiscences of Early Life* by her father, Sir Winston Churchill

Dame Cleo Laine – *The Jazz Revolution* by her husband John Dankworth

Princess Grace of Monaco – plays by George Kelly (her uncle)

Fran Landesman – *Rebel Without Applause* and *Jaywalking* by her husband Jay Landesman

Paul McCartney – *Linda's Pictures* by Linda McCartney (his wife)

Virginia McKenna – *On Playing with Lions* by Bill Travers (her husband)

Sir Torquil Norman – a book of his father's poems and verses

Molly Parkin – *The History of the Colony* by Sophie Parkin (her daughter)

Mary Ure – *The Collected Plays of John Osborne* (her husband)

Isabel Allende chose all the correspondence between her and her mother.

Baroness Scotland chose a bound collection of her family's prose and poetry.

Sylvia Syms chose her husband's handwritten limericks.

CASTAWAYS WHO CHOSE POETRY

A COLLECTION OR AN ANTHOLOGY (NOT BY A SPECIFIC POET)

Jenny Agutter, Honor Blackman, Julian Bream, Sir Robin Day, Dame Ninette de Valois, Diana Dors, Geraint Evans, Lewis Gilbert, Len Goodman, Sir Alec Guinness, Mike Harding, John Humphrys, Douglas Hurd, Howard Jacobson, Thomas Keneally, Laurie Lee, Frank McCourt, Trevor McDonald, Naomi Mitchison, Sir John Mortimer, Dr David Owen, Nicholas Parsons, Harold Pinter, Anna Scher, Vikram Seth,* John Smith, Dorothy Squires, Joanna Trollope, Chad Varah, Penelope Wilton

* To include ones by the Chinese poet Du Fu.

... BY A SPECIFIC POET

Martin Amis – the complete works of John Milton

Kingsley Amis – the collected poetry of Robert Graves

Paddy Ashdown – the collected works of John Donne

Rowan Atkinson – a collection of W. H. Auden poems

John Barry – *Eternal Echoes* by John O'Donohue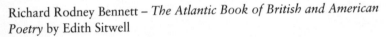

Lionel Bart – *Under Milk Wood* by Dylan Thomas

Richard Rodney Bennett – *The Atlantic Book of British and American Poetry* by Edith Sitwell

John Bird (actor and comedian) – the collected works of Wallace Stevens

David Blunkett – an anthology of verse by Robert Graves

Rob Brydon – the collected works of Dylan Thomas

Dr George Carey – *Four Quartets* by T. S. Eliot

David Croft – the collected poems of Sir John Betjeman

Charles Dance – *A Dream in the Luxembourg* by Richard Aldington

Colin Dexter – the collected works of A. E. Housman

Monty Don – the collected poems of Henry Vaughan

Greg Dyke – the complete works of Dylan Thomas

Gareth Edwards – the collected works of Dylan Thomas

Maria Ewing – the collected poems of John Donne

Anne Fine – the collected poems of Philip Larkin

George Foreman – an anthology of poems, including the poem 'Waiting' by John Burroughs

Bruce Forsyth – *The Rubáiyát of Omar Khayyám* (the second time he was on the show he chose the collected works of Omar Khayyám)

Rumer Godden – *The Atlantic Book of British and American Poetry* by Edith Sitwell

Books

Lord Healey – poetry by W. B. Yeats (on his second appearance he chose *The Faber Book of English Verse*, edited by by John Hayward)

Jack Higgins – *Four Quartets* by T. S. Eliot

Maxwell Hutchinson – *Four Quartets* by T. S. Eliot

Nicholas Hytner – the collected works of Samuel Taylor Coleridge

Ludovic Kennedy – the poems of George Herbert and John Donne

Imran Khan – *Bang-e-Dara* by Muhammad Iqbal

Nicole Kidman – the collected poems of Emily Dickinson

Stephen King – the collected poetry of W. H. Auden

Nigel Lawson – the poetry of John Donne

Herbert Lom – the nonsense rhymes by Edward Lear

Alexander McCall Smith – a collection of W. H. Auden's works

Andrew Motion – *The Prelude* by William Wordsworth

Mo Mowlam – the collected works of Seamus Heaney

Cardinal Cormac Murphy-O'Connor – *Lifelines* by Seamus Heaney

Christopher Ondaatje – Robert Service's *Anthology of Poetry*

Alan Parker – the collected poems of Sir John Betjeman

Paco Peña – anthology of poetry by José Bergua

Mary Portas – the poetry of Rumi

Anthony Quayle – the complete works of Edward Lear

Nelson Riddle – the collected poetry of Robert Frost

~~~~~

Reginald Goodall, Sir Alec Guinness and Dame Marie Rambert each chose John Milton's *Paradise Lost*.

(CASTAWAYS WHO CHOSE POETRY BY A SPECIFIC POET – *cont.*)

Michael Rosen – the complete poems of Carl Sandburg

Patricia Routledge – the collected works of John Donne

Bernice Rubens – *Poems for Joy* and *Sermons for Solace* by John Donne

Ken Russell – *The Prelude* by William Wordsworth

Alex Salmond – the complete works of Robert Burns

Peter Scudamore – a book of verse by Rudyard Kipling

Ravi Shankar – the poems of Rabindranath Tagore

Rod Steiger – a complete book of poetry by e. e. cummings

Juliet Stevenson – the complete works of W. B. Yeats

Alice Thomas Ellis – *Come Hither*, an anthology by Walter de la Mare

E. P. Thompson – *Songs of Innocence and Experience* by William Blake

Michael Tilson Thomas – the collected poems of Rainer Maria Rilke

Ron Todd – the collected works of Robert Burns

Mark Tully – the major works by Gerard Manley Hopkins

David Walliams – the collected poems of Philip Larkin

Charlie Watts – *Collected Poems 1934–52* of Dylan Thomas

Kaye Webb – the poetry of Naomi Lewis

Ann Widdecombe – the collected poems of Thomas Gray

Dr Rowan Williams – a collection of W. H. Auden poems

Baroness Shirley Williams – the collected poems of W. B. Yeats (on her subsequent appearance she chose the collected works of W. H. Auden)

Jeanette Winterson – *Four Quartets* by T. S. Eliot

Benjamin Zephaniah – the poetical works of Shelley

Whoopie Goldberg chose *Letters to a Young Poet* by Rainer Maria Rilke.

CASTAWAYS WHO CHOSE . . .
A FOREIGN LANGUAGE COURSE
OR DICTIONARY

Richard Branson – Japanese

Sir Colin Davis – Persian

Edward Downes – Chinese

Robert Hardy – French

Nigel Hawthorne – French

Arthur Haynes – French

Anthony Horowitz – French

Cath Kidston – French

Hugh Laurie – Italian

Sir Peter Maxwell Davies – Sanskrit

Hephzibah Menuhin – Chinese

Margaret Powell – Tahitian

Prunella Scales – Russian

Frank Skinner – French

Suggs – Italian, specifically a concise book of Italian verbs

David Wilkie – Spanish

Joan Collins chose a teach-yourself manual of the principal foreign languages.

Benny Hill chose a collection of language courses.

Leslie Phillips chose the rudiments of several useful languages.

. . . A BOOK IN LATIN

Sir Harrison Birtwistle, Frederic Raphael, Willy Russell, Fay Weldon (both times she was on the programme)

MOST POPULAR NOVELISTS

Charles Dickens – chosen by 61 castaways

Leo Tolstoy – 50

Marcel Proust – 48

Jane Austen – 27

P. G. Wodehouse – 24

Dante Alighieri – 18

Kenneth Grahame – 18 (all *The Wind in the Willows*)

Lewis Carroll – 17

J. R. R. Tolkien – 17 (16 of which were *The Lord of the Rings*)

James Joyce – 16

Daniel Defoe – 12 (all *Robinson Crusoe*)

Johann von Goethe – 12

Oscar Wilde – 12

Anthony Trollope – 11

CHOSEN BY 10 CASTAWAYS

Fyodor Dostoyevsky, Jerome K. Jerome (all *Three Men in a Boat*)

CHOSEN BY 9

Sir Arthur Conan Doyle, Thomas Hardy, W. Somerset Maugham

CHOSEN BY 8

George Eliot (all *Middlemarch*), A. A. Milne

CHOSEN BY 7

Rudyard Kipling, Evelyn Waugh, H. G. Wells

CHOSEN BY 6

Miguel de Cervantes (all *Don Quixote*), Giuseppe di Lampedusa (all *The Leopard*), Gabriel García Márquez, Margaret Mitchell (all *Gone with the Wind*), Laurence Sterne (all *Tristram Shandy*), Robert Louis Stevenson

CHOSEN BY 5

Antoine de Saint-Exupéry (all *The Little Prince*), F. Scott Fitzgerald, Joseph Heller (all *Catch 22*), Ernest Hemingway, Victor Hugo, Aldous Huxley, Anthony Powell, William Makepeace Thackeray (all *Vanity Fair*), Mark Twain

CHOSEN BY 4

E. M. Forster, John Galsworthy, Herman Hesse, Henry James, C. S. Lewis, Thomas Mann, Herman Melville (all *Moby-Dick*), Patrick O'Brian, Beatrix Potter, James Thurber, Voltaire, Johann Wyss (all *The Swiss Family Robinson*)

CHOSEN BY 3

Douglas Adams, Honoré de Balzac, Charlotte Brontë, Paulo Coelho, Lawrence Durrell, Gustave Flaubert, George and Weedon Grossmith, Mervyn Peake, Aleksander Pushkin, Saki, Sir Walter Scott, John Steinbeck, Jonathan Swift (all *Gulliver's Travels*), T. H. White, Virginia Woolf

CHOSEN BY 2

Peter Ackroyd, Woody Allen, Richard Bach, Alan Bennett, Jorge Luis Borges, Emily Brontë, John Buchan, John Bunyan, Lord Byron, John Le Carré, Raymond Chandler, G. K. Chesterton, Agatha Christie, James Clavell, Dame Daphne du Maurier, Gerald Durrell, William Faulkner, Frederick Forsyth, Stella Gibbons, Georgette Heyer, D. H. Lawrence, Nancy Mitford, Ayn Rand, Harold Robbins, J. D. Salinger, Dorothy L. Sayers, Tom Sharpe, Nevil Shute, Stendhal, James Stephens, Isaac Walton, Thomas Wolfe

CHOSEN BY 1

Louisa May Alcott, Kingsley Amis, James Baldwin, Iain Banks, Samuel Beckett, Saul Bellow, Arnold Bennett, Ronald Blythe, Richard Brautigan, Edward Bulwer-Lytton, Anthony Burgess, Italo Calvino, Albert Camus, Louis-Ferdinand Céline, Sid Chaplin, Leslie Charteris, Bruce Chatwin, Erskine Childers, Susanna Clarke, Jackie Collins, Wilkie Collins, Pat Conroy, Bernard Cornwell, John Cowper Powys, Michael Crichton, Don DeLillo, J. P. Donleavy, Theodore Dreiser, Dorothy Dunnett, Emily Eden, J. Meade Falkner, Edward Fitzgerald, Ian Fleming, Ken Follett, Ford Madox Ford, C. S. Forester, John Fowles, Neil Gaiman, Paul Gallico, Frank Grassic Gibbon, Giovannino Guareschi, Pedro Juan Gutiérrez, H. Rider Haggard, Thomas Harris, G. A. Henty, Jack Higgins, James Hilton, Christopher Isherwood, Jack Kerouac, Harper Lee, Laurie Lee, Doris Lessing, George MacDonald Fraser, Colin MacInnes, Naguib Mahfouz, Katherine Mansfield, Frederick Marryat, Guy de Maupassant, Cormac McCarthy, James Michener, Dan Millman, Alice Munro, Robert Musil, Vladimir Nabokov, V. S. Naipaul, Mary Norton, Flann O'Brien, George Orwell, Alan Paton, Philip Pullman, Mario Puzo, Jean Renoir, Anne Rice, Henry Handel Richardson, Alain Robbe-Grillet, J. K. Rowling, Salman

Rushdie, Paul Scott, Vikram Seth, Sam Shepard, Wilbur Smith, Olaf
Stapledon, Wallace Stegner, Randolph Stow, August Strindberg, Henry
David Thoreau, Robert Tressell, Ivan Turgenev, Jules Verne, Kurt
Vonnegut, Henry Williamson, Kathleen Winsor, P. C. Wren, John
Wyndham, Marion Zimmer Bradley, Émile Zola

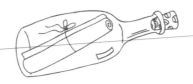

NOT CHOSEN BY *ANY* CASTAWAYS

There are some surprising absentees.

Kathy Acker, Mitch Albom, Monica Ali, Isabel Allende, Eric Ambler,
Martin Amis, Maya Angelou, Jeffrey Archer, Isaac Asimov, Margaret
Atwood, David Baldacci, J. G. Ballard, Pat Barker, Julian Barnes,
Brendan Behan, Aphra Behn, Louis De Bernières, Enid Blyton,
Heinrich Böll, John Braine, Bertolt Brecht, Anne Brontë, Dan Brown,
Edgar Rice Burroughs, William Burroughs, Samuel Butler, A. S.
Byatt, James M. Cain, Truman Capote, Peter Carey, Angela Carter,
Barbara Cartland, Jung Chang, Lee Child, Arthur C. Clarke, Harlan
Coben, Jean Cocteau, Jonathan Coe, J. M. Coetzee, Joseph Conrad,
Catherine Cookson, James Fenimore Cooper, Jilly Cooper, Roald
Dahl, Philip K. Dick, E. L. Doctorow, Margaret Drabble, Alexandre
Dumas, Umberto Eco, Bret Easton Ellis, Ben Elton, J. G. Farrell,
Sebastian Faulks, Henry Fielding, Jonathan Franzen, Esther Freud,
Elizabeth Gaskell, André Gide, George Gissing, William Golding,
Nadine Gordimer, Maxim Gorky, Günter Grass, Graham Greene,
John Grisham, Mark Haddon, Arthur Hailey, Radclyffe Hall, Dashiell
Hammett, L. P. Hartley, Nathaniel Hawthorne, Zoe Heller, Patricia
Highsmith, Khaled Hosseini, Hammond Innes, John Irving, Kazuo
Ishiguro, Erica Jong, Franz Kafka, Thomas Keneally, Ken Kesey,
Stephen King, Charles Kingsley, Dean Koontz, Hanif Kureishi, Stieg
Larsson, Elmore Leonard, Andrea Levy, Sinclair Lewis, Wyndham
Lewis, Hugh Lofting, Jack London, Malcolm Lowry, Robert Ludlum,
Ian McEwan, Stephanie Meyer, Henry Miller, Yukio Mishima, Toni
Morrison, Iris Murdoch, Anaïs Nin, Edna O'Brien, Michael Ondaatje,
Boris Pasternak, James Patterson, Jodi Picoult, Luigi Pirandello,

Sylvia Plath, Edgar Allan Poe, Terry Pratchett, Thomas Pynchon, Erich Maria Remarque, Jean Rhys, Samuel Richardson, Philip Roth, Arundhati Roy, Françoise Sagan, Sidney Sheldon, Mary Shelley, Lionel Shriver, Alan Sillitoe, Georges Simenon, Upton Sinclair, Zadie Smith, Aleksandr Isayevich Solzhenitsyn, Muriel Spark, Danielle Steel, Gertrude Stein, Bram Stoker, Rex Stout, Harriet Beecher Stowe, Patrick Süskind, Graham Swift, Hunter S. Thompson, John Kennedy Toole, John Updike, Gore Vidal, Alice Walker, Irving Wallace, Lew Wallace, Keith Waterhouse, Irvine Welsh, Rebecca West, Nathanael West, Edith Wharton, Angus Wilson, Tom Wolfe

THE BOOKER PRIZE

Sixteen Booker prizewinners have appeared as castaways on *Desert Island Discs*, but not one of them has ever chosen a Booker Prize-winning novel. The 16 were:

Kingsley Amis	Thomas Keneally (twice)
Margaret Atwood	Penelope Lively
Pat Barker	Ian McEwan
A. S. Byatt	V. S. Naipaul
Julian Barnes	Ruth Prawer Jhabvala
Peter Carey	Philip Pullman
Howard Jacobson	Bernice Rubens
Kazuo Ishiguro	Salman Rushdie

CHARLES DICKENS

These are all the (specific) Dickens novels chosen. *The Pickwick Papers* is clearly the most popular Dickens title. However, this list is marred – and thus rendered slightly misleading – by the fact that many castaways chose the complete works of Dickens and two castaways (Sir Learie Constantine and Sir Hugh Casson) were allowed to choose more than one Dickens book.

The Pickwick Papers – chosen by 15 castaways, including Griff Rhys Jones, Robert Robinson, Sir Harry Secombe, Peter Sellers and Timothy Spall

David Copperfield – 6, including Frankie Howerd, Leonard Sachs and John Sessions

Great Expectations – 6, including Richard Briers, Tom Courtenay and Terry O'Neill

Bleak House – 4, including Harry Enfield, Jonathon Porritt and Julian Symons

Nicholas Nickleby – 3, including Hugh Masekela

Oliver Twist – 3, including Dilys Powell

A Tale of Two Cities – 3, including Richard Dreyfuss, and Jack Warner, who chose it in English and in French

A Christmas Carol – 2, Dick Emery and Chris Evans

Barnaby Rudge – 2, Eric Clapton and Nick Hornby

Little Dorrit – 2, including Miriam Margolyes

Martin Chuzzlewit – 1, Heather Jenner

The Mystery of Edwin Drood – 1, Ernie Wise

The Old Curiosity Shop – 1, Sir Learie Constantine

No one (specifically) chose *Dombey and Son*, *Hard Times* or *Our Mutual Friend*.

JANE AUSTEN

Jane Austen novels were chosen by 27 castaways, and 12 of them, including Richard Baker, Cecil Day-Lewis, Dame Daphne du Maurier, Maureen Lipman, Ann Mallalieu and Sir Ian McKellen, chose *all* her books. Of those who expressed a preference, these were, in order of the most popular:

Pride and Prejudice: 7, including Karren Brady, Marguerite Patten and Angela Rippon

Emma: 4, including Kathleen Turner and Esther Rantzen

Persuasion: 2, Dame Janet Baker and Glenda Jackson

Mansfield Park: 1, Graham Norton

Sense and Sensibility: 1, Kristin Scott Thomas

Northanger Abbey has never been chosen.

CASTAWAYS WHO CHOSE WORKS BY SHAKESPEARE
(EVEN THOUGH ALL CASTAWAYS ARE GIVEN *THE COMPLETE WORKS OF SHAKESPEARE*)

Maurice Saatchi – *Hamlet*, the 1897 edition

Prunella Scales – the complete works in German

Before castaways were automatically given *The Complete Works of Shakespeare*, Laurence Harvey, Bernard Miles, Kenneth More and Donald Sinden all chose it.

Phil Redmond asked for the collected works of Charles Dickens instead of Shakespeare.

CASTAWAYS WHO CHOSE . . .

WORKS BY HOMER

Eleanor Bron, James Burke, Quintin Hogg (Lord Hailsham), Boris Johnson (who chose an Indian paper edition to translate), Elia Kazan, Bernard Miles, Richard Rogers, Most Rev. Robert Runcie, Erich Segal, Emma Thompson, Sir Michael Tippett, Sir Laurens van der Post

ARABIAN NIGHTS

Eve Arnold, Margaret Atwood, Dr Desmond Morris, Salman Rushdie

WORKS BY OSCAR WILDE

The Complete Works: chosen by Anthony Andrews, Stuart Burrows, Paulo Coelho, Wendy Craig, Joan Heal, Morrissey, Peggy Mount

The Ballad of Reading Gaol – Dave Allen

The Happy Prince and Other Tales – Coral Browne

The Picture of Dorian Gray – Joan Collins, Anita Dobson

The Selfish Giant – Ruthie Henshall

LEO TOLSTOY'S *WAR AND PEACE*

Forty-three castaways chose this novel, including: Dame Joan Bakewell, Christabel Bielenberg, John and Roy Boulting, Sir James Callaghan, Ian Carmichael, George Clooney, Jack de Manio, Ian Fleming (in German), Susan Hampshire, Debbie Harry, Frankie Howerd, Gloria Hunniford, P. D. James, Martha Lane Fox, Princess Margaret, Richard Noble, Egon Ronay, Julian Slade, Kiri Te Kanawa, Ted Willis, Sir Terry Wogan, Franco Zeffirelli, Fred Zinnemann

LEO TOLSTOY'S *ANNA KARENINA*

Rachel Billington, Melvyn Bragg, Anthony Julius, Vanessa Redgrave, Sir Sacheverell Sitwell, Rick Stein

CHAUCER

Kate Adie, Howard Brenton, Leon Brittan, Sir David Frost, Terry Jones

A HAROLD ROBBINS BOOK

Ambrose – *The Carpetbaggers*

Matt Munro – *The Adventurers*

MERVYN PEAKE'S *GORMENGHAST*

Sir Ranulph Fiennes, Keith Floyd

THE WORKS OF BEACHCOMBER

Raymond Briggs (on both of his appearances), Harry Corbett

A THOMAS HARDY NOVEL

Jane Asher, Jill Balcon, Josephine Barstow, David Mellor, Jean Rook, Twiggy

THE WORKS OF JAMES THURBER

Elvis Costello, Humphrey Lyttelton, Sir Claus Moser, Nyree Dawn Porter

GIUSEPPE DI LAMPEDUSA'S *THE LEOPARD*

Nick Clegg, John Fortune (in Italian and in English), Dr Susan Greenfield, Peter Mayle, Simon Schama

WORKS BY H. G. WELLS

Sir Terence Conran, Benny Green, James Herbert, Armando Iannucci, Robin Knox-Johnston, Valerie Singleton

PLAYS BY GEORGE BERNARD SHAW

Francis Durbridge, Paul Jones, Felicity Kendal, Thomas Keneally, Philip Larkin, Dandy Nichols, Sir Brian Rix, John Slater, Johnny Speight, Rita Tushingham, Kenneth Williams

A NOVEL BY AYN RAND

Sir Michael Caine, Suzi Quatro

AN UNFINISHED NOVEL

Professor A. C. Grayling: *The Man Without Qualities* by Robert Musil

Ernie Wise: *The Mystery of Edwin Drood* by Charles Dickens

Josephine Cox chose 'a book which is in my head about my brother'.

THOMAS MALORY'S *LE MORTE D'ARTHUR*

Robert Fisk, Timothy West

J. D. SALINGER'S *THE CATCHER IN THE RYE*

Diane Cilento, Michael Winner

LEWIS CARROLL'S *ALICE'S ADVENTURES IN WONDERLAND*

Angela Baddeley, Cilla Black, John and Roy Boulting, Lord Carrington, Paul Gallico, Alfred Marks, Bob Monkhouse, David Nixon

John Hurt and Sir Tim Rice chose the complete works of Lewis Carroll.

WORKS BY ERNEST HEMINGWAY

Stewart Granger, Graham Hill, Bill Nighy, Michael Parkinson, Taki

WORKS BY J. B. PRIESTLEY

Kenneth Connor, Barry Cryer

DANTE'S *INFERNO*

Tom Stoppard (in two languages), Franco Zeffirelli

DANTE'S *DIVINE COMEDY*

Claudio Abbado, The Amadeus String Quartet, Rocco Forte, Nigella Lawson (in Italian), Randy Newman, Luciano Pavarotti

JAMES JOYCE'S *ULYSSES*

Peter Blake, Seamus Heaney, David Lodge, Sir Peter Maxwell Davies, Ian McEwan, Jimmy McGovern, Edna O'Brien, Derek Walcott

A. A. MILNE'S *WINNIE THE POOH*

Dick Clement and Ian La Frenais, Christopher Plummer, Oliver Reed

JOHANN WYSS'S *THE SWISS FAMILY ROBINSON*

Sir Arthur Bliss, Dirk Bogarde, Gwen Ffrangcon-Davies, Cliff Richard

GEORGE ELIOT'S *MIDDLEMARCH*

Tina Brown, Stephen Hawking, P. D. James, Jancis Robinson, Tony Robinson

A DOSTOYEVSKY NOVEL

Tony Bennett, Jan Morris, Itzhak Perlman, Donald Pleasence, Ruth Prawer Jhabvala, Vidal Sassoon, Martin Sheen

P. G. WODEHOUSE BOOKS

Douglas Adams, Rowan Atkinson, Henry Blofeld, Robert Bolt, George Chisholm, Professor Richard Dawkins, Stephen Fry, Elspeth Huxley, Jonathan Lynn, Arthur Marshall, Jimmy Mulville, Barry Norman, Lord Oaksey, Leonard Rossiter, Peter Sallis, Alan Titchmarsh, Sir Terry Wogan (twice)

AN EVELYN WAUGH NOVEL

Peter Bull – *Brideshead Revisited* (in Greek)

Robert Harris – *Scoop*

Ronald Harwood, David Mitchell – *Decline and Fall*

Sir Peregrine Worsthorne – *Vile Bodies*

Edward Fox chose a selection of Evelyn Waugh novels.

A WORK BY PROUST

Richard Adams, Tariq Ali, The Amadeus String Quartet, Mary Archer, Sir Frederick Ashton, Stan Barstow, Tony Blair, Claire Bloom, A. S. Byatt, John Cole, Cyril Connolly, Margaret Drabble, Sebastian Faulks, Ralph Fiennes, Sir John Gielgud, Christopher Hampton, Sheila Hancock, David Hicks, James Ivory, Neil Jordan, Penelope Keith, Ewan McGregor, George Melly, Sir John Mortimer, Lady Mosley, Dame Joan Plowright, Michael Portillo, Philip Pullman, A. L. Rowse, John Simpson, Dodie Smith, Sir Stephen Spender, David Tennant, John Updike, Sir Arnold Wesker, Vivienne Westwood

CERVANTES'S *DON QUIXOTE*

Placido Domingo, Peter Finch, Sir Christopher Frayling, Sir Simon Rattle

THE LITTLE PRINCE BY ANTOINE DE SAINT-EXUPÉRY

Eva Bartok, Raymond Blanc, Nana Mouskouri, Marty Feldman, Omar Sharif

JOSEPH HELLER'S *CATCH–22*

Alan Bleasdale, Billy Connolly, Lenny Henry, Bob Hoskins, John Pilger

DANIEL DEFOE'S *ROBINSON CRUSOE*

Alan Alda, Rev. W. Awdry, Shirley Bassey, Frank Bruno, Douglas Fairbanks Jr, Marianne Faithfull, Leslie Grantham, Bear Grylls, Anne-Sophie Mutter, James Stewart, Group Captain Peter Townsend, Des Wilson

THE PROPHET BY KAHLIL GIBRAN

Bertice Reading, General Norman Schwarzkopf, Gloria Swanson

KENNETH GRAHAME'S *THE WIND IN THE WILLOWS*

Hermione Baddeley, Acker Bilk, Michael Craig, Sir Anthony Dowell, Michael Grade, Max Hastings, Freddie Jones, Richard Mabey, Magnus Magnusson, Alan Price, John Ridgway, Ronnie Scott, Terence Stamp, John Thaw, Elsie and Doris Waters

JEROME K. JEROME'S *THREE MEN IN A BOAT*

Dora Bryan, Jeremy Lloyd, Robert McCrum, Vic Reeves, Edward Woodward

LAURENCE STERNE'S *TRISTRAM SHANDY*

John Arlott, Steve Coogan, Bamber Gascoigne, Michael Nyman

AN ANTHONY TROLLOPE BOOK

Julian Fellowes, Dame Celia Johnson, Prue Leith, John Major, Sir John Mills

HERMAN MELVILLE'S *MOBY-DICK*

J. G. Ballard, Hugh Fearnley-Whittingstall, Patricia Highsmith, Penelope Lively

TOLKIEN'S *THE LORD OF THE RINGS*

Dame Janet Baker, David Bellamy, James Bolam, Richard Dunwoody, Dr Jane Goodall, Duncan Goodhew, Sir Edmund Hillary

Will Carling chose *The Hobbit*.

GABRIEL GARCÍA MÁRQUEZ'S *ONE HUNDRED YEARS OF SOLITUDE*

Linton Kwesi Johnson, Mike Leigh, Alison Steadman

WORKS BY WOODY ALLEN

Colin Firth, Michael McIntyre

PAULO COELHO'S *THE ALCHEMIST*

Sacha Distel, Nicola Horlick

TOM SHARPE'S *WILT*

Steve Davis, Wendy Richard

WORKS BY CHEKHOV

Jill Bennett, Gyles Brandreth, Sinéad Cusack, Carl Davis, Cecil Day-Lewis, Kazuo Ishiguro, Elijah Moshinsky, André Previn

F. SCOTT FITZGERALD'S *THE GREAT GATSBY*

Jackie Collins, Anthony Hopkins

MARGARET MITCHELL'S *GONE WITH THE WIND*

Hylda Baker, Bob Hope, Johnny Mathis, Dr Ruth Westheimer

FREDERICK FORSYTH'S *THE DAY OF THE JACKAL*

Pam Ayres, Charles Kennedy

COMICS OR COMIC BOOKS

Phil Collins – *Prehistory of the Far Side* by Gary Larson

Kenny Everett – *Eagle Annual*

Hugh Grant – *King Ottokar's Sceptre* (*The Adventures of Tintin* series) by Hergé

Dennis Price – volume of Giles cartoons

Sir Martin Rees – *Collected Cartoons* by Gary Larson

Paul Smith – *The Beano Annual* 1974

Doris Stokes – *The Complete Andy Capp*

E. P. Thompson – *Pogo* comic strips by Walt Kelly

SINGULAR CHOICES (FICTION)

The Scales of Injustice (based on the TV series *Doctor Who*) by Gary Russell – Gok Wan

The collected works of Arthur Marshall – Victoria Wood

A compendium of the world's best science fiction (so he can 'become an expert') – Patrick Stewart

Memoirs of a Midget by Walter de la Mare – Wee Georgie Wood

The complete works of Graham Linehan – Kathy Burke

Through Russian Snows by G. A. Henty – the Duke of Westminster

The complete *Monty Python* television scripts – Iain Banks

An audiobook of Martin Jarvis reading *Just William* by Richmal Crompton – Jan Pienkowski

Yes Minister – Professor Ara Darzi (Lord Darzi)

CASTAWAYS' NON-FICTION CHOICES

EDWARD GIBBON'S *THE HISTORY OF THE DECLINE AND FALL OF THE ROMAN EMPIRE*

Nina Bawden, Jo Brand, Rory Bremner, Professor Asa Briggs, Stephen Frears, Sir Osbert Lancaster, Kenneth More, Nina and Frederik, C. Northcote Parkinson, John Julius Norwich, Raymond Postgate, Peter Shaffer, Jeremy Thorpe, Wilfred Thesiger

SIR WINSTON CHURCHILL'S *HISTORY OF THE ENGLISH-SPEAKING PEOPLES*

Peter Alliss, Sir Chris Bonington, Fanny and Johnnie Cradock, Hubert Gregg, Sir Michael Hordern, Morecambe and Wise, James Prior, Lord Tebbit, Wilson Whineray

Leslie Crowther, Birgit Nilsson and Zena Skinner chose *The Second World War* by Sir Winston Churchill.

AN ENGLISH DICTIONARY

Joss Ackland, Kingsley Amis, Brenda Blethyn, Wilfrid Brambell, Simon Callow, Kim Cattrall, Billy Connolly, Alan Coren, David Dimbleby, Sacha Distel, Ken Dodd, John Freeman, Terry Gilliam*, Germaine Greer, Deborah Kerr, John Laurie, Tom Lehrer, Shirley Maclaine, George MacDonald Fraser, Wilbur Smith, Colin Welland

* Gilliam said he would hollow out some pages in order to conceal a pistol so that when he got bored with his own company he could shoot himself.

A DICTIONARY OF QUOTATIONS

Basil Boothroyd, Sir Robin Day, Julia Foster, Christopher Fry, Sir John Gielgud, Doris Hare, Hattie Jacques, Carla Lane, Ian Richardson, Dame Cicely Saunders, Minette Walters

A THESAURUS

John Paddy Carstairs, Bing Crosby, Monica Dickens, Jacqueline du Pré, Noel Edmonds, Garrison Keillor, Andrea Levy, Shirley Maclaine, Hayley Mills, Sir Bobby Robson, Vidal Sassoon

THE DICTIONARY OF NATIONAL BIOGRAPHY

Finlay Currie, Felix Dennis, Norris McWhirter.

A BOOK ON ART OR PAINTING

Sir Ken Adam, Gordon Brown, Ian Dury, James Fox, Ricky Gervais, Edward Heath, Tom Keating, Esmond Knight, Grayson Perry, André Previn, Rev. David Sheppard, Dame Veronica Wedgwood, Mike Yarwood

A TELEPHONE DIRECTORY

Umberto Eco, Marvin Hamlisch, Posy Simmonds

WORKS BY VIRGIL

Lady Antonia Fraser, Helena Kennedy, Hugh Trevor-Roper (Lord Dacre)

A BOOK ON WINE

Michael Bogdanov, David Gower, Geoffrey Smith

A BOOK BY OR ABOUT PLATO

John Huston, Miriam Karlin, Robert Maxwell

THE BOOK OF KELLS

Dame Judi Dench, Christina Noble

A BOOK ABOUT PHYSICS

Pauline Collins – a teach-yourself physics book

Professor Brian Cox – *Classical Electrodynamics* by John David Jackson

Clare Francis – a volume on physics

Sir Fred Hoyle – a handbook of physics

THE *I CHING*

Katherine Hamnett, Burl Ives, Glynis Johns, Jane Lapotaire, Keith Michell, Sarah Miles, Nina and Frederik, Sir Simon Rattle

OTHER MEN'S FLOWERS BY LORD A. P. WAVELL

Sir John Glubb, Jocelyn Stevens, Auberon Waugh

SPINOZA'S *ETHICS*

Daniel Barenboim, Tracey Emin

A BOOK ON MYTHOLOGY

Ralph Steadman – (New) *Larousse Encyclopaedia of Mythology*

Fanny and Johnnie Cradock – *Smith's Dictionary of Greek and Roman Biography and Mythology*

AN INSTRUCTION BOOK ON GOLF

Arthur Askey – a golf instruction book (on his second of four appearances)

Sir Clive Woodward – *Short Game of Golf* by Dave Pelz

Dickie Henderson – *How to Play Your Best Golf All the Time*

THE POWER OF POSITIVE THINKING BY NORMAN VINCENT PEALE

Virginia Ironside, Mary Peters, Willard White

A PIANO TUTOR OR MANUAL

Eddie Calvert, Alan Howard

BLANK BOOKS (plus pen or pencil)

Vladimir Ashkenazy, Michael Flanders, Hugh Griffith, Emmylou Harris, Dr Thor Heyerdahl, Frank Ifield, Madhur Jaffrey, Patrick Lichfield, Sir Robert Mayer, Antony Sher, Sir Michael Tippett, P. L. Travers, Peter Ustinov, Kenneth Wolstenholme

Dame Edna Everage chose a Filofax.

Jamie Oliver doesn't read books but requested notepaper and pens in order to write recipes.

SCOUTING FOR BOYS BY ROBERT BADEN-POWELL

Moira Anderson, Siân Phillips

Sheila Hancock chose *The Girl Guides' Handbook*.

THE EXCHANGE AND MART
John Dankworth, Keith Waterhouse

BOOKS BY BENNY GREEN
Sebastian Coe, Jeremy Isaacs, David Puttnam, Dennis Skinner

LAROUSSE GASTRONOMIQUE
David Hare, Barbara Murray, Marjorie Proops, Janet Street-Porter, Dr Roy Strong

~~~~~~

Norman Del Mar chose *Le Petit Larousse Illustré*.

MRS BEETON'S HOUSEHOLD MANAGEMENT
Hermione Gingold, Alfred Hitchcock, Stanley Holloway, Zandra Rhodes, Virginia Wade

A BOOK ABOUT ASTRONOMY
Sir Arthur Bliss, Dame Celia Johnson, Peter Jones, Moira Lister, Imelda Staunton

Virginia Bottomley and Patrick Moore – *Norton's Star Atlas*

Roger McGough – *The Times Atlas of the Night Sky*

Nigel Nicolson – *A Guide to the Universe (Astronomy)*

Wayne Sleep – *Atlas of the Stars*

A BOOK ON MATHEMATICS
Rabbi Lionel Blue – *The Value of Pure Mathematics*

Anna Massey – a book on mathematics

V. S. Naipaul – *Teach Yourself Mathematics*

Lord Rothschild – a book on pure mathematics

Clare Short – a geometry tutor

THE DIARY OF SAMUEL PEPYS

Joss Ackland, Bob Geldof, Alan Johnson, John Le Mesurier, Henry
Longhurst, Claire Tomalin

THE WORKS OF SIGMUND FREUD

Al Alvarez, Michael Green, Hanif Kureishi, Penelope Leach

BOOKS ON CHESS

Dr Jacob Bronowski, John Lill, Sir John Wilson (a chess strategy book
in Braille)

A BOOK ON HISTORY (OR WARFARE)

Jack Ashley, Michael Aspel, Simon Russell Beale, Russell Braddon,
Harold Evans, Georgie Fame, William Hartnell, Thora Hird, Tom Jones,
Herbert Kretzmer, Richard Murdoch, Sir Bobby Robson, Sir Alec Rose,
Tessa Sanderson, Sir Stephen Spender, Jack Straw, Barbara Windsor

ESSAYS BY MICHEL DE MONTAIGNE

Captain Jacques Cousteau, Quentin Crewe, David Dimbleby, Richard
Hoggart, Eric Porter, Michael Powell, Emeric Pressburger, Alan Yentob

WISDEN

Alec Bedser, John Biffen, Dickie Bird, Geoff Boycott, Tony Greig, Nigel
Kennedy, Gary Lineker, David Puttnam, Sir Stuart Rose

THE GUINNESS BOOK OF RECORDS

Arthur Askey, David Essex, Richard Lester, Ron Pickering, Derek Randall, Jackie Stewart

COOKERY BOOKS

Heston Blumenthal, David Cameron (*The River Cottage Cookbook* by Hugh Fearnley-Whittingstall), Robert Carrier, Oz Clarke, John Cleese, Gemma Craven, Len Deighton, Rachael Heyhoe (a book on desert-island cookery), Sue Lawley, Sir Cameron Mackintosh, Kenneth McKellar, Mrs Gladys Mills, Beryl Reid, Albert and Michel Roux, Elisabeth Schwarzkopf, Terence Stamp, Marco Pierre White, Billie Whitelaw

AN ENCYCLOPAEDIA

Dave Brubeck, Charlie Drake, Clive Dunn, Gerald Durrell, Charlton Heston, Dame Kelly Holmes, Sir Michael Hordern, Sidney James, Michael Johnson, Kenneth McKellar, Leo McKern, Edna O'Brien, Des O'Connor, Joseph Rotblat (on CD-Rom), Maggie Smith, Jimmy Tarbuck, Peter Ustinov, Michael Wilding

LEONARDO DA VINCI'S DRAWINGS

Peter Scott, Tony Bennett

AN ATLAS

Dame Judi Dench, Ken Dodd, Gary Glitter, Sir Bernard Ingham, Paul Johnson, Glenys Kinnock, Joanna Lumley, Sir Matthew Pinsent

KENNETH CLARK'S *CIVILISATION*

Ian Hislop, Lynn Seymour

THE DIARY OF ANNE FRANK

Joan Baez, Howard Goodall

STEPHEN HAWKING'S *A BRIEF HISTORY OF TIME*

Vince Cable, Chris Patten, Rose Tremain

A BOOK ON BIRDS

Sir Alec Douglas-Home, Robin Knox-Johnston, Nick Park, Stephen Potter

A HISTORY OF ARCHITECTURE ON THE COMPARATIVE METHOD BY SIR BANISTER FLETCHER

Donald Sinden, Lord Snowdon, Sir Basil Spence

A GARDENING BOOK

Steven Berkoff, David Bryant, Joseph Cotten, Paul Dacre, Michael Heseltine, Glenda Jackson, Gordon Jackson, Alan Pascoe, Gerald Scarfe, Nigel Slater, Lady Tebbit, Percy Thrower, Sir William Walton

A PERSONAL PHOTOGRAPH ALBUM

Lillian Board, Michael Bond, Boy George, Jeremy Clarkson, Arthur Edwards, Ben Elton (his wedding photo album), Lesley Garrett, Graham Hill, Alan Parker, Jerry Springer

A BOOK OF CROSSWORDS

Trevor Brooking, Lionel Blair

A PRAYER, HYMN OR SCRIPTURE BOOK

These choices, unless specified, were in addition to the copy of the Bible given to each castaway.

Ursula Bloom – the Book of Common Prayer

Lord Deedes – in addition to the Bible, he chose the 'original prayer book without any amendments'

Dizzy Gillespie – *Baha'i Prayer Book*

Rev. Ian Paisley – *Foxe's Book of Martyrs*

Enoch Powell – the versions of the Bible chosen: the Old Testament in Hebrew and the New Testament in Greek

Sir Martin Sorrell – the Talmud and the Old Testament (to replace the Bible)

Pamela Stephenson – *Buddhist Scripture* by Dama Pada

George Thomas (Viscount Tonypandy) – *The Methodist Hymn Book*

THE KORAN

James Clavell, David Gilmour, Clive Stafford Smith, Lord Winston

SCIENCE AND HEALTH BY MARY BAKER EDDY

Dame Edith Evans, Joyce Grenfell, Lionel Hampton, Ginger Rogers (all Christian Scientists)

Books

BRIAN KEENAN'S *AN EVIL CRADLING*
David Edgar, Piers Morgan

A BOOK ON PHILOSOPHY
Andrew Cruickshank – *Journal* by Søren Kierkegaard
Ken Follett – *Philosophical Investigations* by Ludwig Wittgenstein
Eric Idle – a compendium of world philosophy
Lang Lang – *The Analects of Confucius*
Gian Carlo Menotti – a book on philosophy by Emmanuel Kant
Yvonne Mitchell – a compilation of works of philosophy

BERTRAND RUSSELL'S *A HISTORY OF WESTERN PHILOSOPHY*
Alan Clark, Rex Harrison, Ben Helfgott, Ron Moody, John Pardoe

NEWSPAPERS OR MAGAZINES
Dennis Brain – back numbers of motor magazines
Fred Dibnah – bound volumes of *The Engineer* magazine
Dorita and Pepe – fashion magazines
Britt Ekland – recent editions of magazines, e.g. *Vanity Fair*, *Vogue*
Molly Keane – bound copies of *The Spectator* magazine
Sir Charles MacLean – volumes of the *Illustrated London News*
Don McCullin – one year of issues of *The Times*
Peter Rogers – a bound volume of *Punch* from the 1960s
Ted Williams – *Horse and Hound* magazine

A BIOGRAPHY

Brian Aldiss – chose a biography of John Osborne

Richard Attenborough – Mahatma Gandhi

Darcey Bussell – Audrey Hepburn

David Kossoff – the Marx Brothers

Paul Merton – Buster Keaton

Leslie Mitchell – Leonardo da Vinci

Ethel Revnell – Bette Davis

Richard Wattis – Benjamin Disraeli

Marguerite Wolff – Franz Liszt

OTHER CHOICES

Nine castaways chose airline, railways or steamer timetables:

  Pietro Annigoni – international timetable of ships and trains

  Ian Hendry – timetable of passing steamers

  Bob and Alf Pearson – ABC railway timetable

  Arnold Ridley, Eddie Waring – *Bradshaw's Railway Timetable*

  John Trevelyan, Alan Whicker, James Loughran – airline timetable

Five chose *Who's Who in the Theatre*:

  Henry Kendall

  Raymond Mander and Joe Mitchenson

  Roy Plomley

  Peter Saunders

  Elisabeth Welch

Four chose *Who's Who*:

  Prince Chula Chakrabongse of Thailand

  Charles Craig

  Lord Goodman

  Gale Pedrick

Books

Four chose Charles Darwin's *On the Origin of Species*:
- Susan Blackmore
- Sir George Christie
- Dr Max Perutz
- Sir Richard Sykes

Four chose Nelson Mandela's *Long Walk to Freedom*:
- Lord Joffe
- Bill Morris
- Sir Gulum Noon
- Thomas Quasthoff

Three castaways chose Sir Thomas More's *Utopia*:
- Professor A. H. Halsey
- Thelma Holt
- Elizabeth, Countess of Longford

Two castaways chose calendars:
- Richard Condon
- Professor George Steiner

Two castaways chose Adam Smith's *The Wealth of Nations*:
- Sir Stanley Kalms
- Andrew Neil

Three castaways chose books of short stories
without specifying an author:
- Anthony Newley
- Patricia Neal
- Philippe Petit

SINGULAR CHOICES
(NON-FICTION)

Apophthegmata Patrum (early writing of Egyptian fathers) – chosen by John Tavener

Air Publication 1234 (RAF manual for navigation) – Alan Sillitoe

Art of Looking Sideways by Alan Fletcher – Viscount Linley

Book of Alcoholics Anonymous – Tony Adams

Book of Lempster (old Irish textbook currently in The Hague) – Paddy Moloney

Book about Hollywood – Barbara Windsor

Book with pictures of pretty women – John Lee Hooker

Cole Porter Songbook – Armistead Maupin

Contingency, Irony and Solidarity by Richard Rorty – Brian Eno

Crying with Laughter by Bob Monkhouse – Pauline Quirke

Culture of the Abdomen: A Cure of Obesity and Constipation by F. A. Hornibrook – Jon Pertwee

Das Kapital by Karl Marx – Tony Benn

Debrett's Peerage – Betty Kenward

Diplomacy and Murder in Tehran: Alexander Griboyedov and the Tsar's Mission to the Shah of Persia by Lawrence Kelly – Elizabeth, Countess Longford

Elected Science by Thomas Merton – Brian Epstein

Elizabethan lyrics from songbooks and dramatists – Geoffrey Household

Essay on population by Thomas Malthus – Patricia Cornwell

Essays on Equality by R. H. Tawney – Neil Kinnock

Everton: The Complete Record by Steve Johnson – Bill Kenwright

Fun in a Chinese Laundry by Josef von Sternberg – Maria Aitken

Giant Book of Mensa Puzzles by Robert Allen – Gene Pitney

Guinness Book of Pop – Richard Curtis

History of Orient Football Club – Julian Lloyd Webber

History of the Derby – Frankie Dettori

How to Win Friends and Influence People by Dale Carnegie – Gerald Harper

A Hundred-and-One Things a Girl Can Do – David Jacobs

In Tune with the Infinite: Fullness of Peace Power by Ralph Waldo Trine – Chili Bouchier

Jane's All the World's Aircraft – Marty Wilde

A joke book – Dennis Taylor

La Première gorgée de bière et autres plaisirs minuscules by Philippe Delerm – Vittorio Radice

Life, Times and Music of an Irish Harper by Donal O'Sullivan – Brian Keenan

London A–Z – Sir David Frost

Magnum Magnum edited by Brigitte Lardinois – David Suchet

Mahler's copy of *The Complete Works of Bach* – Ralph Kohn

A matchbook (as in a book of matches) – Tim Robbins

Medical Care of Merchant Seamen by William Louis Wheeler – Siân Phillips

Melbourne street directory (an old version) – Barry Humphries

Microcosmographia Academica by Francis M. Cornford – Dr David Starkey

Most recent publication of veterinarian medicine – James Herriot

My Method of Singing by Enrico Caruso – Clive James

National Hunt Form Book – Robin Cook

New York Times Film Directory – Mel Tormé

Power of Now by Eckhart Tolle – Annie Lennox

Prisons (Le Carceri): The Complete First and Second States by Giovanni Batista Piranesi – Daniel Libeskind

Olive: The Life and Lore of a Noble Fruit by Mort Rosenblum – James Dyson

Opera di M. Bartolomeo Scappi (recipe book of the Pope's chef in 1525) – Anton Mosimann

Parliamentary Practice by Thomas Erskine-May – Commander Sir Stephen King-Hall

Partridge's Dictionary of Slang – Richard Eyre

Pictures of the English countryside – Tommy Reilly

R.C.T.S. History of Great Western Railway Engines – Pete Waterman

Ripley's Believe It or Not – Eric Sykes

Rules of patience – Robert Morley

Sai-Yu-Ki – Yoko Ono

Scores of all music chosen in a bound volume – Dame Josephine Barnes

Shorthand instruction book with paper and pens – Phil Drabble

1972 Social Register of New York – J. P. Donleavy

Socialist Sixth of the World by Hewlett Johnson – Jimmy Knapp

Songs from the 1880s with piano accompaniment by Franz Schubert – Brian Sewell

Spotlight casting directory – Patrick Cargill

Stand by Your Man (autobiography) by Tammy Wynette – John Cleese

A talking book by Dame Judi Dench – Ronald Eyre

Teach Yourself Bridge – Maeve Binchy

Teach Yourself Mathematics with illustrations of voluptuous women as portrayed by the great artists of the past – John Rutter

Team of Rivals: The Political Genius of Abraham Lincoln by Doris Kearns Goodwin – Jon Snow

Think and Grow Rich and *I'll Teach You Personality* – Al Read

Transcripts from the Watergate hearings – Earl Wild

Tropical plant book in Italian with English gloss – Sir Eduardo Paolozzi

True funny stories in German – Baroness Maria von Trapp

Two photographs (one of his wife Betty; one of 1928 Blackburn Rovers FC team) – Alfred Wainwright

Wild Reckoning: An Anthology Provoked by Rachel Carson's 'Silent Spring' edited by John Burnside and Maurice Riordan – Sir David King

CONSISTENT CASTAWAYS

Sir David Attenborough chose *Shifts and Expedients of Camp Life* by W. B. Lord on his three most recent appearances on the show.

Julie Andrews chose *The Once and Future King* by T. H. White on both occasions she appeared on the show.

Stephen Sondheim chose *The Collected Works of E. B. White* on both of his two appearances on the show.

Fay Weldon chose *Kennedy's Latin Primer* on both occasions she appeared on the show.

Richard Ingrams chose *Teach Yourself Piano Tuning* on the two occasions he appeared on the show.

Susan Hill chose *The Pursuit of Love* by Nancy Mitford on both occasions she appeared on the show.

LISTENERS' CHOICE

THE LISTENERS'
TOP 100 ARTISTS

As voted for by the public in 2011, with, on the right, the number of times the artist has featured in an episode of *Desert Island Discs*.

Listeners' Choice	Castaways' Choice
1. The Beatles	252
2. Bob Dylan	91
3. Ludwig van Beethoven	719
4. Wolfgang Amadeus Mozart	792
5. Pink Floyd	24
6. Johann Sebastian Bach	652
7. The Rolling Stones	54
8. Edward Elgar	328
9. Ralph Vaughan Williams	150
10. Queen	14
11. Led Zeppelin	5
12. David Bowie	32
13. Giacomo Puccini	297
14. George Frideric Handel	283
15. Van Morrison	38
16. Bruce Springsteen	20
17. Leonard Cohen	19
18. Gustav Mahler	133
19. Elvis Presley	73
20. Simon and Garfunkel	38
21. Radiohead	8

Listeners' Choice		Castaways' Choice
22.	The Smiths	8
23.	Pyotr Ilyich Tchaikovsky	318
24.	Frank Sinatra	240
25.	The Beach Boys	22
26.	Joni Mitchell	20
27.	Jimi Hendrix	12
28.	Sergey Vasilevich Rachmaninov	164
29.	Franz Schubert	362
30.	Neil Young	9
31.	Fleetwood Mac	6
32.	The Kinks	10
33.	Dire Straits	16
34.	The Who	8
35.	Abba	17
36.	Miles Davis	44
37.	Bob Marley	36
38.	Kate Bush	8
39.	Giuseppe Verdi	332
40.	U2	9
41.	Oasis	4
42.	Richard Wagner	264
43.	Elton John	33
44.	The Clash	11
45.	Johnny Cash	14
46.	Nina Simone	26
47.	Eric Clapton	22
48.	Hubert Parry	51

Listeners' Choice		Castaways' Choice
49.	John Lennon	37
50.	Stevie Wonder	34
51.	Gustav Holst	50
52.	Johannes Brahms	244
53.	Antonio Vivaldi	71
54.	R. E. M.	4
55.	Ella Fitzgerald	128
56.	Jean Sibelius	151
57.	Richard Strauss	218
58.	Gabriel Fauré	71
59.	The Eagles	14
60.	Genesis	4
61.	Georges Bizet	76
62.	Marvin Gaye	22
63.	Johann Pachelbel	14
64.	Susan Boyle	0
65.	Elbow	2
66.	Louis Armstrong	136
67.	Frédéric Chopin	235
68.	Joy Division	5
69.	Tom Waits	14
70.	Claude Debussy	179
71.	Rod Stewart	19
72.	Coldplay	5
73.	The Stone Roses	2
74.	The Jam	7

Listeners' Choice	Castaways' Choice
75. George Gershwin	77
76. Muse	2
77. Paul Simon	19
78. The Doors	2
79. Dmitri Shostakovich	49
80. Samuel Barber	15
81. Michael Jackson	7
82. Adele	1
83. Electric Light Orchestra	2
84. Otis Redding	10
85. The Cure	1
86. Gregorio Allegri	10
87. John Martyn	7
88. The Killers	2
89. James Taylor	7
90. Dusty Springfield	7
91. Nat King Cole	71
92. Frank Zappa	1
93. Jeff Buckley	4
94. Fairport Convention	0
95. Nirvana	2
96. Antonín Dvořák	111
97. Elvis Costello	10
98. Felix Mendelssohn	152
99. Nick Drake	3
100. Thomas Tallis	47

When it comes to the classical composers, the choices of the listeners tally remarkably closely with those of the castaways – which is perhaps not surprising given that, by its very nature, classical music has withstood the test of time.

Having said that, the following composers have all been selected more than 50 times and yet fail to appear in the public's list: Hector Berlioz, Benjamin Britten, Frederick Delius, César Franck, Edvard Grieg, Joseph Haydn, Franz Liszt, Modest Mussorgsky, Sergei Prokofiev, Henry Purcell, Maurice Ravel, Gioacchino Rossini, Camille Saint-Saens, Robert Schumann, Johann Strauss II, Igor Stravinsky, William Walton.

The really big disconnect between the public's and the castaways' choices is apparent with 'popular' music. This is partly down to the fact that, by its very nature, popular music is much more ephemeral and the public has chosen contemporary favourites over older acts. Interestingly, *none* of the following acts – each of them selected at least fifteen times by the *Desert Island Discs* castaways – made the Listeners' Top 100: Count Basie, Shirley Bassey, Ray Charles, Bing Crosby, Noël Coward, Sammy Davis Jr, Neil Diamond, Duke Ellington, Judy Garland, Billie Holiday, Buddy Holly, Paul Robeson, Artie Shaw, Barbra Streisand, Dionne Warwick.

THE LISTENERS'
TOP 100 TRACKS

As voted for by the public in 2011, with, on the right, the number of times the track has featured in an episode of *Desert Island Discs*.

Listeners' Choice	Castaways' Choice
1. Ralph Vaughan Williams, *The Lark Ascending*	23
2. Edward Elgar, *Enigma Variations*	69
3. Ludwig van Beethoven, *Symphony No. 9 in D Minor 'Choral'*	97
4. Queen, *Bohemian Rhapsody*	4
5. Pink Floyd, *Comfortably Numb*	1
6. Edward Elgar, *Cello Concerto in E Minor*	51
7. George Frideric Handel, *Messiah*	118
8. Gustav Holst, *The Planets*	39
9. Ralph Vaughan Williams, *Fantasia On A Theme By Thomas Tallis*	28
10. Wolfgang Amadeus Mozart, *Requiem in D Minor*	34
11. Led Zeppelin, *Stairway To Heaven*	2
12. Johann Pachelbel, *Canon in D Major*	13
13. Pink Floyd, *Wish You Were Here*	2
14. The Beatles, *Hey Jude*	16
15. Gustav Mahler, *Symphony No. 5 in C Sharp Minor*	28
16. Hubert Parry, *Jerusalem*	34
17. The Kinks, *Waterloo Sunset*	4
18. Sergey Vasilevich Rachmaninov, *Piano Concerto No. 2 in C Minor*	81

Listeners' Choice		Castaways' Choice
19.	The Rolling Stones, *Gimme Shelter*	4
20.	Simon And Garfunkel, *Bridge Over Troubled Water*	11
21.	Gabriel Fauré, *Requiem*	49
22.	Wolfgang Amadeus Mozart, *Clarinet Concerto in A Major*	42
23.	The Beach Boys, *God Only Knows*	4
24.	Samuel Barber, *Adagio for Strings*	10
25.	Bob Dylan, *Like A Rolling Stone*	6
26.	Ludwig van Beethoven, *Symphony No. 6 in F Major 'Pastoral'*	62
27.	The Beatles, *In My Life*	8
28.	Gregorio Allegri, *Miserere*	10
29.	The Beatles, *A Day In The Life*	13
30.	Ludwig van Beethoven, *Piano Concerto No. 5 in E Flat Major 'Emperor'*	56
31.	Pink Floyd, *Shine On You Crazy Diamond*	3
32.	Antonio Vivaldi, *The Four Seasons*	38
33.	Giacomo Puccini, *Turandot: Nessun Dorma*	36
34.	Georges Bizet, *Au Fond Du Temple Saint* (from *The Pearl Fishers*)	20
35.	George Gershwin, *Rhapsody In Blue*	41
36.	Johann Sebastian Bach, *St Matthew Passion*	78
37.	Eric Clapton, *Layla*	9
38.	John Lennon, *Imagine*	19
39.	Jimi Hendrix, *All Along The Watchtower*	3
40.	Ludwig van Beethoven, *Symphony No. 7 in A Major*	54
41.	Thomas Tallis, *Spem In Alium*	16

Listeners' Choice	Castaways' Choice
42. Richard Strauss, *Four Last Songs*	49
43. Claude Debussy, *Suite Bergamasque* (commonly known as *Clair de Lune*)	47
44. The Beatles, *Here Comes The Sun*	6
45. Joaquín Rodrigo, *Concierto de Aranjuez*	24
46. David Bowie, *Life On Mars*	4
47. Electric Light Orchestra, *Mr Blue Sky*	1
48. The Eagles, *Hotel California*	4
49. Elbow, *One Day Like This*	1
50. The Who, *Won't Get Fooled Again*	2
51. Louis Armstrong, *What A Wonderful World*	21
52. Ludwig van Beethoven, *Piano Sonata No. 14 in C Sharp Minor, 'Moonlight Sonata'*	23
53. Johnny Cash, *Hurt*	1
54. Johann Sebastian Bach, *Goldberg Variations*	35
54. Miles Davis, *So What?*	4
56. The Rolling Stones, *Sympathy For The Devil*	6
57. Max Bruch, *Violin Concerto No. 1 in G Minor*	31
58. Bruce Springsteen, *Thunder Road*	0
59. Johann Sebastian Bach, *Mass in B Minor*	57
60. Bruce Springsteen, *Born To Run*	3
61. Gerry Rafferty, *Baker Street*	2
62. Procol Harum, *A Whiter Shade of Pale*	5
63. Joy Division, *Love Will Tear Us Apart*	2
64. Pyotr Ilyich Tchaikovsky, *1812 Overture*	25
65. The Smiths, *There Is A Light That Never Goes Out*	1

Listeners' Choice	Castaways' Choice
66. David Bowie, *Heroes*	3
66. Abba, *Dancing Queen*	5
68. Don McLean, *American Pie*	4
69. Johann Sebastian Bach, *Concerto for Two Violins in D Minor*	53
70. Franz Schubert, *String Quintet in C Major*	71
71. Bob Dylan, *Tangled Up In Blue*	3
71. Carl Orff, *Carmina Burana*	21
73. The Beatles, *Yesterday*	18
73. Marvin Gaye, *I Heard It Through The Grapevine*	7
75. Dave Brubeck, *Take Five*	8
76. The Beatles, *Strawberry Fields Forever*	6
76. Jeff Buckley, *Hallelujah*	3
78. Van Morrison, *Brown-Eyed Girl*	5
79. The Beatles, *Eleanor Rigby*	11
80. Gustav Mahler, *Symphony No. 2 in C Minor 'Resurrection'*	14
81. Otis Redding, *(Sittin' On) The Dock of The Bay*	4
82. Leonard Cohen, *Suzanne*	2
83. The Beatles, *Let It Be*	7
84. The Beach Boys, *Good Vibrations*	4
85. Antonín Dvořák, *Symphony No. 9 in E Minor, 'From The New World'*	41
86. Pulp, *Common People*	5
87. Bob Dylan, *Mr Tambourine Man*	8
88. Jimi Hendrix, *Voodoo Chile*	5
89. Led Zeppelin, *Kashmir*	2

Listeners' Choice	Castaways' Choice
89. Meat Loaf, *Bat Out of Hell*	5
89. The Undertones, *Teenage Kicks*	2
92. Giuseppe Verdi, *Requiem*	70
93. Joni Mitchell, *A Case of You*	6
93. Dire Straits, *Sultans of Swing*	1
95. The Rolling Stones, *Brown Sugar*	3
96. Lynyrd Skynyrd, *Freebird*	0
97. Giuseppe Verdi, *Nabucco: Va Pensiero Sull'ali Dorate (Chorus of The Hebrew Slaves)*	29
97. Henry Purcell, *When I Am Laid In Earth (Dido's Lament, from Dido And Aeneas)*	25
99. Kate Bush, *Wuthering Heights*	1
100. Wolfgang Amadeus Mozart, *Piano Concerto No. 21 in C Major*	32

ADDITIONAL MISCELLANY

One of the (many) joys of researching this book was an introduction to people I'd never come across or heard of: eccentrics, for example, such as Colonel Alfred Wintle (1962) – known as A. D. Wintle. He once sent a letter to the editor of *The Times*:

> Sir,
>
> I have just written you a long letter.
>
> On reading it over, I have thrown it into the waste paper basket.
>
> Hoping this will meet with your approval,
>
> I am, Sir,
>
> Your obedient Servant,
>
> A.D. Wintle

The journalist **Martha Gelhorn** was invited to appear on the programme. However, as she was not prepared to talk about her late husband, Ernest Hemingway, the recording was cancelled.

Jonah Barrington (1942) was a musician and the radio critic of the *Daily Express* during World War II. He helped to create the nickname 'Lord Haw-Haw' for the Nazi radio broadcaster William Joyce. He wrote: 'He speaks English of the haw-haw, damn-it-get-out-of-my-way variety, and his strong suit is gentlemanly indignation.'

Jack Buchanan (1951) was an actor and musical star, and was well known among his friends for his financial generosity to less prosperous colleagues. Every year during the running of the Grand National, Buchanan would cancel that day's performance of his current musical. He would then charter an excursion train to the racetrack and back, supplying meals for the entire cast and crew of his show and giving them £5 each for a bet on a horse.

Muir Mathieson (1951) was a conductor, and the son-in-law of William Nelson Darnborough, who was famous for his success at roulette in Monte Carlo. From 1904 to 1911, he amassed a fortune of $415,000. In one of his most amazing feats, Darnborough bet on the number 5 and won on five successive spins.

Peter Sellers (1957) was the first male to feature on the cover of *Playboy*.

Frankie Vaughan (1958) was born Frank Abelson. The name 'Vaughan' came from a grandmother whose first grandson he was, who used to call Frank 'my number one' grandson, and in whose Russian accent 'one' sounded like 'Vaughan'.

Ursula Bloom (1960), the novelist and journalist, became close friends later on in life with Dr Crippen's love, Ethel Le Neve.

Eddie Calvert (1960), the trumpeter, left the UK for South Africa in the 1960s when his career hit a slump. While there, he recorded a pro-apartheid version of *Amazing Grace*, retitled 'Amazing Race'.

Rowland Emett (1963), the comedy cartoonist, created the elaborate inventions of Caractacus Potts (played by Dick Van Dyke) for the film *Chitty Chitty Bang Bang* – including the car itself.

Richard Wattis (1964), the actor, died of a heart attack in a Kensington restaurant in 1975, aged 62, in the middle of his favourite meal.

Hylda Baker (1969), comedian and actor, was born in Farnworth, near Bolton, and as part of her act developed an exaggerated movement of the lips while speaking. This had its origins in the communication style of Lancashire workers in their noisy cotton mills, where words couldn't be heard and lips were read instead.

David Hughes (1970) fell ill in 1972 while singing the part of Pinkerton in *Madam Butterfly* at the London Coliseum. He collapsed in the wings near the end but managed to complete the final scene. Just before the ambulancemen took him out of the theatre he said, 'I didn't let them down, did I?' He died the following day, from heart failure.

Vidal Sassoon (1970 and 2011) was 20 when he joined the Israeli army, and fought in the 1948 Arab–Israeli War. He recalled, 'When you think of 2,000 years of being put down and suddenly you are a nation rising, it was a wonderful feeling. There were only 600,000 people defending the country against five armies, so everyone had something to do.'

Andy Stewart (1970) had a hit with the song *Donald Where's Your Troosers?* in 1961 and again in 1989. Stewart is said to have written the song in just 10 minutes as he sat, with his trousers down, in a recording studio toilet.

Michael Crawford (1971, 1978 and 1999) was born Michael Patrick Smith. He adopted the name 'Michael Crawford' when taking a bus home after an audition and seeing a lorry with the slogan 'Crawford's Biscuits Are Best'.

Sir Louis Gluckstein MP (1971) was, at 2.02 metres (6 feet 7 and a half inches), believed to have been the tallest Member of Parliament until the election of Daniel Kawczynski in 2005.

Brian Inglis (1974) was a friend and colleague of Bill Grundy, who died on 9 February 1993. Inglis had just finished writing Grundy's obituary when he himself died two days later.

Alan Civil (1975), regarded as one of the world's most accomplished soloists on the French horn, played the horn solo on The Beatles song *For No One* from the *Revolver* album, and was also part of the orchestral crescendo in *A Day In The Life* from the *Sgt Pepper's Lonely Hearts Club Band* album.

Bing Crosby (1975) proposed to the model and actress Pat Sheehan, but she turned him down. She later married his son, Dennis.

Sir Cecil Beaton (1980) was educated at Heath Mount School, where he was bullied by Evelyn Waugh.

Reginald Goodall (1980) was, in the 1930s, a supporter of Oswald Mosley, leader of the British Union of Fascists. According to his biographer, John Lucas, 'Goodall did not try to cover up his Mosleyite past ... His unwillingness in the immediate aftermath of the Second World War to believe the full extent of the atrocities committed by Nazi Germany seems inexplicable and unnerving.'

Helen Mirren's (1982) grandfather was a Russian aristocrat stranded in London after the 1917 Russian Revolution.

Marvin Hamlisch (1983) is one of only 13 people to have been awarded Emmys, Grammys, Oscars and a Tony. He is also one of only two people (the other is Richard Rodgers) to win those awards and a Pulitzer Prize. Hamlisch also won two Golden Globes.

Baroness Shirley Williams (1986 and 2006) screen-tested for the lead role in *National Velvet* that was won by Elizabeth Taylor.

Cecil Lewis (1991) was, at the time of his death in 1997, the last surviving British flying officer of World War I. He was also a co-founder of the BBC.

Sir Robin Butler (1993) was, early in his Civil Service career, occasionally confused with the politician Rab Butler. Memos for Rab Butler would end up on his desk – and vice versa. Eventually, they agreed that all memos ambiguously addressed to 'R. Butler' should go to Rab's office first, and then Rab's office would send on any intended for the other, very much junior R. Butler. One day, the young Butler received a letter that read: 'You have been selected for the Harlequins 1st XV on Saturday. Please be at Twickenham by 2 p.m.' Underneath, in Rab's distinctive handwriting, was the message: 'Dear Robin, I am not free on Saturday. Please could you deputise for me? Rab.'

Lesley Garrett (1993) was 19 when, to earn money in the summer, she washed dishes at the officers' mess at RAF Lindholme. She received two marriage proposals there.

Christopher Lee (1995) was the only member of the cast (and crew) of *The Lord of the Rings* movies to have met J. R. R. Tolkien.

Sir Richard Doll (2001), the epidemiologist, was one of the first people to prove that smoking causes lung cancer and increases the risk of heart disease.

Courtney Pine (2001) appeared as himself in a jazz quartet in the 1988 *Doctor Who* episode 'Silver Nemesis'.

Paul Gambaccini (2002) was at Oxford University at the same time as Bill Clinton. Of the two, it was Gambaccini who was voted 'The American Most Likely To Succeed'.

Patricia Cornwell (2002) is a descendant of the writer Harriet Beecher Stowe.

Jeremy Clarkson's (2003) mother made her fortune from Paddington Bear merchandise.

Bill Cullen (2003), the businessman and writer, is booked to be one of the first passengers to take a flight into space on Richard Branson's Virgin Galactic service.

George Foreman (2003), boxer and businessman, named all five of his sons George.

Vic Reeves's (2003) father and grandfather share his birthday – and his real name of Jim Moir.

Kristin Scott Thomas's (2003) father, a naval pilot, was killed in a crash when she was five. Her mother married another pilot six years later, but he too was killed in similar circumstances.

Sir Ken Adam (2004) was the only German to fight for the RAF in World War II.

Kim Cattrall (2004) appeared in a school play called *Piffle It's Only a Sniffle* in which she took the role of a cold germ that had to infect the other children by tickling them with a feather until they sneezed.

Richard Griffiths' (2006) parents were both deaf, and he learned sign language at an early age in order to communicate with them.

Pianist **Natasha Spender** (2007) gave a concert at the former Bergen-Belsen concentration camp to inmates who were recovering in its hospital wing.

Randy Newman (2008) revealed how his father, a doctor, had treated The Rolling Stones when they were on tour and had commented that they were 'the whitest men' he had ever seen.

CAST OF
CASTAWAYS

This cast list features all the castaways who appear in this book. Here (as throughout the book), a title or honorific is given only when the castaway had already been awarded it at the time of their appearance on the programme.

Abbado, Claudio, conductor

Abbott, Diane, politician

Abbott, Paul, screenwriter

Abicair, Shirley, singer

Abrahams, Harold, athlete

Abse, Dannie, poet

Ackland, Joss, actor

Acosta, Carlos, dancer

Adam, Sir Ken, film designer and director

Adams, Douglas, author

Adams, Richard, writer

Adams, Tony, footballer

Addams, Dawn, actress

Adie, Kate, broadcaster

Adler, Larry, harmonica player

Adshead, Dr Gwen, forensic psychotherapist

Afshar, Haleh, Baroness, academic

Agate, James, critic

Agutter, Jenny, actress

Aitken, Maria, actress

Alda, Alan, actor

Aldiss, Brian, writer

Aleksander, Professor Igor, expert on neural systems engineering

Ali, Tariq, writer

Al-Khalili, Professor Jim, physicist

Allcard, Edward, yachtsman

Allen, Dave, comedian

Allende, Isabel, writer

Alliss, Peter, golf commentator

Allsop, Kenneth, *Tonight* reporter and writer

Alston, Rex, sports commentator

Alvarez, Al, writer

Amadeus String Quartet, The

Ambrose, bandleader

Amies, Hardy, fashion designer

Amis, Kingsley, writer

Amis, Martin, writer

Anderson, Gillian, actress

Anderson, Lindsay, film director

Anderson, Moira, singer

Andrews, Anthony, actor

Andrews, Archie, ventriloquist's dummy

Andrews, Eamonn, TV presenter

Andrews, Julie, actress and singer

Angelou, Maya, writer

Annan, Lord, academic

Annigoni, Pietro, artist

Antonio, dancer

Archer, Jeffrey, writer

Archer, Mary, scientist

Arlott, John, broadcaster and writer

Armatrading, Joan, singer/songwriter

Armstrong, Louis, jazz trumpeter

Armstrong, Sir Thomas, conductor

Arnold, Eve, photographer

Arnold, Malcolm, composer

Cast of Castaways

Arrau, Claudio, pianist

Ashcroft, Dame Peggy, actress

Ashdown, Paddy, politician

Asher, Jane, actress

Ashkenazy, Vladimir, pianist

Ashley, Jack, Lord, politician

Ashton, Sir Frederick, choreographer

Askey, Arthur, comedian

Aspel, Michael, TV presenter

Asquith, Anthony, film director

Atkins, Eileen, actress

Atkins, Robert, actor

Atkinson, Rowan, actor

Attenborough, Sir David, TV natural historian

Attenborough, Richard, actor and director

Atwell, Winifred, pianist

Atwood, Margaret, writer

Awdry, Rev. W., creator of Thomas the Tank Engine

Ayer, Sir A. J., philosopher

Ayres, Pam, poet

Ayrton, Michael, artist and writer

Aznavour, Charles, singer and actor

Bacall, Lauren, actress

Baddeley, Angela, actress

Baddeley, Hermione, actress

Bader, Sir Douglas, World War II RAF pilot

Baez, Joan, singer/songwriter

Bailey, Bill, comedian

Bailey, David, photographer

Baillie, Isobel, opera singer

Bainbridge, Dame Beryl, writer

Baker, Danny, broadcaster

Baker, George, actor

Baker, Hylda, actress

Baker, Dame Janet, opera singer

Baker, Richard, broadcaster

Bakewell, Dame Joan, broadcaster

Balchin, Nigel, writer

Balcon, Jill, actress

Balcon, Sir Michael, film producer

Ball, Michael, singer and actor

Ballard, J. G., writer

Bankhead, Tallulah, actress

Banks, Iain, writer

Bannatyne, Duncan, businessman

Bannister, Sir Roger, doctor and athlete

Barber, Chris, jazz musician

Barber, Lynn, journalist

Barenboim, Daniel, pianist and conductor

Barker, Eric, comedian

Barker, Pat, writer

Barkworth, Peter, actor

Barnard, Dr Christiaan, heart surgeon

Barnes, Dame Josephine, gynaecologist

Barnes, Julian, writer

Barnett, Lady Isobel, broadcaster

Barrington, Jonah, musician

Barry, John, composer

Barstow, Josephine, opera singer

Barstow, Stan, writer

Bart, Lionel, composer

Bartok, Eva, actress

Basie, Count, bandleader

Bassey, Shirley, singer

Bates, Alan, actor

Bates, H. E., writer

Bath, Henry Thynne, 6th Marquess of, owner of Longleat

Bath, Alexander Thynn, 7th Marquess of, owner of Longleat

Bawden, Nina, writer

Baxter, Raymond, TV presenter

Baxter, Stanley, actor and comedian

Beacham, Stephanie, actress

Beale, Simon Russell, actor

Beaton, Sir Cecil, photographer and designer

Beaux Arts Trio, musicians

Bedford, Sybille, journalist and novelist

Bedser, Alec, cricketer

Beecham, Sir Thomas, conductor

Belafonte, Harry, singer

Belita, actress and skater

Bell, Martin, TV journalist and politician

Bellamy, David, botanist

Beningfield, Gordon, artist and designer

Benn, Tony, politician

Bennett, Alan, playwright and actor

Bennett, Jill, actress

Bennett, Joan, actress

Bennett, Richard Rodney, composer

Bennett, Tony, singer

Benson, Ivy, bandleader

Bentine, Michael, writer and comedian

Bentley, Dick, comedian

Berberian, Cathy, singer

Berkoff, Steven, actor

Berlin, Sir Isaiah, philosopher

Bernard, Jeffrey, writer

Betjeman, Sir John, Poet Laureate

Beverley Sisters, The

Bhaskar, Sanjeev, actor and comedian

Bielenberg, Christabel, writer

Biffen, John, politician

Bilimoria, Karan, businessman

Bilk, Acker, musician

Billington, Rachel, writer

Binchy, Maeve, writer

Bird, Dickie, cricket umpire

Bird, John, actor and comedian

Bird, John, editor of *The Big Issue*

Birtwistle, Sir Harrison, composer

Black, Cilla, singer and TV presenter

Black, Conrad, newspaper proprietor

Black, Don, lyricist

Blackman, Honor, actress

Blackmore, Susan, psychologist

Blackstone, Baroness, academic and politician

Blair, Betsy, actress

Blair, Lionel, dancer and entertainer

Blair, Tony, Leader of the Opposition (became prime minister in 1997)

Blake, Peter, artist

Blake, Quentin, book illustrator

Blakemore, Professor Colin, neurobiologist

Blanc, Raymond, chef

Blanchflower, Danny, footballer

Bland, Sir Christopher, chairman of British Telecom

Blashford-Snell, Lieutenant-Colonel John, explorer

Bleasdale, Alan, playwright

Blessed, Brian, actor

Blethyn, Brenda, actress

Bliss, Sir Arthur, Master of the Queen's Music

Blofeld, Henry, cricket commentator

Bloom, Claire, actress

Bloom, Ursula, writer

Blue, Lionel, Rabbi, broadcaster

Blumberg, Professor Baruch, chemist and Nobel prizewinner

Blumenthal, Heston, chef

Blunkett, David, politician

Blyth, Chay, yachtsman

Board, Lillian, athlete

Boe, Alfie, opera singer

Bogarde, Dirk, actor and writer

Bogdanov, Michael, theatre director

Bolam, James, actor

Bolt, Robert, playwright

Bond, Michael, creator of Paddington Bear

Bonfield, Sir Peter, chief executive of British Telecom

Bonington, Sir Chris, mountaineer

Boorman, John, film director

Booth, Webster, singer

Boothby, Lord, politician and journalist

Boothroyd, Basil, writer

Boothroyd, Betty, politician

Borge, Victor, humorist

Botham, Ian, cricketer

Bottomley, Virginia, politician

Bouchier, Chili, actress

Bough, Frank, TV presenter

Boult, Sir Adrian, conductor

Boulting, John, filmmaker

Boulting, Roy, filmmaker

Bourne, Matthew, choreographer

Boyce, Max, comedian

Boycott, Geoffrey, cricketer

Boyer, Ronnie, ballroom dancer

Boyle, Sir Edward, politician

Brabazon of Tara, Lord, aviation pioneer and politician

Brabham, Jack, Formula One racing driver

Bradbury, Malcolm, writer

Braddon, Russell, writer

Braden, Bernard, broadcaster

Brady, Karren, businesswoman

Bragg, Melvyn, writer and broadcaster

Brain, Dennis, French horn player

Braine, John, writer

Brambell, Wilfrid, actor

Bramwell-Booth, Catherine, Salvation Army commissioner

Brand, Jo, comedian

Brandreth, Gyles, writer, broadcaster and politician

Brannigan, Owen, opera singer, bass

Branson, Richard, businessman

Brasher, Chris, athlete

Bratby, John, painter

Bream, Julian, classical guitarist

Brearley, Mike, cricketer

Breasley, Scobie, jockey

Bremner, Rory, impressionist

Brendel, Alfred, concert pianist

Brenton, Howard, playwright

Briers, Richard, actor

Briggs, Professor Asa, social historian

Briggs, Barry, speedway rider

Briggs, Raymond, writer and illustrator

Brightwell, Robbie, athlete

Brittan, Leon, politician

Britten, Valentine, BBC gramophone librarian

Britton, Tony, actor

Brome, Vincent, writer

Bron, Eleanor, actress

Bronowski, Dr Jacob, scientist and broadcaster

Brooke-Little, John, Richmond Herald of Arms

Brooking, Trevor, footballer

Brooks, Mel, film director and writer

Broome, David, showjumper

Brough, Peter, ventriloquist

Brown, Derek, director of the Michelin Red Guides

Brown, Gordon, Shadow Chancellor (became prime minister in 2007)

Brown, Pamela, actress

Brown, Tina, magazine editor

Browne, Coral, actress

Brubeck, Dave, jazz pianist

Bruce, Brenda, actor

Bruce, Christopher, choreographer

Brunius, Jacques, actor and director

Bruno, Frank, boxer

Bryan, Dora, actress

Bryant, Sir Arthur, historian

Bryant, David, bowls champion

Brydon, Rob, comedian and actor

Bryson, Bill, writer

Buchanan, Jack, actor

Bugner, Joe, boxer

Bull, Peter, actor and teddy bear expert

Bullock, Alan, historian

Bumbry, Grace, opera singer

Burgess, Anthony, writer

Burke, James, TV science presenter

Burke, Kathy, actress and director

Burrows, Eva, general of the Salvation Army

Burrows, Stuart, opera singer

Busch, N., member of the London Philharmonic
Orchestra

Bussell, Darcey, ballerina

Butler, Sir Robin, civil servant

Butlin, Billy, holiday camp pioneer

Buxton, Cindy, film-maker and photographer

Byatt, A. S., writer

Bygraves, Max, singer and comedian

Caballé, Montserrat, opera singer

Cable, Vince, politician

Cadbury, Sir Adrian, businessman

Cahn, Sammy, lyricist

Caine, Marti, comedian

Caine, Sir Michael, actor

Cairoli, Charlie, clown

Cale, John, rock musician

Callaghan, Sir James, former prime minister

Callil, Carmen, publisher

Callow, Simon, actor

Calvert, Eddie, trumpeter

Calvert, Phyllis, actress

Cameron, David, Leader of the Conservative Party (became prime minister 2010)

Campbell, Commander, mariner and explorer

Campbell, Donald, land and water speed record-holder

Campbell, Sir Menzies, politician

Campbell, Nina, interior designer

Camps, Professor Francis, expert on forensic medicine

Cardus, Sir Neville, cricket writer

Carey, Most Rev. Dr George, Archbishop of Canterbury

Carey, Peter, writer

Cargill, Patrick, actor

Carling, Will, Rugby Union player

Carluccio, Antonio, chef

Carman, George, QC

Carmichael, Ian, actor

Caro, Sir Anthony, sculptor

Caron, Leslie, actress

Carpenter, Harry, boxing commentator

Carrier, Robert, chef

Carrington, Lord, politician

Carse, Duncan, actor and explorer

Carson, Jean, actress

Carstairs, John Paddy, film director

Cartland, Barbara, writer

Casson, Sir Hugh, architect, designer

Casson, Sir Lewis, actor and director

Castle, Barbara, politician

Castle, Roy, entertainer

Cattrall, Kim, actress

Cecil, Lord David, man of letters, biographer and teacher

Cecil, Henry, racehorse trainer

Chakrabarti, Shami, director of Liberty

Chamberlain, Richard, actor

Champion, Bob, jockey

Chang, Jung, writer

Channing, Carol, actress

Chapman, Edward, actor

Charlton, Jackie, footballer

Chataway, Christopher, athlete and politician

Cheshire, Group Captain Leonard, founder of Cheshire Homes for the Sick

Chester, Charlie, comedian and broadcaster

Chisholm, George, jazz trombonist

Christie, Sir George, chairman of Glyndebourne

Chula Chakrabongse of Thailand, Prince

Churchill, Sarah, actress

Cilento, Diane, actress

Civil, Alan, French horn player

Clapton, Eric, rock guitarist

Clark, Alan, politician and historian

Clark, Jim, racing driver

Clark, Petula, singer and actress

Clarke, Arthur C., science fiction writer

Clarke, Kenneth, politician

Clarke, Oz, wine expert

Clarke, T. E. B., screenwriter

Clarkson, Jeremy, writer and TV presenter

Clary, Julian, comedian

Clavell, James, writer

Cleese, John, actor, comedian

Clegg, Nick, politician

Clement, Dick, writer

Clements, John, actor and producer

Clifford, Timothy, director-general of the National Galleries of Scotland

Clooney, George, actor

Clunes, Martin, actor

Coates, Eric, composer

Cobbold, David, Lord, owner of Knebworth House

Cobham, Sir Alan, aviation pioneer

Cochran, C. B., showman

Cocker, Jarvis, singer/songwriter

Coe, Sebastian, athlete and politician

Coelho, Paulo, writer

Cogan, Alma, singer

Cole, George, actor

Cole, John, TV political reporter

Collins, Jackie, writer

Collins, Joan, actress

Collins, Pauline, actress

Collins, Phil, singer/songwriter

Coltrane, Robbie, actor

Compton, Denis, cricketer

Compton, Fay, actress

Condon, Richard, writer

Connolly, Billy, comedian and actor

Connolly, Cyril, literary critic

Connor, Kenneth, actor

Conran, Jasper, fashion designer

Conran, Shirley, writer

Conran, Sir Terence, designer and retailer

Constantine, Sir Learie, cricketer

Conteh, John, boxer

Conti, Tom, actor

Conway, Russ, pianist

Coogan, Steve, actor and comedian

Cook, Robin, politician

Cooke, Alistair, broadcaster

Cookson, Dame Catherine, writer

Cooney, Ray, playwright and theatre producer

Cooper, Alice, rock star

Cooper, Lady Diana, writer

Cooper, Dame Gladys, actress

Cooper, Henry, boxer

Cooper, Jilly, writer

Cooper, Joseph, broadcaster and pianist

Copland, Aaron, composer

Corbett, Harry, puppeteer (creator of Sooty and Sweep)

Corbett, Ronnie, comedian and actor

Coren, Alan, writer and humorist

Cornwell, Bernard, writer

Cornwell, Patricia, writer

Costello, Elvis, singer/songwriter

Cotten, Joseph, actor

Cottle, Gerry, circus owner

Cotton, Billy, bandleader

Cottrell Boyce, Frank, writer

Courtenay, Tom, actor

Courtneidge, Cicely, actress

Cousins, Robin, ice-skater

Cousteau, Captain Jacques, underwater explorer

Coutts, General Frederick, international leader of the Salvation Army

Coward, Noël, actor and playwright

Cowdrey, Colin, cricketer

Cowell, Simon, record producer and TV presenter

Cox, Professor Brian, scientist

Cox, Josephine, writer

Cradock, Fanny, TV cookery presenter

Cradock, Johnnie, food and wine expert

Craig, Charles, opera singer

Craig, Michael, actor

Craig, Wendy, actress

Craven, Gemma, actress

Crawford, Michael, actor

Crewe, Quentin, writer

Cribbins, Bernard, actor

Critchley, Julian, politician

Croft, David, TV producer and writer

Crosby, Bing, singer and actor

Crowther, Leslie, TV presenter

Cruickshank, Andrew, actor

Cryer, Barry, writer and comedian

Cullen, Bill, TV gameshow presenter

Cummings, Constance, actress

Cummins, Peggy, actress

Cuneo, Terence, painter

Currie, Finlay, actor

Curry, John, ice-skater

Curtis, Richard, screenwriter and film director

Curzon, Sir Clifford, pianist

Cusack, Sinéad, actress

Cushing, Peter, actor

Cutforth, René, broadcaster

Dacre, Paul, newspaper editor

Dahl, Roald, writer

Dahrendorf, Sir Ralf, academic

Dallaglio, Lawrence, Rugby Union player

Dance, Charles, actor

Dangerfield, Stanley, dog show judge

Daniel, Paul, conductor

Daniels, Bebe, actress

Dankworth, John, jazz musician

Darzi, Professor Ara, Lord, surgeon and politician

Davies, Andrew, screenwriter

Davies, George, clothing designer and retailer

Davies, Professor Dame Kay, geneticist

Davies, Rupert, actor

Davis, Andrew, conductor

Davis, Carl, composer and conductor

Davis, Sir Colin, conductor

Davis, David, politician

Davis, Joe, snooker player

Davis, Steve, snooker player

Davis, William, magazine editor

Dawkins, Professor Richard, biologist and writer

Dawson, Les, comedian

Day, Frances, actor

Day, Sir Robin, TV political interviewer

Day-Lewis, Cecil, Poet Laureate

de Burgh, Chris, singer

de Casalis, Jeanne, actress

de Gurr St George, Vivian, Piccadilly shoeblack

de los Ángeles, Victoria, opera singer

de Manio, Jack, broadcaster

de Valois, Dame Ninette, ballerina

Dean, Basil, theatre producer

Deedes, William, Lord, journalist and politician

Deeley, Michael, film producer

Deighton, Len, writer

Del Mar, Norman, conductor

Delderfield, R. F., writer

Delfont, Sir Bernard, theatre impresario

Dench, Dame Judi, actress

Denis, Armand, explorer

Denis, Michaela, explorer

Denison, Michael, actor

Denning, Alfred Thompson, Lord, judge

Dennis, Felix, publisher

Dettori, Frankie, jockey

Devonshire, Duchess of, chatelaine of Chatsworth

Devonshire, Duke of, owner of Chatsworth

Dexter, Colin, writer

di Stefano, Giuseppe, opera singer

Dibnah, Fred, steeplejack

Dickens, Monica, writer

Dickson, Barbara, singer and actress

Dickson, Dorothy, actress and singer

Dickson Wright, Clarissa, TV presenter

Dietrich, Marlene, actress and singer

Dimbleby, David, broadcaster and journalist

Dimbleby, Richard, broadcaster and journalist

Dingle, Captain, explorer

Distel, Sacha, singer and musician

Djerassi, Carl, inventor of the contraceptive pill and writer

Dobson, Anita, actress

Dodd, Ken, comedian

Dolin, Sir Anton, ballet dancer and choreographer

Doll, Sir Richard, epidemiologist

Domingo, Placido, opera singer

Dominica, Sister Frances, pioneer of the hospice movement

Don, Monty, TV gardening presenter

Donlan, Yolande, actress

Donleavy, J. P., writer

Donoughue, Lord, politician and businessman

Doonican, Val, singer and TV presenter

Dorati, Antal, conductor

Dorita, Latin-American folk singer

Dors, Diana, actress

Dotrice, Roy, actor

Dougall, Robert, TV newsreader

Douglas-Home, Sir Alec, former prime minister

Douglas-Home, William, playwright

Dove, Rita, poet

Dowell, Sir Anthony, ballet dancer

Downes, Edward, conductor

Drabble, Margaret, writer

Drabble, Phil, naturalist

Drake, Charlie, actor and comedian

Dreyfuss, Richard, actor

Driberg, Tom, politician and journalist

Driver, Betty, actress

du Maurier, Dame Daphne, writer

du Pré, Jacqueline, cellist

Duncan Smith, Iain, politician

Dunn, Clive, actor

Dunn, Lieutenant-Colonel Sir Vivian, music
director of Royal Marines

Dunwoody, Richard, jockey

Durbridge, Francis, playwright

Durrell, Gerald, writer

Dury, Ian, singer/songwriter

Dyall, Valentine, actor

Dyke, Greg, BBC director-general

Dyson, James, businessman

Eavis, Michael, Glastonbury Festival founder

Eco, Umberto, writer

Eddington, Paul, actor

Edelmann, Anton, chef

Edgar, David, playwright

Edmonds, Frances, writer

Edmonds, Noel, TV presenter

Edmonds, Phil, cricketer and businessman

Edrich, Bill, cricketer

Edwards, Arthur, newspaper photographer

Edwards, Gareth, Rugby Union player

Edwards, Jimmy, comedian and actor

Edwards, Percy, animal imitator

Ekland, Britt, actress

Elder, Mark, director of English National Opera

Elkins, Michael, foreign correspondent

Elliott, Denholm, actor

Elliott, Rev. Canon W. H., Precentor of the Chapels Royal

Ellis, Mary, actress and singer

Ellison, Rt Hon. and Rt Rev. Gerald, Bishop of London

Ellroy, James, writer

Elton, Ben, writer and comedian

Emery, Dick, comedian and actor

Emett, Rowland, cartoonist

Emin, Tracey, artist

Emney, Fred, actor

Enfield, Harry, comedian and writer

English, Arthur, actor

Eno, Brian, musician

Epstein, Brian, manager of The Beatles

Essex, David, singer and actor

Esteve-Coll, Elizabeth, director of the Victoria and Albert Museum

Evans, Chris, broadcaster

Evans, Dame Edith, actress

Evans, Geraint, opera singer

Evans, Harold, newspaper editor

Everage, Dame Edna, housewife and superstar

Everett, Kenny, DJ and comedian

Ewing, Maria, opera singer

Eyre, Richard, theatre director

Eyre, Ronald, playwright

Fabian, Robert, police detective

Fairbairn, T. C., impresario

Fairbanks Jr, Douglas, actor

Faith, Adam, singer and actor

Faithfull, Marianne, singer

Fame, Georgie, singer

Farrar, David, actor

Fassett, Kaffe, artist

Faulks, Sebastian, writer

Fearnley-Whittingstall, Hugh, food writer

Feldman, Marty, actor

Fellowes, Julian, actor and writer

Fenton, Professor James, poet

Ffrangcon-Davies, Gwen, actress

Field, Shirley Anne, actress

Fielding, Fenella, actress

Fields, Dame Gracie, actress and singer

Fiennes, Ralph, actor

Fiennes, Sir Ranulph, explorer

Finch, Peter, actor

Fine, Anne, writer

Firth, Colin, actor

Fisk, Robert, foreign correspondent

Flanagan, Bud, singer and comedian

Flanders, Michael, actor and songwriter

Fleming, Ian, writer

Fleming, Peter, writer and explorer

Fleming, Renée, opera singer

Fletcher, Cyril, TV presenter

Floyd, Keith, TV cookery presenter

Fluck, Peter, co-creator of *Spitting Image*

Fogle, Bruce, vet

Follett, Ken, writer

Fontaine, Joan, actress

Fonteyn, Dame Margot, ballerina

Foot, Michael, politician

Forbes, Bryan, actor

Foreman, George, boxer

Forman, Sir Denis, chairman of Granada TV

Formby, George, comedian and ukulele player

Forster, Margaret, writer

Forsyth, Bruce, TV presenter and entertainer

Forsyth, Frederick, writer

Forte, Rocco, hotelier

Fortune, John, actor and comedian

Foster, Brendan, athlete

Foster, Julia, actress

Fowler, Eileen, physical exercise instructor

Fowles, John, writer

Fox, Edward, actor

Fox, James, actor

Foyle, Christina, businesswoman and bookseller

Francis, Clare, yachtswoman and writer

Francis, Dick, writer

Fraser, Lady Antonia, writer

Fraser, Bill, actor

Frayling, Sir Christopher, rector of the Royal College of Art

Frears, Stephen, film director

Frederik, singer

Freeman, John, TV presenter, diplomat and politician

Freni, Mirella, opera singer

Freud, Clement, broadcaster and politician

Frink, Elisabeth, sculptor

Frost, Sir David, TV presenter

Frost, Sir Terry, painter

Fry, Christopher, playwright

Fry, Stephen, actor and writer

Fuller, Rosalinde, actress

Gable, Christopher, actor

Galbraith, Professor J. K., economist

Gallico, Paul, writer

Galway, James, classical flautist

Gambaccini, Paul, broadcaster

Gambon, Michael, actor

Gardiner, John Eliot, conductor

Gardner, Frank, BBC security correspondent

Garrett, Lesley, opera singer

Gascoigne, Bamber, writer and broadcaster

Gaskin, Catherine, writer

Gatiss, Mark, actor and comedian

Gedda, Nicolai, opera singer

Geldof, Bob, musician and campaigner

Genn, Leo, actor

George, Boy, singer

George, Susan, actress

Gervais, Ricky, actor, comedian and writer

Gibberd, Sir Frederick, engineer and architect

Gibson, Wing Commander Guy, VC,
World War II RAF pilot

Gibson, William, writer

Gielgud, Sir John, actor

Gielgud, Val, head of BBC Radio Drama

Gilbert, Lewis, film director

Gilbert, Martin, historian

Gill, A. A., critic and columnist

Gillespie, Dizzy, jazz trumpeter

Gilliam, Terry, animator and film director

Gilliat, Sidney, film-maker

Gilmour, David, rock guitarist

Gingold, Hermione, actress

Glendenning, Raymond, sports commentator

Glennie, Evelyn, percussionist

Glitter, Gary, singer

Glover, Brian, actor

Glover, Jane, conductor

Glubb, Sir John, soldier

Gluckstein, Sir Louis, president of Royal
Albert Hall

Gobbi, Tito, opera singer

Godden, Rumer, writer

Godfree, Kitty, tennis player

Goldberg, Whoopi, actress

Goldsmith, Harvey, impresario and promoter

Gollancz, Victor, publisher

Goodall, Howard, composer

Goodall, Dr Jane, primatologist and naturalist

Goodall, Reginald, conductor

Goodhew, Duncan, swimmer

Goodman, Len, dance instructor

Goodman, Lord, lawyer

Goodwin, Denis, comedy scriptwriter

Goodwin, Ron, musician and composer

Goossens, Sidonie, harpist

Gordievsky, Oleg, KGB colonel

Gordon, Richard, doctor and writer

Goring, Marius, actor

Gormley, Anthony, sculptor

Gower, David, cricketer and broadcaster

Grace of Monaco, Princess, actress and member of Monaco royal family

Grade, Sir Lew, TV executive

Grade, Michael, TV executive

Graham, Rev. John, crossword compiler

Graham, Winston, writer

Grainer, Ron, composer

Granger, Stewart, actor

Grant, Hugh, actor

Grantham, Leslie, actor

Grappelli, Stephane, violinist

Gray, Dulcie, actress

Gray, Linda Esther, opera singer

Grayling, Professor A. C., philosopher

Greco, Juliette, singer

Green, Benny, writer and broadcaster

Green, Felicity, fashion journalist

Green, Hughie, TV presenter

Green, Michael, TV executive

Greene, Sir Hugh, former director-general of the BBC

Greenfield, Dr Susan, neuroscientist

Greenwood, Joan, actress

Greer, Germaine, writer and academic

Gregg, Hubert, actor and playwright

Gregson, John, actor

Greig, Tony, cricketer

Grenfell, Joyce, actress and writer

Grey, Anthony, foreign correspondent

Grey, Dame Beryl, ballerina

Grey Thompson, Tanni, paralympian, athlete, gold medallist

Griffith, Hugh, actor

Griffiths, Richard, actor

Grigson, Geoffrey, poet and critic

Grigson, Jane, cookery writer

Cast of Castaways

Grimshaw, Sir Nicholas, architect

Grinham, Judy, swimmer

Grisewood, Frederick, broadcaster

Grossman, Loyd, writer and TV presenter

Grylls, Bear, explorer and broadcaster

Gryn, Rabbi Hugo, Holocaust survivor

Guest, George, organist

Guinness, Sir Alec, actor

Guthrie, Tyrone, theatre director

Guyler, Deryck, actor

Hacker, Alan, clarinettist, composer and conductor

Hackett, General Sir John, soldier and writer

Hadow, Pen, explorer

Hague, William, politician

Hailey, Arthur, writer

Hale, Binnie, actress and musician

Hale, Kathleen, children's writer and illustrator

Hale, Lionel, critic, broadcaster and playwright

Hale, Sonnie, actor, writer and director

Hall, Adelaide, jazz singer

Hall, Henry, bandleader

Hall, Sir Peter, theatre director

Halsley, Professor A. H., sociologist

Hamilton, Andy, comedian and writer

Hamlisch, Marvin, composer

Hammond, Joan, opera singer

Hammond, Kay, actress

Hamnett, Katherine, fashion designer

Hampshire, Susan, actress

Hampton, Christopher, playwright

Hampton, Lionel, jazz musician

Hanbury-Tenison, Robert, explorer

Hancock, Sheila, actress

Hancock, Tony, comedian and actor

Handl, Irene, actress

Hands, Terry, theatre director and producer

Hanff, Helene, writer

Hansford Johnson, Pamela, novelist and
broadcaster

Hardcastle, William, journalist and broadcaster

Harding, Mike, musician and comedian

Hardwicke, Sir Cedric, actor

Hardy, Robert, actor

Hare, David, playwright

Hare, Doris, actress

Hare, Robertson, actor

Harewood, Earl of, managing director of the ENO

Harker, Gordon, actor

Harle, John, saxophonist

Harper, Gerald, actor

Harper, Heather, opera singer

Harris, Emmylou, singer

Harris, Mollie, actress and writer

Harris, Robert, writer

Harris, Rolf, artist, singer and TV presenter

Harrison, Kathleen, actress

Harrison, Rex, actor

Harrison, Rosina, Lady Astor's lady's maid

Harrisson, Tom, anthropologist

Harry, Debbie, singer

Hartnell, William, actor

Harty, Russell, TV presenter

Harvey, Laurence, actor

Harvey-Jones, Sir John, businessman

Harwood, Ronald, playwright

Haskins, Chris, businessman

Haslam, Nicky, interior designer

Hastings, MacDonald, journalist and broadcaster

Hastings, Max, newspaper editor and journalist

Hathaway, Dame Sybil, Dame of Sark

Hattersley, Roy, politician and writer

Hawking, Professor Stephen, physicist

Hawkins, Desmond, founder of BBC Natural History Unit

Hawthorne, Nigel, actor

Hay, Roy, horticulturalist

Haydon-Jones, Ann, tennis player

Hayes, Patricia, actress

Haynes, Arthur, comedian

Heal, Joan, actor and comedian

Healey, Denis, Lord, politician

Heaney, Seamus, writer

Heath, Edward, former prime minister

Hegarty, John, advertising executive

Helfgott, Ben, athlete and Holocaust campaigner

Helpmann, Sir Robert, ballet dancer and choreographer

Hemmings, David, actor

Hempleman Adams, David, explorer

Henderson, Dickie, comedian

Henderson, Sir Nicholas, diplomat

Hendry, Ian, actor

Henriques, Robert, novelist and broadcaster

Henry, Lenny, actor and comedian

Henshall, Ruthie, actress

Herbage, Julian, musicologist

Herbert, Sir Alan P., writer and politician

Herbert, James, writer

Herbert, Wally, polar explorer

Herman, Woody, bandleader

Herriot, James, vet and writer

Heseltine, Michael, politician

Heston, Charlton, actor

Heyerdahl, Dr Thor, anthropologist and writer

Heyhoe, Rachael, cricketer

Heywood, Anne, actress

Hicks, David, interior designer

Higgins, Jack, writer

Highsmith, Patricia, writer

Hildegarde, cabaret singer

Hill, Benny, comedian and actor

Hill, Graham, Formula One racing driver

Hill, Susan, writer

Hillary, Sir Edmund, mountaineer

Hiller, Dame Wendy, actress

Hillier, Bevis, writer

Hines, Earl, 'Fatha', jazz pianist

Hird, Thora, actress

Hislop, Ian, *Private Eye* editor and satirist

Hitchcock, Alfred, film director

Hobson, Harold, drama critic

Hobson, Valerie, actress

Hockney, David, artist

Hodge, Patricia, actress

Hoffnung, Gerard, artist, comedian and musician

Hogg, Quintin (Lord Hailsham), Conservative politician

Hoggart, Richard, academic and writer

Holgate, Virginia, equestrian

Holland, Jools, musician

Holloway, Stanley, actor and comedian

Holmes, Dame Kelly, athlete

Holroyd, Michael, writer

Holst, Imogen, conductor and musicologist

Holt, Thelma, theatre producer

Hooker, John Lee, blues guitarist

Hope, Bob, actor and singer

Hopkins, Anthony, actor

Hopper, Christopher, manager of the Royal Albert Hall

Hordern, Sir Michael, actor

Horlick, Nicola, businesswoman

Hornby, Nick, writer

Horne, Kenneth, comedian

Horowitz, Anthony, writer

Horrocks, Jane, actress

Hosking, Eric, ornithologist and photographer

Hoskins, Bob, actor

Household, Geoffrey, writer

Houston, Renée, actress

Howard, Alan, actor

Howard, Anthony, broadcaster

Howard, Elizabeth Jane, writer

Howard, Leslie, actor

Howard, Michael, politician

Howard, Trevor, actor

Howe, Sir Geoffrey, politician

Howerd, Frankie, comedian

Howes, Bobby, actor and comedian

Howes, Sally Ann, actress

Hoyle, Sir Fred, astrophysicist and astronomer

Hudd, Roy, actor and comedian

Huddleston, Bishop Trevor, president of the Anti-Apartheid Movement

Hughes, David, opera singer

Hughes, Shirley, children's writer and illustrator

Hulbert, Jack, actor

Hull, Rod, comedian

Humperdinck, Engelbert, singer

Humphries, Barry, comedian and performer

Humphrys, John, broadcaster

Hunniford, Gloria, TV presenter

Hunter, Rita, opera singer

Hurd, Douglas, politician

Hurt, John, actor

Huston, John, film director

Hutchinson, Maxwell, architect

Hutton, Sir Leonard, cricketer

Huxley, Elspeth, writer

Hyde-White, Wilfrid, actor

Hylton, Jack, bandleader

Hytner, Nicholas, theatre director

Iannucci, Armando, director and writer

Idle, Eric, *Monty Python* comedian

Ifield, Frank, singer

Illingworth, Leslie Gilbert, artist and political cartoonist

Imrie, Celia, actress

Ingham, Sir Bernard, Margaret Thatcher's press secretary

Inglis, Brian, writer and broadcaster

Ingrams, Richard, editor and writer

Innes, Hammond, writer

Irons, Jeremy, actor

Ironside, Virginia, agony aunt

Irvine, Lucy, explorer and writer

Isaacs, Jeremy, TV executive

Ishiguro, Kazuo, writer

Isserlis, Steven, cellist

Ives, Burl, singer and actor

Iveson, Tony, World War II RAF pilot

Ivory, James, film director

Jackson, Betty, fashion designer

Jackson, Glenda, actress and politician

Jackson, Gordon, actor

Jackson, Jack, bandleader, radio presenter

Jacobi, Derek, actor

Jacobs, David, broadcaster

Jacobson, Howard, writer

Jacobson, Maurice, music festivals adjudicator

Jacques, Hattie, actress

Jacques, Dr Reginald, conductor and musicologist

Jaeger, Lieutenant Colonel C.H., senior director of music, Brigade of Guards

Jaffrey, Madhur, cookery writer and actress

Jaffrey, Saeed, actor

James, Clive, broadcaster and writer

James, Geraldine, actress

James, P. D., writer

James, Sidney, actor

Jameson, Derek, journalist and broadcaster

Jason, David, actor

Jay, Joan, fashion glamour girl

Jeans, Isabel, actress

Jeans, Ursula, actress

Jefford, Barbara, actress

Jenkins, Clive, trade unionist

Jenkins, Karl, jazz musician and composer

Jenkins, Roy, politician

Jenner, Heather, owner of a marriage bureau

Jewel, Jimmy, comedian and actor

Joffe, Lord, lawyer and Labour peer

John, Barry, Rugby Union player

John, Elton, singer/songwriter

Johns, Glynis, actress

Johns, Stratford, actor

Johnson, Alan, politician

Johnson, Boris, politician

Johnson, Dame Celia, actress

Johnson, Linton Kwesi, poet

Johnson, Michael, athlete

Johnson, Paul, writer and historian

Johnston, Brian, broadcaster

Johnston, Sue, actor

Jonas, Peter, director of the ENO

Jones, Alan, racing driver

Jones, Sir Digby, director-general of the CBI

Jones, Freddie, actor

Jones, Paul, singer and musician

Jones, Peter, actor

Jones, Dr Steve, geneticist and broadcaster

Jones, Terry, comedian, writer

Jones, Tom, singer

Jones, Tristan, sailor

Jordan, Neil, film director

Joyce, C. A., prison worker

Joyce, Eileen, concert pianist

Julius, Anthony, lawyer and writer

Kalms, Sir Stanley, businessman

Karlin, Miriam, actress

Karsavina, Tamara, ballerina

Kavanagh, P. J., writer

Kavanagh, Ted, writer

Kaye, Gorden, actor

Kaye, M. M., writer

Kaye, Stubby, actor

Kazan, Elia, film director

Keane, Molly, writer

Keating, Tom, painter and restorer

Keegan, John, military historian

Keenan, Brian, writer and former hostage

Keillor, Garrison, writer and broadcaster

Keith, Alan, broadcaster

Keith, Penelope, actress

Kellino, Pamela, actress and writer

Kelly, Barbara, broadcaster

Kelly, Margaret – Miss Bluebell, dancer

Kempson, Rachel, Lady Redgrave, actress

Kendal, Felicity, actress

Kendall, Henry, actor and director

Keneally, Thomas, writer

Kennedy, Charles, politician

Kennedy, Helena, human rights lawyer

Kennedy, Ludovic, TV presenter

Kennedy, Nigel, violinist

Kent, Duchess of, member of the royal family

Kent, Jean, actress

Kentner, Louis, concert pianist

Kenton, Stan, bandleader

Kenward, Betty, magazine journalist

Kenwright, Bill, theatre producer

Kermode, Sir Frank, literary critic

Kerr, Deborah, actress

Kerr, Graham, chef and broadcaster

Kerr, Judith, children's writer and illustrator

Kershaw, Andy, broadcaster

Khan, Imran, cricketer and politician

Kidman, Nicole, actress

Kidston, Cath, fashion designer

Killanin, Lord, Olympics administrator

King, Dave, comedian and actor

King, Sir David, chief scientific adviser

King, Hetty, comedian

King, Lord, head of British Airways

King, Stephen, writer

King-Hall, Commander Sir Stephen, sailor
and writer

Kingsley, Ben, actor

Kinnock, Glenys, politician

Kinnock, Neil, politician

Kipnis, Igor, harpsichordist

Kirkwood, Pat, actress

Kitt, Eartha, actress and singer

Knapp, Jimmy, trade unionist

Knight, Esmond, actor

Knox-Johnston, Robin, yachtsman

Koch, Dr Ludwig, scientist and ornithologist

Kohn, Ralph, businessman and singer

Kossoff, David, actor and broadcaster

Kretzmer, Herbert, journalist and lyricist

Kuchmy, J., member of the London Philharmonic
Orchestra

Kureishi, Hanif, writer

La Frenais, Ian, writer

La Plante, Lynda, TV screenwriter

La Rue, Danny, entertainer

Ladenis, Nico, chef

Laine, Dame Cleo, singer

Laird, Gavin, trade unionist

Laker, Jim, cricketer

Lambton, Lady Lucinda, photographer

Lancaster, Sir Osbert, cartoonist

Landen, Dinsdale, actor

Landesman, Fran, poet

Lane, Carla, writer, comedian

Lane, Lupino, comedian

Lane Fox, Martha, businesswoman

Lang Lang, pianist

Lapotaire, Jane, actress

Larkin, Philip, poet

Lasdun, Sir Denys, architect

Laski, Marghanita, critic and writer

Launder, Frank, filmmaker

Laurie, Hugh, actor, comedian

Laurie, John, actor

Leith, Prue, cookery writer

Lejeune, C. A., critic

Lemmon, Jack, actor

Lennox, Annie, singer

Leppard, Raymond, conductor

Lerner, Alan Jay, composer

Leslie, Ann, journalist

Lessing, Doris, writer

Lester, Richard, film director

Levin, Bernard, journalist

Levy, Andrea, writer

Lewis, Cecil, writer and explorer

Liberace, pianist and entertainer

Libeskind, Daniel, engineer and architect

Lichfield, Patrick, photographer

Liddell, Alvar, broadcaster

Lill, John, concert pianist

Lillie, Beatrice, actress

Lindsay, Robert, actor

Lineker, Gary, footballer

Linley, Viscount, furniture maker

Lipman, Maureen, actress and writer

Lister, Moira, actress

Little, Tasmin, violinist

Lively, Penelope, writer

Livesey, Roger, actor

Livingstone, Ken, politician

Lloyd, George, composer

Lloyd, Hugh, actor

Lloyd, Jeremy, TV situation comedy writer

Lloyd Webber, Sir Andrew, composer

Lloyd Webber, Julian, cellist

Loach, Ken, film director

Lockwood, Margaret, actress

Lodge, David, academic and writer

Lom, Herbert, actor

Loman, Harry, stage-door keeper

Longford, Elizabeth, Countess of, writer and biographer

Longford, Lord, politician and campaigner

Longhurst, Henry, journalist and golf expert

Loss, Joe, bandleader

Loughran, James, conductor

Loussier, Jacques, pianist

Lovell, Sir Bernard, director of the Jodrell Bank Experimental Station

Lovelock, James, Gaia scientist

Lowe, Arthur, actor

Lubbock, Mark, conductor and composer

Lucas, Matt, comedian and actor

Lulu, singer and actress

Lumley, Joanna, actress

Lustgarten, Edgar, crime writer

Lyall, Gavin, writer

Lympany, Moura, pianist

Lynam, Des, broadcaster

Lynn, Jonathan, writer, film director and actor

Lynn, Dame Vera, singer

Lyon, Ben, comedian

Lyttelton, Humphrey, jazz trumpeter and broadcaster

Maazel, Lorin, conductor

Mabey, Richard, naturalist and writer

MacArthur, Dame Ellen, round-the-world yachtswoman

MacDonald Fraser, George, writer

MacGregor, Joanna, concert pianist

MacGregor, Sue, broadcaster

MacGregor-Hastie, Roy, historian and writer

Mackenzie, Sir Compton, writer

Mackerras, Sir Charles, conductor

Mackintosh, Sir Cameron, theatre producer

Maclaine, Shirley, actress

MacLean, Sir Charles, chief scout of the Commonwealth

MacLean, Sir Fitzroy, soldier, diplomat and writer

MacManus, Emily, retired matron

MacMillan, Sir Kenneth, choreographer

MacPherson, Sandy, theatre organist

Madeley, Richard, TV presenter

Magnusson, Magnus, broadcaster

Mailer, Norman, writer

Major, John, prime minister

Major, Dame Norma, wife of the former prime minister and writer

Makarova, Natalia, ballerina

Malcolm, George, harpsichordist, conductor and organist

Malkovich, John, actor

Mallalieu, Ann, QC, politician and lawyer

Mander, Raymond, theatre historian

Manilow, Barry, singer

Manning, Olivia, writer

Manningham-Buller, Dame Elizabeth, head of MI5

Mansfield, Michael, QC, barrister

Mansfield, Sir Peter, physicist

Mantovani, musician

Marceau, Marcel, mime artist

Margaret, Princess, member of the royal family

Margolyes, Miriam, actress

Mark, Sir Robert, head of the Metropolitan Police

Markova, Dame Alicia, ballerina

Marks, Alfred, actor

Marsh, Dame Ngaio, writer

Marshall, Arthur, broadcaster

Marshall, Wayne, organist, conductor and composer

Martin, George, record producer

Martin, Mary, actress and singer

Martin, Millicent, singer and actress

Marx, Robert, underwater archaeologist

Maschler, Fay, restaurant critic

Maschwitz, Eric, musician and lyricist

Masekela, Hugh, trumpeter

Maskell, Dan, tennis commentator

Mason, James, actor

Mason, Monica, director of the Royal Ballet

Massey, Anna, actress

Massey, Daniel, actor

Mathieson, Muir, conductor

Mathis, Johnny, singer

Matthews, Jessie, actress and singer

Maupin, Armistead, writer

Maxwell Davies, Sir Peter, composer

Maxwell, Robert, businessman

May, Brian, rock guitarist

Mayer, Sir Robert, music patron

Mayerl, Billy, pianist

Mayle, Peter, writer

Mays, Raymond, car designer and racing driver

McBain, Ed, writer

McCall Smith, Alexander, writer

McCartney, Paul, singer/songwriter

McCormack, Mark, sports agent

McCourt, Frank, writer

McCowen, Alec, actor

McCrum, Robert, writer

McCullin, Don, news photographer

McDonald, Trevor, TV news reader

McEwan, Geraldine, actress

McEwan, Ian, writer

McGough, Roger, poet

McGovern, Jimmy, writer

McGregor, Ewan, actor

McIntyre, Michael, comedian

McKellar, Kenneth, singer

McKellen, Sir Ian, actor

McKenna, Paul, hypnotist and writer

McKenna, Virginia, actress

McKenzie, Julia, actress and singer

McKern, Leo, actor

McMillan, Ian, stand-up poet

McNab, Andy, soldier and writer

McWhirter, Norris, *Guinness Book of Records* co–creator

Mehta, Zubin, conductor

Melchett, Peter, executive director of Greenpeace

Mellor, David, politician

Melly, George, jazz musician

Menotti, Gian Carlo, composer

Menuhin, Hephzibah, concert pianist

Menuhin, Yehudi, violinist

Merchant, Ismail, film producer

Merton, Paul, comedian

Messel, Oliver, stage designer

Meyer, Sir Christopher, diplomat

Michael, George, singer/songwriter

Michael of Kent, Princess, member of the royal family

Michell, Keith, actor

Miles, Bernard, actor

Miles, Sarah, actress

Miller, Sir Jonathan, doctor, writer and director

Miller, Max, comedian

Miller, Mitch, oboist

Miller, Ruby, actress

Milligan, Spike, writer and comedian

Mills, Cyril, circus director

Mills, Freddie, boxer

Mills, Mrs Gladys, pianist

Mills, Hayley, actress

Mills, Sir John, actor

Milnes, Sherrill, opera singer

Milnes-Walker, Nicolette, sailor

Minghella, Anthony, film director

Minter, Alan, boxer

Moore, Christy, singer/songwriter

Moore, Dudley, actor, comedian and musician

Moore, Gerald, pianist

Moore, Sir Patrick, astronomer

Moore, Roger, actor

More, Kenneth, actor

Morecambe, Eric, comedian

Morgan, Cliff, Rugby Union player and broadcaster

Morgan, Piers, broadcaster and journalist

Morley, Robert, actor

Morley, Sheridan, critic and writer

Morpurgo, Michael, writer

Morris, Bill, trade unionist

Morris, Dr Desmond, anthropologist and writer

Morris, Jan, writer

Morris, Johnny, broadcaster and traveller

Morrissey, singer/songwriter

Mortimer, Sir John, lawyer and writer

Moser, Sir Claus, academic and public servant

Moshinsky, Elijah, film director

Mosimann, Anton, chef

Mosley, Diana, Lady, Mitford sister
(widow of Sir Oswald Mosley)

Moss, Pat, showjumper and rally driver

Moss, Stirling, motor racing driver

Motion, Andrew, poet and biographer

Moult, Ted, farmer and broadcaster

Mount, Peggy, actress

Mouskouri, Nana, singer

Mowlam, Mo, politician

Muggeridge, Malcolm, writer and broadcaster

Muir, Frank, broadcaster and TV presenter

Mullen, Barbara, actress

Mulville, Jimmy, comedian and actor

Munro, Matt, singer

Murdoch, Richard, comedian

Murphy-O'Connor, Most Rev. Cardinal Cormac,
Archbishop of Westminster,

Murray, Barbara, actress

Murray, Les, poet

Mutter, Anne-Sophie, violinist

Naipaul, V. S., writer

Neagle, Anna, actress

Neal, Patricia, actress

Neel, Boyd, conductor

Negus, Arthur, antiques expert

Neil, Andrew, broadcaster

Nesbitt, Cathleen, actress

Nesbitt, James, actor

Neville, John, actor

Newby, Eric, travel writer

Newley, Anthony, actor and singer

Newman, Andrea, writer

Newman, Randy, singer/songwriter

Nicholls, Agnes, opera singer

Nichols, Beverley, writer

Nichols, Dandy, actress

Nichols, Joy, actress

Nichols, Peter, playwright

Nickalls, G. O., oarsman

Nicolson, Nigel, politician and writer

Nighy, Bill, actor

Nilsson, Birgit, opera singer

Nimmo, Derek, actor and broadcaster

Nina, singer

Niven, David, actor

Nixon, David, magician

Noakes, John, TV presenter

Noble, Adrian, theatre director

Noble, Christina, children's campaigner

Noble, Dennis, opera singer

Noble, Richard, land speed record-breaker

Noon, Sir Gulam, businessman

Norden, Denis, writer and TV presenter

Norman, Archie, businessman

Norman, Barry, broadcaster and writer

Norman, Jessye, opera singer

Norman, Sir Torquil, aviator and inventor

Northcote Parkinson, C., historian

Norton, Graham, TV presenter and comedian

Norwich, John Julius, writer and broadcaster

Nunn, Sir Trevor, theatre director

Nyman, Michael, composer

O'Brien, Edna, writer

O'Connor, Des, singer and entertainer

O'Grady, Paul, comedian and TV presenter

O'Hanlon, Redmond, explorer and writer

O'Hara, Mary, singer

O'Neill, Terry, photographer

O'Shea, Tessie, singer

O'Sullevan, Sir Peter, horseracing commentator

O'Sullivan, Maureen, actress

Oaksey, Lord, horseracing writer and commentator

Ogdon, John, concert pianist

Oldfield, Bruce, fashion designer

Oliver, Jamie, chef

Oliver, Vic, comedian

Ondaatje, Christopher, writer

Ono, Yoko, artist and musician

Osborne, John, playwright

Owen, Dr David, politician

Oz, Frank, *Muppet Show* performer

Paige, Elaine, actress and singer

Paisley, Rev. Ian, politician

Palin, Michael, comedian and TV presenter

Palmer, Geoffrey, actor

Palmer, Lilli, actress

Palmer, Rex, broadcaster

Paolozzi, Sir Eduardo, sculptor

Pappano, Antonio, conductor

Pardoe, John, politician

Park, Nick, animator

Parker, Alan, film director

Parker, Cecil, actor

Parker, Cornelia, artist

Parker, Sir Peter, head of British Rail

Parkin, Molly, writer

Parkinson, Michael, TV presenter

Parnell, Jack, bandleader

Parry, M., member of the London
Philharmonic Orchestra

Parsons, Nicholas, broadcaster

Pascoe, Alan, athlete

Patrick, Nigel, actor

Patten, Chris, politician and former governor of Hong Kong

Patten, Marguerite, cookery writer and broadcaster

Paul, June, athlete

Pavarotti, Luciano, opera singer

Pears, Sir Peter, opera singer

Pearson, Alf, singer

Pearson, Bob, singer

Pedrick, Gale, journalist and scriptwriter

Peel, John, broadcaster

Pegler, Alan, owner of the *Flying Scotsman*

Peña, Paco, flamenco guitarist

Penhaligon, David, politician

Penrose, Sir Roger, mathematician

Pepe, Latin-American folk singer

Perlman, Itzhak, violinist

Perry, Frances, horticulturalist

Perry, Grayson, potter

Pertwee, Jon, actor

Perutz, Dr Max, chemist and molecular biologist

Peters, Mary, athlete

Petit, Philippe, high-wire artist and acrobat

Phillips, Arlene, dancer and choreographer

Phillips, Leslie, actor

Phillips, Siân, actress

Philpott, Trevor, journalist and TV reporter

Pickering, Ron, TV sports commentator

Pickles, Wilfred, actor and radio presenter

Pienkowski, Jan, illustrator

Pilbeam, Nova, actress

Pilger, John, journalist and broadcaster

Pillinger, Professor Colin, planetary scientist

Pine, Courtney, jazz saxophonist

Pinsent, Sir Matthew, oarsman

Pinter, Harold, playwright

Pipe, Martin, horseracing trainer

Piper, John, artist

Pirie, Gordon, athlete

Pitman, Jenny, racehorse trainer

Pitney, Gene, singer

Plaidy, Jean, writer and historian

Plater, Alan, playwright

Pleasance, Donald, actor

Plomley, Roy, *Desert Island Discs* creator

Plowright, Dame Joan, actress

Plowright, Rosalind, opera singer

Plummer, Christopher, actor

Poliakoff, Nicolai, Coco the Clown

Poliakoff, Stephen, playwright

Pollard, Eve, journalist

Poole, Quentin, head chorister

Porritt, Jonathon, environmentalist

Portas, Mary, retail expert

Porter, Eric, actor

Porter, Nyree Dawn, actress

Porter, Dame Shirley, politician

Portillo, Michael, politician

Postgate, Oliver, Bagpuss creator

Postgate, Raymond, writer and historian

Potter, Dennis, TV playwright

Potter, Stephen, author of *The Theory and Practice of Gamesmanship*

Powell, Anthony, writer

Powell, Dilys, film critic

Powell, Enoch, politician

Powell, Margaret, author of *Below Stairs*

Powell, Michael, film director

Powell, Robert, actor

Powell, Sandy, comedian

Power, Tyrone, actor

Pratchett, Terry, writer

Prawer Jhabvala, Ruth, screenwriter

Preminger, Otto, film director

Press, Percy, Punch and Judy puppeteer

Pressburger, Emeric, screenplay writer

Previn, André, composer and conductor

Price, Alan, musician

Price, Annie, filmmaker and photographer

Price, Dennis, actor

Price, Leontyne, opera singer

Price, Vincent, actor

Prince, Hal, theatre director

Prior, Allan, writer

Prior, James, politician

Proops, Marjorie, agony aunt

Pryce, Jonathan, actor

Pullman, Philip, writer

Puttnam, David, film producer

Pyke, Dr Magnus, scientist and broadcaster

Pym, Barbara, writer

Quasthoff, Thomas, opera singer

Quatro, Suzi, rock musician and singer

Quayle, Anthony, actor

Quinn, Michael, chef

Quirke, Pauline, actress

Race, Steve, pianist and broadcaster

Radice, Vittorio, businessman

Raeburn, Anna, broadcaster

Rainer, Luise, actress

Rambert, Dame Marie, ballet dancer

Rampling, Charlotte, actress

Ramsay, Gordon, chef and TV presenter

Randall, Derek, cricketer

Rankin, Ian, writer

Rantzen, Esther, TV presenter

Raphael, Frederic, writer

Rattigan, Sir Terence, playwright

Rattle, Sir Simon, conductor

Ravel, Jeanne, ballroom dancer

Rawsthorne, Noel, organist

Ray, Cyril, wine expert

Ray, Robin, actor and broadcaster

Ray, Ted, actor and comedian

Rayner, Claire, agony aunt and writer

Read, Al, comedian

Reader, Ralph, theatre director and writer

Reading, Bertice, singer

Reardon, Ray, snooker player

Redgrave, Lynn, actress

Redgrave, Sir Michael, actor

Redgrave, Lady (Rachel Kempton), actress

Redgrave, Vanessa, actress

Redmond, Phil, TV screenwriter

Reece, Brian, actor

Reed, Oliver, actor

Rees, Sir Martin, Astronomer Royal

Reeve, Christopher, actor

Reeves, Vic, comedian

Reid, Beryl, actress

Reilly, Tommy, harmonica player

Revnel, Ethel, comedian

Reynolds, Quentin, journalist

Rhodes, Zandra, fashion designer

Rhys Jones, Griff, actor and comedian

Rice, Sir Tim, lyricist

Rich, Buddy, drummer

Richard, Alison, academic and anthropologist

Richard, Cliff, pop singer

Richard, Wendy, actress

Richardson, Ian, actor

Richardson, Sir Ralph, actor

Riddle, Nelson, bandleader

Ridgway, John, explorer

Ridley, Arnold, actor and playwright

Rippon, Angela, broadcaster

Ritchie, June, actress

Ritter, Tex, singer and actor

Rix, Sir Brian, actor and campaigner

Robbins, Tim, actor

Robens, Lord, chairman of the National Coal Board

Robertson, Alec, broadcaster

Robertson, Fyfe, broadcaster and journalist

Robertson Justice, James, actor

Robeson, Paul, singer and actor

Robinson, Eric, conductor

Robinson, Gerry, businessman

Robinson, Jancis, wine expert

Robinson, Robert, broadcaster

Robinson, T. R., horologist

Robinson, Tony, actor and TV presenter

Robles, Marisa, harpist

Robson, Sir Bobby, footballer and manager

Robson, Flora, actress

Roddick, Anita, businesswoman

Rodgers, Clodagh, singer

Rogers, Ginger, actress

Rogers, Paul, actor

Rogers, Peter, film producer

Rogers, Richard, architect

Rolfe Johnson, Anthony, opera singer

Roll, Lord, academic public servant and banker

Ronay, Egon, food and wine expert

Rook, Jean, newspaper columnist

Ros, Edmundo, bandleader

Rose, Sir Alec, yachtsman

Rose, Sir Stuart, businessman

Rosen, Michael, poet

Rosenthal, Jack, writer

Rosoman, Leonard, artist

Ross, Annie, actress and singer

Rossiter, Leonard, actor

Rotblat, Joseph, physicist

Rothermere, Viscount, newspaper publisher

Rothschild, Miriam, doctor and writer

Rothschild, Lord, academic and businessman

Rous, Sir Stanley, football administrator

Routledge, Patricia, actress

Roux, Albert, chef

Roux, Michel, chef

Rowling, J. K., writer

Rowse, A. L., historian

Rubens, Bernice, writer

Rubinstein, Artur, classical pianist

Runcie, Most Rev. Robert, Archbishop of
Canterbury

Rushdie, Salman, writer

Rushton, Willie, cartoonist and actor

Russell, Ken, film director

Russell, Willy, playwright

Rutherford, Margaret, actress

Rutter, John, composer

Ryder, Sue, campaigner

Saatchi, Maurice, advertising executive

Sachs, Albie, judge and campaigner

Sachs, Leonard, actor

Sacks, Oliver, neurologist and writer

Sagan, Carl, astronomer

Sainsbury, Lord, businessman and politician

Sallis, Peter, actor

Salmond, Alex, politician

Sanderson, Tessa, athlete

Sargent, Sir Malcolm, conductor

Sarony, Leslie, actor, comedian and songwriter

Sassoon, Vidal, hairdresser

Saunders, Dame Cicely, founder of hospice movement

Saunders, Jennifer, actress and writer

Saunders, Peter, theatre impresario

Savile, Jimmy, DJ and TV presenter

Scales, Prunella, actress

Scarfe, Gerald, cartoonist

Scargill, Arthur, trade unionist

Schama, Simon, historian

Scher, Anna, drama teacher

Schiff, Andras, classical pianist

Schlesinger, John, film director

Schönberg, Claude-Michel, composer

Schumann, Elisabeth, opera singer

Schwarzkopf, Elisabeth, opera singer

Schwarzkopf, General H. Norman, soldier

Scotland, Baroness, politician

Scott, Janette, actress

Scott, Peter, naturalist

Scott, Ronnie, jazz musician

Scott, Selina, TV presenter

Scott, Sheila, pilot

Scott, Terry, actor

Scott-James, Anne, gardening writer

Scott Thomas, Kristin, actress

Scotto, Renata, opera singer

Scudamore, Peter, jockey

Seal, Elizabeth, actress and singer

Searle, Ronald, illustrator

Secombe, Sir Harry, actor, singer and comedian

Seeger, Peggy, singer/songwriter

Segal, Erich, writer

Sekers, Sir Nicholas, businessman and industrialist

Sellers, Peter, actor

Sellick, Phyllis, pianist

Sentamu, Rt Rev. John, Bishop of Birmingham

Sessions, John, actor

Seth, Vikram, writer

Sewell, Brian, art critic

Seyler, Athene, actress

Seymour, Lynn, ballerina

Shaffer, Peter, playwright

Shand, Jimmy, danceband leader

Shankar, Ravi, musician

Shankly, Bill, football manager

Sharif, Omar, actor

Sharpe, Tom, writer

Shaw, Martin, actor

Shaw, Sandie, singer

Shearer, Moira, ballerina and actress

Shearing, George, jazz pianist

Sheen, Martin, actor

Sheene, Barry, motorcycle racer

Shelton, Anne, singer

Shephard, Gillian, politician

Shepherd, David, wildlife artist

Sheppard, Rev. David, cricketer and clergyman

Sher, Antony, actor

Sherriff, R. C., playwright

Sherrin, Ned, broadcaster

Shinwell, Manny, Lord, politician

Shipton, Eric, explorer and mountaineer

Short, Clare, politician

Shulman, Milton, critic

Sibley, Antoinette, ballerina

Sillitoe, Alan, writer

Silvester, Victor, bandleader

Sim, Sheila, actress

Simmonds, Posy, cartoonist and writer

Simmons, Jean, actress

Simon, Francesca, children's writer

Simon, Neil, playwright

Simpson, John, TV foreign correspondent

Simpson, Tommy, cyclist

Sinden, Donald, actor

Singleton, Valerie, TV presenter

Sitwell, Sir Sacheverell, poet

Skinner, Dennis, politician

Skinner, Frank, comedian

Skinner, Zena, cookery expert

Slade, Julian, composer

Slater, John, actor

Slater, Nigel, cookery writer and broadcaster

Slatkin, Leonard, conductor

Slaughter, Tod, actor

Sleep, Wayne, dancer

Smit, Tim, founder of the Eden Project

Smith, Cyril, musician

Smith, Delia, cookery writer and broadcaster

Smith, Dodie, writer

Smith, Geoffrey, gardener

Smith, Harvey, showjumper

Smith, John, politician

Smith, Liz, actress

Smith, Maggie, actress

Smith, Paul, fashion designer

Smith, T. Dan, politician

Smith, Wilbur, writer

Smythe, Pat, showjumper

Snagge, John, broadcaster

Snow, C. P., writer and physicist

Snow, Jon, TV news anchor

Snowdon, Earl of, photographer

Soames, Mary, Lady, writer and historian

Söderström, Elisabeth, opera singer

Solomons, Jack, boxing promoter

Solti, Georg, conductor

Somes, Michael, dancer

Sondheim, Stephen, composer

Soper, Lord, Methodist minister

Sorrell, Sir Martin, advertising executive

Sowerbutts, Bill, horticulturalist

Spall, Timothy, actor

Spear, Ruskin, artist

Speight, Johnny, TV writer

Spence, Sir Basil, architect

Spencer, June, actress

Spender, Natasha, pianist

Spender, Sir Stephen, poet

Springer, Jerry, TV presenter

Squires, Dorothy, actress

St John Stevas, Norman, politician

Stafford Smith, Clive, death-row lawyer

Stamp, Terence, actor

Stark, Dame Freya, explorer and travel writer

Starkey, Dr David, historian and broadcaster

Staunton, Imelda, actress

Steadman, Alison, actress

Steadman, Ralph, cartoonist

Steafel, Sheila, actress

Steel, Anthony, actor

Steel, David, politician

Steele, Tommy, actor and singer

Steiger, Rod, actor

Stein, Marion, pianist

Stein, Rick, chef

Steiner, Professor George, academic
and critic

Stephens, Robert, actor

Stephenson, Pamela, actress and psychologist

Stern, Isasc, violinist

Stevens, Jocelyn, businessman and publisher

Stevens, John, Lord, head of the Metropolitan
Police

Stevenson, Juliet, actress

Stewart, Andy, singer

Stewart, Ian, mathematician

Stewart, Jackie, motor-racing driver

Stewart, James, actor

Stewart, Patrick, actor

Stokes, Doris, medium

Stokowski, Leopold, conductor

Stone, Christopher, broadcaster

Stoppard, Tom, playwright

Storey, David, playwright

Straw, Jack, politician

Street-Porter, Janet, journalist and broadcaster

Streatfeild, Noel, children's writer

Strong, Patience, poet

Strong, Dr Roy, director of the National Portrait Gallery

Styne, Jule, songwriter

Suchet, David, actor

Suggs, singer/songwriter

Sulston, Sir John, biologist

Sutherland, Donald, actor

Sutherland, Joan, opera singer

Suzman, Janet, actress

Suzuki, Pat, actress and singer

Swan, Robert, explorer and environmentalist

Swann, Donald, singer and entertainer

Swanson, Gloria, actress

Swinburne, Nora, actress

Swinnerton, Frank, critic and novelist

Swinton, Professor W. E., expert on prehistoric animals

Syal, Meera, actress and comedian

Sykes, Eric, comedian and actor

Sykes, Sir Richard, businessman

Symons, Julian, crime writer

Syms, Sylvia, actress

Taki, columnist

Tallis, Professor Raymond, philosopher
and physician

Tarbuck, Jimmy, comedian

Tarrant, Chris, TV presenter

Tavener, John, composer

Taylor, Dennis, snooker player

Taylor Bradford, Barbara, writer

Taylor-Wood, Sam, artist and film director

Teagarden, Jack, jazz trombonist

Tebbit, Margaret, Lady, wife of Norman Tebbit

Tebbit, Norman, Lord, politician

Te Kanawa, Kiri, opera singer, soprano

Tennant, David, actor

Tennant, Neil, singer/songwriter

Terfel, Bryn, opera singer

Testino, Mario, photographer

Teyte, Dame Maggie, opera singer

Thatcher, Margaret, Leader of the Opposition (became prime minister in 1979)

Thaw, John, actor

Thebom, Blanche, opera singer

Thelwell, Norman, cartoonist

Theroux, Paul, writer

Thesiger, Ernest, actor

Thesiger, Wilfred, explorer and writer

Thomas, George (Viscount Tonypandy), speaker of the House of Commons

Thomas, Irene, *Brain of Britain* radio personality

Thomas, Leslie, writer

Thomas, Terry, actor and comedian

Thomas Ellis, Alice, writer

Thompson, Daley, decathlete

Thompson, Don, athlete

Thompson, E. P., historian and campaigner

Thompson, Emma, actress and writer

Thompson, Eric, actor, producer and presenter

Thorburn, June, actress

Thorndike, Dame Sybil, actress

Thorpe, Jeremy, politician

Thrower, Percy, TV gardening presenter

Thubron, Colin, writer

Tilson Thomas, Michael, conductor

Tippett, Sir Michael, composer

Titchmarsh, Alan, gardener and broadcaster

Todd, Richard, actor

Todd, Ron, trade unionist

Tomalin, Claire, writer

Tomlinson, David, actor

Tomlinson, John, opera singer

Topol, actor and singer

Tormé, Mel, singer

Tortelier, Paul, cellist and composer

Townsend, Group Captain Peter, writer
and explorer

Townsend, Sue, writer

Toye, Wendy, dancer and choreographer

Tracey, Stan, jazz pianist

Travers, Ben, playwright

Travers, P. L., writer

Tremain, Rose, writer

Trethowan, Sir Ian, journalist, broadcaster

Trevelyan, John, film censor

Trevelyan Oman, Julia, set designer

Trevor-Roper, Hugh, Lord Dacre, historian

Trollope, Joanna, writer

Trueman, Fred, cricketer

Trumpington, Baroness, politician

Tubb, Carrie, opera singer

Tucker, Sophie, singer

Tulloh, Bruce, athlete

Tully, Mark, broadcaster

Turner, Dame Eva, opera singer

Turner, Kathleen, actress

Tushingham, Rita, actress

Tutin, Dorothy, actress

Tutu, Most Rev. Desmond, Archbishop of
Cape Town

Twiggy, model and actor

Tynan, Kenneth, theatre critic

Uchida, Mitsuko, pianist

Unwin, Stanley, comedian and inventor of nonsense language

Updike, John, writer

Ure, Mary, actress

Ustinov, Peter, actor, writer and raconteur

Vadim, Roger, film director

Valentine, Dickie, singer

Van Der Post, Sir Laurens, writer and explorer

Varah, Chad, founder of the Samaritans

Vaughan, Frankie, singer

Vaughan, Sarah, singer

Vaughan-Thomas, Wynford, war correspondent and broadcaster

Vayne, Kyra, opera singer

Vegas, Johnny, comedian

Vettriano, Jack, artist

Vickers, Jon, opera singer

von Trapp, Baroness Maria, inspiration for *The Sound of Music*

Wade, Virginia, tennis player

Wain, John, writer and critic

Wainwright, Alfred, guidebook author

Waite, Terry, missionary, humanitarian

Walbrook, Anton, actor

Walcott, Derek, poet and playwright

Wall, Max, comedian and actor

Wallace, Ian, opera singer

Walliams, David, comedian

Walter, Dame Harriet, actress

Walter, Dr W. Grey, roboticist

Walters, Julie, actress

Walters, Minette, writer

Walton, Susana, Lady, horticulturalist

Walton, Sir William, composer

Wan, Gok, TV fashion presenter

Wanamaker, Zoe, actress

Waring, Eddie, Rugby League commentator

Warner, Jack, actor

Warren, Frank, boxing promoter

Waterhouse, Keith, writer

Waterman, Dame Fanny, piano teacher

Waterman, Pete, record producer

Waters, Doris, entertainer

Waters, Elsie, entertainer

Waters, Roger, rock musician

Wattis, Richard, actor

Watts, Charlie, rock drummer

Watts, Helen, opera singer

Waugh, Alec, writer

Waugh, Auberon, writer

Wax, Ruby, actress and comedian

Webb, Kaye, publisher

Webb, Lizbeth, opera singer

Webb, Marti, actress and singer

Wedgwood, Dame Veronica, historian

Weedon, Bert, guitarist

Weidenfeld, George, publisher

Welch, Elisabeth, singer

Welch, Leslie, memory expert

Weldon, Fay, writer

Welland, Colin, actor

Weller, Paul, singer/songwriter

Wesker, Sir Arnold, playwright

Wesley, Mary, writer

West, Peter, broadcaster

West, Dame Rebecca, writer

West, Timothy, actor

Westheimer, Dr Ruth, sex therapist

Westminster, Duke of, landowner and property developer

Weston, Simon, Falklands War veteran

Westwood, Vivienne, fashion designer

Whately, Kevin, actor

Whicker, Alan, broadcaster

Whineray, Wilson, Rugby Union player

White, Marco Pierre, chef

White, Michael, film and theatre producer

White, Willard, opera singer

Whitehorn, Katharine, writer

Whitehouse, Paul, comedian and actor

Whitelaw, Billie, actress

Whitelaw, William, politician

Whitfield, June, actress

Whitlohn, Sir Harry, theatrical manager (April Fool's joke)

Widdecombe, Ann, politician

Wilcox, Herbert, film producer and director

Wild, Earl, concert pianist

Wilde, Marty, pop singer

Wilder, Gene, actor

Wilding, Michael, actor

Wilkie, David, swimmer

Williams, Dorian, showjumping commentator

Williams, Emlyn, writer and actor

Williams, Hugh, actor

Williams, John, classical guitarist

Williams, Kenneth, actor

Williams, Most Rev. Dr Rowan, Archbishop of Canterbury elect

Williams, Baroness Shirley, politician

Williams, Ted, equestrian

Williams, Tennessee, playwright

Williamson, Henry, writer

Williamson, Malcolm, Master of the Queen's Music

Willis, Ted, writer

Wilson, A. N., writer

Wilson, Angus, writer

Wilson, Des, director of Shelter

Wilson, Jacqueline, writer

Wilson, Sir John, scientist and blindness campaigner

Wilson, M., member of the London Philharmonic Orchestra

Wilson, Mary, prime minister's wife and poet

Wilton, Penelope, actress

Windsor, Barbara, actress

Winn, Godfrey, journalist

Winner, Michael, film director and restaurant critic

Winston, Professor Robert, human fertility expert

Winterson, Jeanette, writer

Wintle, Colonel A. D., soldier and writer

Wisdom, Sir Norman, comedian and actor

Wise, Ernie, comedian

Withers, Googie, actress

Wogan, Sir Terry, TV and radio presenter

Wolfenden, Sir John, director of the British Museum

Wolff, Professor Heinz, scientist

Wolff, Marguerite, pianist

Wolfit, Donald, actor

Wolstenholme, Kenneth, football commentator

Wood, Frances, historian

Wood, Natalie, actress

Wood, Victoria, writer and actress

Wood, Wee Georgie, music hall artist

Woodhouse, Barbara, dog trainer

Woodruff, Maurice, psychic, clairvoyant
and astrologer

Woodward, Sir Clive, Rugby Union player and coach

Woodward, Edward, actor

Woolley, Sir Richard, Astronomer Royal

Worrell, Frank, cricketer

Worsthorne, Sir Peregrine, journalist

Worth, Irene, actress

Worth, Joy, radio presenter

Wynne, David, sculptor

Yacoub, Sir Magdi, surgeon

Yarwood, Mike, comedian

Yentob, Alan, TV executive and broadcaster

York, Michael, actor

York, Susannah, actress

Young, Gladys, actress and radio personality

Young, Lavinia, matron of Westminster Hospital

Young, Brigadier Peter, soldier and military historian

Zec, Donald, journalist

Zeffirelli, Franco, film director

Zephaniah, Benjamin, poet

Zetterling, Mai, actress

Zinnemann, Fred, film director

ACKNOWLEDGEMENTS

This book was a labour of love but it wasn't a solo act.

Firstly, it's my pleasure to thank Brenda Kimber, my warm and wonderful editor, who was encouraging and nurturing in equal measure.

My thanks also to Sally Gaminara, publisher and editor of the companion volume to this book – *Desert Island Discs: 70 Years of Castaways* – for her valuable support, Mari Roberts for her fine copyediting, and author Sean Magee, who compiled and edited *Castaways*. He's a fine man and I've very much enjoyed collaborating with him.

I'd also like to thank my three dedicatees: my wife Penny and our sons, Jack and Charlie. They more than deserve these thanks for, as well as being utterly gorgeous in every way (well, *sometimes*), they also helped me research this book.

Finally, my thanks go to the BBC, the *Desert Island Discs* team and, most of all, the people who compiled the fabulous database. If I've done half as good a job as they did, I'll be very happy.